Private Property and the Origins of Nationalism in the United States and Norway

Eirik Magnus Fuglestad

Private Property and the Origins of Nationalism in the United States and Norway

The Making of Propertied Communities

palgrave
macmillan

Eirik Magnus Fuglestad
Ruralis—Institute for Rural
and Regional Research
Trondheim, Norway

ISBN 978-3-030-07902-4 ISBN 978-3-319-89950-3 (eBook)
https://doi.org/10.1007/978-3-319-89950-3

Softcover re-print of the Hardcover 1st edition 2018

Cover credit: *Eidsvoll 1814* by Oscar Wergeland/Archives of the Storting

Printed on acid-free paper

This Palgrave Macmillan imprint is published by the registered company Springer International Publishing AG part of Springer Nature
The registered company address is: Gewerbestrasse 11, 6330 Cham, Switzerland

For my parents, Tom and Brit Fuglestad, and to the smallholding farm of Langeli, where I grew up

Foreword

Debates about the origins of modern nationalism have tended to revolve around questions of the relative importance of pre-existing ethnic and cultural identities, the impact of new communication technologies, and the functional demands of industrial economics and centralized states for more unified and integrated populations. Eirik Fuglestad brings a new perspective on these debates by focussing on a crucial but often neglected issue—the role of private property in this process.

This approach enables him to do two novel things. One is to get beneath treatments of nationalism as a general effect of capitalism or class-based politics, to explore the formal connections between concepts of property and sovereignty that were transforming together in the same historical context. It turns out the ideas of citizens securely owning their own property, and citizens collectively "owning" their common territory and government, are connected in a broader pattern of legitimacy. Within this he traces an historical shift (c.1760–1880) from an emphasis on ownership of land as a criterion of political membership, to one on the ownership of one's own labor. From national communities of landholders, to national communities of workers. This points to his other achievement, which is to clarify that the shift from agrarian to industrial society that was basic to Ernest Gellner's influential explanation of nationalism involved, at least in some early cases, a transitional phase. Before full industrialization, the role of an independent landholding class of small to large farmers involved in commercial agriculture turns out to have provided one of the key seedbeds for nationalist ideas in the late eighteenth and early nineteenth centuries.

Added to these innovations, people rarely think of comparing the US and Norway as cases of nationalism. For Dr. Fuglestad this counterintuitive research strategy pays off. These two cases neatly illustrate the underlying pattern of evolving property rights and nationalist ideas, while also demonstrating the very different ways this played out in different historical, economic and political contexts. Altogether this book provides a new and provocative way of thinking about the emergence of modern nationalism, one that deserves to be read and debated.

Scotland, UK

Jonathan Hearn
Professor of Political and Historical Sociology
University of Edinburgh

Preface

All Western states today define themselves as nation-states, and all of these states have a political and economic structure in which an individual's right to own private property is an underlying and pervasive feature. Drawing on examples from the historical trajectories of the US and Norway between c.1760 and 1880, this book explores the development of nation-states and the role of private property rights in this development. The book seeks to demonstrate the fundamental role both of the idea of private property for the ideology of nationalism, and of the significance of a particular kind of property regime (widespread landowning) for the emergence and development of nationalism as an historical phenomenon.

This book is historical and particular in nature—it deals with events and ideas in specific places of the distant past—but the purpose of this book is to understand the world in which we live today. This book might thus be placed in the tradition of thinkers such as Karl Marx, Emile Durkheim and Max Weber; it is essentially an attempt to understand the preconditions for, and the origins of, the modern world of nation-states with a broad historical view, and to thus illuminate structural historical processes in their making. The first basic assumption to this approach is the banal but important historical insight that society is not static: the institutions, ideas and material relations of the present have evolved out of earlier forms. The present is historically laden: to understand it, we must understand from where it came. A second basic insight or assumption that these approaches have in common is the recognition that changes in what we might call the material world—that is, changes in forms of property, population swings, wars, access to resources, changes in ways of production and appropriation, etc.—have a decisive effect on social forms and dominant ideas in society. To understand social change, we must take into account the material forces that shape the lives of people. Karl Marx was one of those who first strongly accentuated changes in the material world as a driving force, as it were, in history; and Marx's emphasis on changes in the mode of production—specifically changes in property regimes—for the formation of new ideas and social forms is the basis on which this book is built. The book focusses specifically on how the property regime in societies is related to the idea and ideology of nationalism. It is the institution and idea of private property, and its role in the national ideology, that is the central aspect of this book. The claim is made that the existence of a particular type of property regime (those to be found, for example, in the US and Norway in the early nineteenth century) was particularly favourable for the formation of nationalism. A second central claim is that landed property rights was also an integral part of the ideology of nationalism.

The main points that the book makes are that it was the emergence of more widespread smallholding of land that was one of the most decisive preconditions for the emergence of nationalism in the US and Norway. It is furthermore suggested that widespread ownership of land resulted in the emergence of a form of nationalism in which ownership of landed property was crucial because it became tied up with the idea of national popular sovereignty. Put in a simplified way: sovereignty was popular because property was popular (widespread). This connection was made mainly, on the one hand, from the real historical tie between ownership of land, juridical sovereignty and political powers and, on the other hand, from the more conceptual similarity between property rights or ownership and sovereignty.

The book identifies two forms of nationalism based on the way that property was understood in the national ideology. Hence, the book is organized in two main parts. Part I deals with what we can call the agrarian moment, and it deals with the independence movements of the North American British colonies and the Kingdom of Norway in the late eighteenth century and the early nineteenth century. This part describes an agrarian phase or moment of nationalism where it was real landed property that was seen to be crucial to the creation of national sovereignty. Part II of the book looks at what we can call the industrial moment in the history of nationalism. With the coming of industrial property and the expansion of wage labour, landed property lost its significance, and instead the right to the fruits of one's labour was understood as the most important part of the property right. I have called this a shift from land to labour, or a *transvaluation of property.*

This property rights perspective on nationalism in the US and Norway contributes to a new understanding of nationalism not only in these places but perhaps also in the Western world in general. Developments in the US and Norway can be seen in the wider context of the decline of feudalism and absolutism and the emergence of democratic, industrial societies in the Western world. The landed, agrarian form of nationalism might in effect be a "missing link" between pre- or proto-national forms of society (feudal, religious, absolutist, mercantilist, etc.), and the fully modern industrial form identified, for example, by Ernest Gellner. It is the connection between property (from land to labour) and sovereignty that unites them.

In the broadest sense this book is about the world in which we live, and it deals with the development of the United States and Norway into modern societies, but it is to debates in nationalism studies that this book is intended to contribute first and foremost. The Ph.D. dissertation on which this book is based was conceived and written in the stimulating milieu of nationalism scholars and students at the School of Social and Political Science at the University of Edinburgh, UK; and it is very much a product of this experience. My first year in Edinburgh as a graduate student on the MSc in nationalism studies deeply inspired me to think about nationalism, its origins and its nature. Of course, I also brought with me some baggage from home, as it were. Being myself the son of a Norwegian farmer, and having studied the Norwegian national narrative with its focus on the free smallholder at the University of Stavanger, I met the international theories of nationalism and its students with this particular background. One of the things that struck me early on, when my own knowledge met with the international theories and students in Edinburgh, was the lack of literature on landed property rights and nationalism. It seemed to me, from my knowledge of Norwegian nationalism, that this was a central aspect of nationalism. Yet it was difficult to find literature that dealt with, or acknowledged, what seemed to me a clear and present connection between the early emergence of nationalism and landed property rights. Thus began my own inquiry into this topic as a graduate student during my MSc degree. When I completed my

MSc, I was able to apply for funding from the Norwegian fund for education, *Statens Lånekasse*, to do a Ph.D. and was accepted for the Ph.D. programme at the School of Social and Political Science at the University of Edinburgh.

Writing the Ph.D. dissertation that became the basis of this book turned out to be a bit of an intellectual odyssey, going back and forth across the enormous, stormy Atlantic Ocean, so to speak, between the North American British colonies and the Norwegian province of the Danish Oldenburg Empire in the eighteenth century at first. Following these two societies as they changed from agrarian provinces of great empires to becoming independent burgeoning industrial nations by the close of the nineteenth century. Jumping from revolutionary American debates on liberty and independence, to the Norwegian declaration of independence in the shade of the Napoleonic wars. Going from the American "irrepressible conflict" over slavery and the civil war, to the Norwegian movement for parliamentary democracy. It seemed overwhelming and almost impossible to try to find some kind of order and system in these seemingly different and idiosyncratic events. Some people will say that this is indeed impossible and futile, and that generalizations cannot be made, but I had excellent guidance from two inspiring and competent sociologists and nationalism scholars—Professor Jonathan Hearn and Dr. James Kennedy. They wisely guided me through my quest for knowledge, and helped me discover and organize the patterns and trends of social change that this book aims to display. On that note, I want to thank the people who have helped and inspired me during the process of writing this book.

The largest intellectual debt and gratitude I owe to Professor Jonathan Hearn and Dr. James Kennedy. I would not have been able to write this book without the inspired comments and wise guidance from these two great scholars. I would like to thank also the examiners who oversaw the viva of this text, when it was a Ph.D. dissertation: Professor Sinisa Malesevic and Professor Frank Cogliano both gave inspiring comments and thought-provoking discussion on my thesis.

Many thanks go to my peers and friends at the University of Edinburgh, especially my friends and colleagues in ENNIN (Edinburgh's Ethnicity, Nationalism and National Identity Network). I have had countless inspired conversations with the many wonderful people involved here, and not the least have they (as well as all other friends) provided me with wonderful moments of leisure and good fun. This has been a great source of renewed energy to keep me working of my research. In this regard I would like to thank Shruti Chaudhry for walks and chats and drinks and movie nights, Ceren Sengul for Jägermeister shots, Heddwyn Loyd Fletcher for being my beer buddy, Marie Eve Hamel for being my Ph.D. buddy and flat-mate Dani Cetra for hangouts in the flat. I would also like to thank the band *The Chilli Dogs* for providing music many a Thursday night at the Cannons Gait pub.

Thanks also to my family and to my always encouraging wife Alin Ake Kob for support during the years of work and writing. Alin also read and commented on an early draft of this book, I owe her a great debt for that.

Special thanks go to my friends Erin Hughes and Jamie Mitchel who in addition to being great friends during all my years of study also proofread and commented on the final draft of the thesis (Erin), and who helped me format the text (Jamie). Jamie proofread and gave me comments on the book manuscript as well. Taylor Sawyer also helped proofread the final manuscript; I am indebted to her for that. The librarians at *Bjerkreim Folkebibliotek* (the public library in Bjerkreim, Norway) deserve special thanks as well; they have been extremely helpful and understanding in ordering books and sources that I have used during my research.

I would like to thank my editor at Palgrave— Megan Laddusaw—for making this book a reality, and for her patience and advice during the process of preparing the book. Christine Pardue, secretary at Palgrave, was also most helpful and understanding in the process. The book manuscript was sent for anonymous review before it was published, and I got helpful comments from that process, so thanks to my reviewer also. Finally, I would like to thank *Ruralis* (Institute for Rural and Regional Research, Trondheim, Norway) for providing time and resources for me to finish the final write-up of the book.

The people and institutions that I have thanked here have been of great help and inspiration during the writing of this book. I myself am solely responsible for any shortcomings or faults in the text.

Trondheim, Norway
March 2018

Eirik Magnus Fuglestad

Contents

Part III Conclusions

CHAPTER 1

Introduction: A Property Rights Perspective to the Study of Nationalism

This book offers an historical sociological analysis of the emergence and development of nationalism in the US and Norway between 1762 and 1884. Both the US and Norway were agrarian societies at the beginning of this time period, and had a property structure that was marked by relatively widespread smallholdings of land. This fact became crucial for the development of national ideology, as ideas of popular sovereignty and individual freedom became tied up with widespread individual ownership of landed property. This book offers an analysis of the relationship between landed property rights and nationalism in these cases, and the development of this relationship with the coming of industrialization. I believe I have arrived at a novel understanding of nationalism, one which reveals the fundamental role of private, landed property rights to the emergence, nature, and development of nationalism, and which illuminates how the agrarian origins of nationalism adapted to its industrial future.

The book uses Charles Tilly's concept of universalizing comparison[1] to generalize development in these countries into a theory of nationalism. One could also refer to Skocpol and Somers' parallel demonstration

[1] Tilly, Charles, *Big Structures, Large Processes, Huge Comparisons*, Russell Sage Foundation, New York (1984), pp. 82–83.

E. M. Fuglestad, *Private Property and the Origins of Nationalism in the United States and Norway*,
https://doi.org/10.1007/978-3-319-89950-3_1

of theory, and to their concept of macro-analytical comparison.[2] Another way of explaining the way in which this book builds its argument is through Miroslav Hroch's term synchronic historical comparison: in other words establishing similar historical processes that happened roughly during the same time period in different places:

> If we can establish that the objects of comparison went through roughly the same stages of development, we can compare these analogous events, even if from the standpoint of absolute chronological they occurred at different times.[3]

Why the cases of the US and Norway? It might seem like an odd comparison. There are, however, good reasons for choosing these cases. The point of departure for my comparison between the US and Norway was the similar distribution of landed property in these cases at their respective revolutionary moments. According to classical Marxian materialist assumptions, similar relations of property should result in largely similar developments of ideology and the state. The US and Norway represented the actual existence of a form of relatively widespread private property at an early stage, and before the emergence of a political national movement or the creation of a nation-state. As the initial question that led to the writing of this book was the role of private property in national ideology, such material relations seemed a fruitful starting point. Indeed, these nations did establish very early on private property regimes and democracies based on widespread landholding. Both did this in opposition to imperial states. What happened in the US and Norway was similar, and many Norwegian scholars, as well as Norwegians at the time of the national revolution, have pointed to this similarity. The historian Sigmund Skard wrote about the Norwegian revolution of 1814 and its similarity to America's: "The historical situation has been felt as parallel: two small nations arose heroically up against great powers. There was a commonality in their spirit which went

[2] Skocpol, Theda, and Margaret Somers, "The use of comparative history in macro social inquiry," *Comparative Studies in Society and History*, Vol. 22 (1980).

[3] Hroch, Miroslav, *Social Preconditions of National Revival in Europe: A Comparative Analysis of the Social Composition of Patriotic Groups in the Smaller European Nations*, Cambridge University Press, Cambridge (1985), p. 20.

deeper than their differences."[4] Francis Sejersted—another Norwegian historian—has also noted the similarity between the two societies at the outset of the nineteenth century, and points specifically to the idea that both societies were very much akin to a Lockean ideal society—that is to say, societies constituted in large part of individual proprietors of land participating freely in relations with each other and in government.[5] This sounds very idealistic, but this fundamental similarity, the "commonality in spirit" constituted by the relative widespread ownership of land and similar liberal constitutions, can serve as a fruitful point of departure for comparison.

There is also a point in accentuating the differences between the US and Norway. One was situated in the New World, the other in the Old World, and there was a giant ocean between them. One marked the start of the age of revolution, and the other was close to its end. In the US there existed four million chattel slaves (understood in most respects to be a form of property) at the time of the revolution; in Norway nothing of the kind had existed for almost 1000 years. In America huge areas of land were taken from the native populations by force or expulsion by the settlers, thus providing the settlers with new land. In Norway there were few possibilities to acquire new land. The US became a republic and Norway remained a constitutional monarchy. These differences might actually strengthen the fundamental comparability of these cases. Despite enormous difference in space, and almost a quarter of a century of difference in time between their national revolutions—and despite the difference in social structure created by the institution of slavery and availability of land in America—what happened was similar. Even despite the different state forms of a republic and a monarchy, there was a fundamental and pervasive similarity in the new states that became established and in the philosophy to which they adhered. This might indicate that similar property regimes in land indeed strongly influenced the ideology. Furthermore, this also points to the common intellectual milieu of which nationalists in the US and Norway were a part of. The way these cases developed was not isolated; moreover, although these cases were peculiar in certain

[4] Skard, Sigmund, *USA i Norsk historie: 1000–1776–1976*, Det Norske Samlaget, Oslo (1976), p. 56 (my translation).

[5] Sejersted, Francis, *Demokrati og rettsstat*, Pax Forlag, Oslo (2002), pp. 348–349.

ways, they were part of something broader. Nationalism in these cases did not emerge in a vacuum. In fact, the national revolutions of the US and Norway mark the beginning (the US) and the end (Norway) of a series of nationalist revolutions in the Western Hemisphere. The US and Norway were part of what Jonathan Hearn has called "the North Atlantic interaction sphere."[6] Starting with the American revolution, expressions of nationalism in the form of liberation movements promoting liberal constitutions emerged in a spatial sphere covering North America and Western Europe, as well large parts of Latin America in the years between 1776 and 1814. The French revolution of 1789 is perhaps the most commonly used example of this. In addition, we might include the Haitian revolution of 1791 (and its constitution of 1801), the Venezuelan Constitution of 1811, the Mexican rising of 1810, and the Spanish Constitution of 1812. One might also mention the Napoleonic code (1804) with its strong emphasis on the right to property. In the German states in particular, nationalism emerged as a reaction to the rule of Napoleon. All these occurrences and many more may be seen to constitute the age of revolution or the age of nationalism, in which the emergence of nationalism in my cases was a part.[7] The geographical position and general characteristics of their ideologies place my cases in this context, within the tradition of what Hans Kohn called "western nationalism"—an individualistic, liberal, democratic and essentially capitalist worldview.[8] After Kohn, others have developed similar typologies without the historical and geographical specificities of Kohn's distinction between Western and Eastern nationalism, but which nevertheless are extensions and modifications of these categories. We might thus also label the nationalism of our cases civic nationalism as opposed to ethnic and individualistic or "authoritarian/

[6] Hearn, Jonathan, "The origins of modern nationalism in the North Atlantic interaction sphere," *Sociological Review Online*, Vol. 14, No. 5 (2009).

[7] The accounts that I have primarily relied on for the sociopolitical development of the Western world in this time period are: Hobsbawm, Eric, *The Age of Revolution: Europe 1789–1848*, Weidenfeld & Nicolson, London (1962); Merriman, John, *A History of Modern Europe: From the Renaissance to the Present*, W. W. Norton & Co., New York and London (1996); Palmer, R.R., *The Age of Democratic Revolution: A Political History of Europe and America*, Vol. 1, Princeton University Press, Princeton and London (1959); and Palmer, R.R., *The Age of Democratic Revolution: A Political History of Europe and America*, Vol. 2, Princeton University Press, Princeton and London (1964). It is also from these accounts (and specifically Hobsbawm) that I borrow the term "age of revolution."

[8] Kohn, Hans, *The Idea of Nationalism: A Study in Its Origins and Background*, Transaction Publishers, New Brunswick (2005) [1944].

collectivistic". What is important to recognize is that the nationalism that emerged in the US and Norway was one specific breed, as it were, of the larger category of nationalism, which was nevertheless brought forth by specific historical and social conditions—specifically, the widespread ownership of land. It must, however, be emphasized that the widespread ownership structure found in the US and Norway was, even though it was relatively unusual, a symptom of a broader historical trend in Western Europe, where land and property rights became more individual and disconnected from feudalistic or feudal-like structures. Thus, although the argument of this book concerns the specific property structures of the US and Norway, they are used here as very clear examples of a kind of property structure that emerged in many places in Western Europe during and after this time period.

A New Theory of Nationalism

Nationalism, Property and Agrarian Society

In the 1980s Ernest Gellner put forth a theory of nationalism that has since been definitive and influential for all subsequent studies of nationalism. His theory still defines much of the debate around nationalism, as well as the understanding of it. It will be useful to employ Gellner's theory as a springboard for the argument of this book. Gellner held that nationalism was "primarily a political principle, which holds that the political and the national unit should be congruent."[9] He believed that nationalism emerged with industrial society in Europe. "The age of transition to industrialism was bound, according to our model, also to be an age of nationalism," wrote Gellner. Here, industrialism created nationalism because it brought to the world a "homogeneity imposed by objective, inescapable, imperative [which] eventually appears on the surface in the form of nationalism."[10] Although Gellner, tongue-in-cheek, held his argument to be Euclidian in its logic,[11] many have since shown that nationalism did in fact emerge long before industrialization. While this book sees the origins of nationalism before industrialization, the book

[9] Gellner, Ernest, *Nations and Nationalism*, Blackwell, Oxford (2006) [1983], p. 1.

[10] Gellner (2006), p. 38.

[11] Gellner, Ernest, "The coming of nationalism and its interpretation: The myths of nation and class," in Gopal Balakrishnan (ed.), *Mapping the Nation*, Verso, London (1999) [1996], p. 111.

also holds that nationalism and industrial society not only have an elective affinity, but that nationalism became, to use the Marxian term, the superstructure of the industrial mode of production. How then is it that nationalism, a pre-industrial phenomena, is so well suited to industrial society? The answer, this book suggests, lies in the initial connection between nationalism and landed private property rights.

This book locates the origins of nationalism in changes of property structures within agrarian societies, and points to how the principles of nationalism were at first understood in relation to, and emerged from, agrarian conditions of landed property (the agrarian moment), and how nationalism thus became the foundation for industrial society (industrial moment). In short, nationalism was originally a result of a transformation of notions of property and sovereignty within agrarian societies, brought forth by changes in landed property regimes. Hence, the structural shift that according to Gellner makes nationalism possible, and which he saw as one between agrarian and industrial society, was in fact a change within agrarian society. The structural change was a change that saw the emergence of more widespread smallholdings of land, as opposed to large manorial landholding based on aristocratic privilege. When landholding became more widely distributed, it posed changes to the political power structure through which property as universal right was introduced. Gellner said that the age of nationalism was one of ***universal high culture***, where every man is a Mamluk[12]; this book argues that to understand nationalism properly, we must see it also as an age of ***universal property ownership***. To invoke the Hegelian image of the master–slave dialectic, history, up until the age of nationalism, was one of slave (propertyless) versus master (owners). In the age of nationalism, all are masters, the dialectic is fulfilled—all are equally recognized as individuals with the right to property.[13]

The Hegelian statement is only an exaggerated image of course, but it does point to something fundamental about the novelty of nationalism as historical phenomena as presented in this book: since the first civilizations, property ownership has been confined to the few, whereas the masses

[12]Gellner (2006), p. 18.

[13]Hegel's dialectic is often understood metaphysically. But Susan Buck-Morrs has suggested and convincingly shown that Hegel had this image from real and contemporary issues of slaves and masters. See Buck-Morss, Susan, "Hegel and Haiti," *Critical Inquiry*, Vol. 26, No. 4 (Summer, 2000). The master–slave dialectic understood in literal terms has special relevance for understanding nationalism in the US and Norway, as we shall see.

were confined to poverty.[14] In ancient Greece and Rome, for example, it was citizens or aristocrats who had property over slaves and land. In the European feudal age, it was lords and kings that had it over serfs and land. The natural order of things was master and slave. This changes with the age of nationalism, under its aegis, as stated in the American *Declaration of Independence*, "all men" are granted "the right to life, liberty and the pursuit of happiness." To invoke another image: at first, none had property, then some had property, and finally all have property.[15] Again, this is only in theory, but this was the theory by which the members of the national movements in the US and Norway legitimized their cause—it was their *raison d'être*. This became so due to the landed property relations in these cases: the property structures in the US and Norway reinforced a style of thought where the image of master and slave, envisioned as propertied versus propertyless, became a central image.[16] One fundamental principle of nationalism was individual freedom through ownership as opposed to slavery.[17] Nationalism was a way of understanding and organizing the world in which the freedom of the individual was the fundamental goal. Nationalists sought to realize their vision of freedom by creating a national sovereignty based on the property of every member of the nation. Thus was the propertied freedom of each individual seen to be safe, and the nation became a propertied community.

The Freedom in Property and Its Transvaluation

The more general philosophical points made above should not be interpreted as a form of idealism in the approach of the book. On the

[14] I am generalizing here as well. For an overview of the diversity of land law in the ancient world see, for example, Ellickson, Robert C., and Charles Thorland, "Ancient Land Law, Mesopotamia, Egypt, Israel," *Yale Law School Legal Scholarship Repository* (01.01.1995).

[15] This is inspired by Gellner's paraphrase of Hegel talking about the state. Gellner was talking in the abstract about historical stages and the development of the state. He wrote "once none had the state, then some had it, and finally all have it": Gellner (2006), p. 5.

[16] I shall elaborate on this in the next chapter and in the conclusion, and it will be a recurring theme throughout the book.

[17] The institution of chattel slavery remained, of course, a pervasive institution in the US all the way up until 1861. But this did not mean that it could not be claimed that America was a land of freedom. I discuss the relationship of slavery and propertied freedom throughout this dissertation.

contrary, this book may be seen as Marxian materialist, and the materialism of its approach is based on changes in property regimes. Put crudely, it was the forms of property and the mode of production that made the idea of nationalism conceivable—it was not the idea of nationalism that conceived the mode of production and the property regime to which it corresponded.[18]

There were two major changes in property regimes during the time period that this book covers. The first change was the emergence of more widespread smallholding mentioned above—*the agrarian moment*. It was this that set the preconditions for the emergence of nationalism. The agrarian moment spawned what I have called *the first form of the nation*. The *first form of the nation* alludes to an agrarian society and an agrarian ideology of nationalism. There was a relatively small state, and the state was dominated by landed interests along with some commercial interests. The main political expression of this form was a landed democracy ideologically based on the sovereignty of the people. Because nationalism emerged in agrarian societies, it was a strengthening of landed private property rights that was the driving motor of nationalist development in this initial phase: the idea of sovereignty of the people became inseparably bound up with the political rule of the landowning class, and freedom inseparably bound up with the ownership of landed property. The second change was one away from an agricultural economy, which saw the rise of industrial property and capital—*the industrial moment*. The industrial moment led to a change in the form of the nation, or what I have called *the second form of the nation*. This alludes to a society and an ideology of nationalism that is in the process of industrialization. There are relatively more people working in wage-based jobs, and politics is increasingly dominated by professional politicians leading constituencies dominated by workers and city professionals. The state becomes bigger in this form, and the main political expression of this form is universal male suffrage, although in America I have exemplified this through the abolition of slavery.

With the coming of industrial society, there was what this book terms a *transvaluation of property*. This can also be stated as a shift from land

[18]Or as Marx and Engels put it in more abstract terms, talking about the relationship between consciousness and the material world: "life is not determined by consciousness, but consciousness by life." See Marx, Karl, and Frederick Engels, *The German Ideology*, Lawrence & Wishart, London (1970) [1846–1847], p. 47.

to labor as a principle of political inclusion, and it was driven by a shift in the property structure that saw the emergence of a proletariat (larger classes of wage earners) and thus a relative decline in ownership of landed property. The term *transvaluation*, was used by Liah Greenfeld in her study of nationalism, and she in turn got the term from Nietzsche. A transvaluation basically means a radical reevaluation of values—to turn them on their head.[19] What this refers to, specifically when speaking of *a transvaluation of property* in this book, is how propertied freedom went from being understood primarily as landed or real property to meaning property in one's labour. This was a transvaluation because after this change happened the individual was seen as free if he or she owned his or her own labour and/or had property in his or her person. Before the transvaluation, labourers without landed or real property were seen as dependent or unfree, on similar footing to that of a slave. The transvaluation adjusted the sovereignty and property concepts to include a broader stratum of people in political power: since the essential future of property was now understood to be the labour of the individual (instead of land), all who laboured were seen as free and could now partake in political power. In this way popular sovereignty became disconnected from landed property and connected instead to all the labouring individuals of the nation. This legitimized capitalist labour relations as all individuals were now seen as free by having property in one's labour, be it the propertied capitalist or the industrial wage labourer.

The Emergence of Nationalism and Landed Private Property

Theories of Nationalism and the Omission of Property

New theories of nationalism since Gellner released his book in 1983 have of course been produced, and it will be useful to place the argument of this book within this wider context too. This book focusses on claims to property rights by what can be understood as political actors. Similar approaches have been applied by scholars such as Michael Mann,

[19]The concept is used in Greenfeld (1993), p. 16. Nietzsche wrote about this concept: "there is a transvaluation of values, and the concepts 'true' and 'false' are forced to change places." See Nietzsche, Frederick, *The Antichrist*, Project Gutenberg EBook (2006), p. 8. http://archive.org/stream/theantichrist19322gut/19322.txt (accessed 06.03.2015).

Miroslav Hroch, and Eric Hobsbawm. Hobsbawm, in typical Marxian fashion, has stressed that nationalism is carried by the petit bourgeoisie and the bourgeoisie,[20] while Mann has specifically pointed to an alliance between modernizing traditional elites and the petit bourgeoisie.[21] Hroch has pointed out the more complex and diverse class composition of the carriers of national sentiment.[22] Similarly Mann again has pointed to the importance of a quite diverse middle class, careerists and professionals in the new state bureaucracies for the mid–nineteenth century consolidation of European nationalism.[23] All three of these theorists do indirectly, or sometimes arbitrarily, touch upon the subject of property ownership through their class analysis, or in discussions on capitalism and the development of the state. The approach taken in this book, however, differs from and expands upon the reflections of Mann, Hobsbawm, and Hroch because it focusses: (1) on property and nationalism as ideology; and (2) on the importance of different kinds of property regimes for the emergence and formation of that ideology. This book is not so much trying to identify which political actors are the carriers of nationalism, but to show how nationalism as ideology is constituted largely through assertions and assumptions about property—which are informed by something close to objective, structural changes in property regimes.

The Two Schools of Nationalism Studies

Since the 1970s a huge body of literature has been produced on the subject of nationalism.[24] This literature can be roughly divided into two main groups or schools based on how nationalism is viewed and understood: ethnosymbolists and modernists. These two views offer quite different and often conflicting ways of understanding nationalism; the

[20] Hobsbawm, Eric, *Nations and Nationalism Since 1780: Program, Myth, Reality*, Cambridge University Press, Cambridge (1992).

[21] Mann, Michael, *The Sources of Social Power, Vol. 2: The Rise of Classes and Nation States 1760–1914*, Cambridge University Press, Cambridge (1993).

[22] Hroch (1985).

[23] Mann (1993). For a good, clear and concise general overview of Mann and Hobsbawm see Hearn, Jonathan, *Rethinking Nationalism: A Critical Introduction*, Palgrave Macmillan, Basingstoke (2006), pp. 70–71 and 141–142.

[24] There is a good summary of the historiography of the research on nationalism in Hearn (2006).

ethnosymbolists tend to emphasize long-term cultural processes and attachment of meaning,[25] while modernists generally focus more on the constructed and purely modern (political, economic, etc.) nature of nationalism.[26] This book advances a modernist understanding of nationalism. Although, as will become evident, parts of the argument advanced have a slight ethnosymbolist quality to them, and can be described with reference to ethnosymbolists John Armstrong and Anthony Smith's understandings of nationalism. Two central concepts in these two scholars' understanding of nationalism are the concepts of *mythomoteurs* and *ethnie*. Armstrong uses the concept of *mythomoteur* to describe the myth that gives a nation its sense of purpose and which constitutes the symbolical core of the nation.[27] Smith advances a similar understanding to this by applying the concept of *ethnie*.[28] A key point with both these concepts is that the nation is seen to have a symbolical core constituted by a mythologized narrative about past peoples. In the cases investigated in this book the mythical element took the form of narratives of ancient freedoms based on ownership of property. The idea of ancient freedoms had different sources in the two cases: in colonial America it was the tradition of Anglo-Saxon freedoms inherited from the British tradition of

[25] For some such accounts see, for example: Armstrong, John, *Nations Before Nationalism*, University of North Carolina Press, Chapel Hill (1982); and Grosby, Steven, *Biblical Ideas of Nationality: Ancient and Modern*, Eisenbrauns, Winona Lake (2002). A medieval argument for the origins of nationalism is proposed in Hastings, Adrian, *The Construction of Nationhood: Ethnicity, Religion and Nationhood*, Cambridge University Press, Cambridge (1997). For an early modernist argument see Gorski, Philip S., "The mosaic moment: An early modernist critique of modernist theories of nationalism," *American Journal of Sociology*, Vol. 150, No. 5 (March, 2000), pp. 1459–1460.

[26] The classic account on nationalism and modern society is Gellner (2006). Some accounts focussing on nationalism and the state are: Mann (1993); Marx, Anthony, *Faith in Nation: Exclusionary Origins of Nationalism*, Oxford University Press, Oxford (2003); and Breuilly, John, *Nationalism and the State*, Manchester University Press, Manchester (1993). Karl Deutsch focussed on communication in Deutsch, Karl, *Nationalism and Social Communication: An Inquiry into the Foundations of Nationality*, New York (1953). Benedict Anderson is also a modernist and famous for his focus on print capitalism and for understanding the nation as an "imagined community." See Anderson, Benedict, *Imagined Communities: Reflections on the Origins and Spread of Nationalism*, Verso, London (2006) [1983].

[27] Armstrong (1982).

[28] Anthony Smith is the most prominent figure here. See, for example, Smith, Anthony, *National Identity*, Penguin, London (1991).

political thought that was invoked, while in Norway the ancient freedoms were based on historiographical traditions that suggested that there had existed a unique Nordic freedom in ancient times. In both cases these narratives became important for how the political national movement emerged. The way that these narratives were used, however, is perhaps more similar to how modernists Hobsbawm and Terrence Ranger describe the idea of *invented tradition*.[29] The idea of *invented tradition* implies more of a conscious and direct construction of traditions and myths for the purpose of legitimizing political national claims. In the cases presented in this book the historical narrative is not directly constructed, but it has a modern form and was used in a distinctly political ideological way as a mode of justifying certain material relations of property. Neither Armstrong, Smith, nor Hobsbawm and Ranger pay any attention to the role of private property rights in these narratives, or of property regimes for the importance of the emergence of such narratives. It seems to me that the property aspect is central to why such narratives emerge, as well as to how they are made up. More importantly, I think that this property rights element of nationalism makes it, although agrarian, fully modern.

The Coming of Modernity

The emergence of widespread private landed property and popular sovereignty emerged and could come to constitute nationalism only with the transformations that happened in the Western world from the sixteenth century onwards. Nationalism is not possible without the material and cognitive preconditions that developed there, and which were, it must be stressed, unique in the history of humanity.

Everybody knows of course that all societies and all historical epochs are unique in some sense. Nevertheless, it must be allowed, for analytical purposes, to impose models on social development so that we can speak of analogous historical developments: one can see the development of different places in relation to each other both spatially and temporally, and thus observe certain developments at certain points as novel or unique in relation to what has occurred before. For example, one might

[29] Hobsbawm, Eric, and Terrence Ranger, *The Invention of Tradition*, Cambridge University Press, Cambridge (1983).

apply the Marxian model with different modes of production, such as a slave economy, feudalism and capitalism; or one could use Ernest Gellner's model, operating with hunter–gatherer societies, agrarian, societies and industrial societies.[30] The point about the West is that it was the first place where material relations provided the basis for a transition or a transformation to industrial society.[31] Gellner writes about the uniqueness of this development:

> The event was unique: no imitative industrialization can be treated as an event of the same kind as the original industrialization, simply in [*sic*] virtue of the fact that all others were indeed imitative, were performed in the light of the now established knowledge that the thing could be done and had certain blatant conspicuous advantages.[32]

Gellner here points specifically to industrialization. This industrialization was the product of unique developments that had transformed Western Europe at least since the fifteenth century.[33] Changes in agrarian

[30]For the Marxian typology see, for example, Marx, Karl, and Frederick Engels, *The German Ideology*, Lawrence & Wishart, London (1970) [1846–1847], pp. 43–48. For Gellner's typology see, for example, Gellner, Ernest, *Plow, Sword and Book: The Structure of Human History*, Paladin, London (1988).

[31]It is of course a fundamental fact that this development could happen in the West only, or at least largely because of Western exploitation of large parts of the rest of the world in the early phases of this development. One interesting discussion of the interconnectedness of the process of modernization can be found in Wolf, Eric, *Europe and the People Without History*, University of California Press, Berkeley (1982). See also Wallerstein, Immanuel, *The Modern World-System: Capitalist Agriculture and the Origins of the European World-Economy*, Academic Press, New York (1974); and Wallerstein, Immanuel, *The Modern World-System: Mercantilism and the Consolidation of the European World-Economy*, Academic Press, New York (1980).

[32]Gellner (2006), p. 19.

[33]We could call the precondition for industrial society, as Weber did, "the spirit of capitalism." See Weber, Max, *The Protestant Ethic and the Spirit of Capitalism*, Routledge, London (2001) [1930]. But I must accentuate the importance in transformations of agrarian property regimes for this spirit to come about. This was pointed out in Wood, Ellen Meiksins, *The Pristine Culture of Capitalism: A Historical Essay on Old Regimes and Modern States*, Verso, London and New York (1991), pp. 2–11. Some reflections on changes in landed property regimes for the emergence of industrial society are given in Polanyi, Karl, *The Great Transformation*, Beacon Press, Boston (1957) [1944], pp. 68–76. The classic statement on this is of course to be found in one of Marx's many works. A simple and forceful statement can be found in Marx, Karl and Frederick Engels, *Manifesto of the Communist Party*, New York Labour News, New York (1908) [1848], although Marx did not properly recognize the agrarian landed developments of capitalism, as pointed out in Wood (1991), pp. 2–11.

property regimes might have been particularly important.[34] When I use Gellner's quote here, I see industrialization as a symptom of the unique material and cognitive developments that happened in the West, and which preceded industrialization: there had been everywhere hunter–gatherer societies, and everywhere traditional agrarian societies. In most places there had been various forms of dynastic or religious rule and roughly similar ways of organizing appropriation and property, but nowhere else did preconditions for industrial societies develop (or "sprout" in Marx's term).[35] There is general agreement that the changes that brought about the preconditions for industrial society started happening gradually in the West between the fifteenth and the eighteenth centuries, and that they comprise:

> Economic, political and cultural characteristics, uniting capitalism (what classical political economists liked to call commercial society), legal rational political authority (perhaps, but not necessarily, with a preference for its liberal democratic form), and technological progress – or "rationalization," in its various aspects as manifest in markets, states, secularism and scientific knowledge.[36]

This nexus of ideas and conditions constitute modernity, and it was as part of these developments that nationalism emerged and formed in symbiosis with private landed property. We can point especially to what Gellner calls the modern cognition. The modern is defined, says Gellner,

[34]See, for example, the classical Brenner debate in Aston, T.H., and C.H.E. Philpin, *The Brenner Debate: Agrarian Class Structure and Economic Development in Pre-industrial Europe*, Cambridge University Press, Cambridge (1985). I am also influenced by Wood (1991).

[35]I am aware that this is a complex and contested issue. It could, for example, point to industrialization of Indian textile industry in the seventeenth and eighteenth century. See Mukund, Kanakalatha, "Indian textile industry in 17th and 18th centuries: Structure, organisation and responses," *Economic and Political Weekly*, Vol. 22, No. 38 (1992), pp. 2057–2065; and Wolf (1982), pp. 287–288. It is nevertheless the case that it was in the West where capitalist development had the strongest impact on the whole of society at the earliest stage.

[36]Wood, Ellen Meiksins, *Liberty and Property: A Social History of Western Political Thought from the Renaissance to the Present* (2012), p. 2.

by "the vision of the world as homogeneous, subject to systematic, indiscriminate laws, and open to interminable exploration …" While the Old Worlds were:

> On the one hand, each of them, a cosmos: purposive, hierarchical "meaningful"; and on the other hand, not quite unified, consisting of subworlds, each with its own idiom and logic, not subsumable under a single overall orderliness.[37]

This he contrasts to the modern world:

> The New World was on the one hand morally inert, and on the other, unitary … nothing is inherently connected with anything else. The actual connection of this world can only be established by first separating in thought everything that can be separated.[38]

This modern way of seeing the world is crucial because it allows for the vision of society as secular and atomistic (that it can be broken down to component parts, which may be connected in various and, in theory, infinite ways). Only with this vision is it possible to conceive of a world where "the people" may be vested with ultimate sovereignty (not god), and where sovereignty of the people is seen as a composite of an (in theory) infinite number of individuals with the right to property—which is the central organizing principle of society.

Property as Sovereignty

There are certain central features of landed property that gave it its important role in the formation of nationalism in its first agrarian phase. We might note, contrary to what one might assume, that property is *not* primarily a thing (although, of course, landed property, in itself is a tangible thing), but rather a *right*.[39] It might be said that all societies

[37] Gellner (2006), pp. 22–23.

[38] Gellner (2006), pp. 22–23.

[39] I have derived my theories of property primarily from the following books: Macpherson, C.B., *Property: Mainstream and Critical Positions*, Blackwell, Oxford (1978); Macpherson, C.B., *The Political Theory of Possessive Individualism: Hobbes to Locke*, Clarendon Press, Oxford (1962); Hallowell, Irving, *Culture and Experience*, University of

must have some system of possession because it is necessary to organize relations between humans and things, and relations between humans. For the emergence of nationalism, though, it was the historically specific property *right* that came to be important. To have a right to private property is to have an individual, exclusive, enforceable claim to the use or benefit of something. There are two important implications of this: (1) private property is essentially a political claim and is thus different from possessions in that property is socially enforced by society or the state through laws, custom, or convention and (2) private property is a social relation, because private property implies the right of one person in relation to another—in other words A owns B against C. For these reasons, the right to property always implies a power relation; it represents an exclusionary relationship between individuals, and therefore makes the individual sovereign. This has been pointed out by thinkers from Rousseau onwards—and for Marx, for example, there was always an implicit relationship between property and power—but this relationship has perhaps most clearly been pointed out by the early–twentieth century American Lawyer Morris Cohen, who asserted that "property is sovereignty." Cohen explained:

> The essence of private property is always the right to exclude others … if, then, somebody else wants to use the food, the house, the land or the plough that the law calls mine, he has to get my consent. To the extent that these things are necessary to the life of my neighbor, the law thus confers on me power, limited but real, to make him do what I want. If Laban has the sole disposal of his daughters and his cattle, Jacob must serve him if he desires to possess them. In a regime where land is the principal source of livelihood, he who has the legal right over the land receives homage and service from those who wish to live on it … Property law does more. It determines what men shall acquire. Thus, protecting the property rights of a landlord means giving him the right to collect rent, protecting the property of a railroad or a public-service corporation means giving it the right to make certain charges. Hence the ownership of land and machinery, with

Pennsylvania Press (1955); Reeve, Andrew, *Property*, Macmillan, London (1986); Paul, Ellen Frankel, Fred D. Miller Jr., and Jeffery Paul, *Property Rights*, Cambridge University Press, Cambridge (1994); and Skinner, Quinten, and Peter Garnsey, *Thinking About Property: From Antiquity to the Age of Revolution*, Cambridge University Press, Cambridge (2007).

the rights of drawing rent, interest, etc., determines the future distributions of the good that will come into being.[40]

It is because the right to property confers these kinds of powers on individuals over those who do not have property that private property resembles sovereignty. It was largely for this reason that it became, in the national ideology of my cases, connected to individual freedom and popular sovereignty during the agrarian phase of modern development. In an agrarian world, self-ownership over landed property meant independence, power, and freedom: independence because it provided economic security, power because it gave control over resources, and freedom because there was no one laying bonds on the individual and his use of the land or the surplus produced from it. These three aspects are interwoven, related to the fundamental power structure of agrarian societies and based on the general connection between wealth and power.[41] There are, of course, forms of rule and domination that are not directly based on the accumulation of wealth, but economic interests and rule are almost always interrelated. Wealth is almost always the means by which more power may be acquired, either in the form of prestige or actual military or economic force. Since land, in agrarian societies, is by far the largest source of wealth, there is a strong connection between ownership of it and power.

There is also another way in which landed property is related to power and comes more directly to resemble sovereignty. Andrew Reeve has noted how landed property and state territory have a similarity:

Land provides the territorial dimension of the political unit. Modern states, at least, are defined in part by legal jurisdiction which they claim

[40] Cohen, Morris, "Property and sovereignty," in Macpherson (ed.) (1978), pp. 159–160.

[41] This proposed connection between wealth and government is a fairly standard one. Arendt, for example, claims that it goes back to antiquity: "The connection between wealth and government in any given country, and the insight that forms of government are interconnected with the distribution of wealth, the suspicion that political power may simply follow economic power ... all this is of course not the invention of Marx, nor for that matter Harrington: 'dominion is property, real or personal'; or of Rohan: the kings command the people and interests commands kings. If one wants to blame any single author for the so called materialist view of history, one must go as far back as Aristotle." See Arendt, Hannah, *On Revolution*, Penguin Books, London (1990) [1963], p. 22.

> over a particular territory ... land mediates, in this sense, between political power and individuals subject to it.[42]

Furthermore, landed property is concrete, fixed, and stable. It is for these reasons that the landowner has a particular interest in maintaining the state because landed property cannot be moved—the wealth in land is tied to a specific place, as opposed to the wealth of a merchant.[43] The fixity of landed wealth and its territorial dimension provides a direct link with political sovereignty in agrarian societies: the way in which most European medieval states grew from the landed property of kings is a case in point.[44] In addition to the sovereignty/power connection, Reeve notes also that landed property has a connection to freedom because all action has a spatial dimension; land may thus provide the spatial dimension for action. Metzer and Engerman have also noted this connection between property in land, sovereignty and nationalism through the kind of property-based democracy that the American and Norwegian nation-states established at their emergence. They write:

> While the ownership of land as prerequisite for enfranchisement has long been abandoned in modern democratic states ... this may reflect some kind of an accommodation between nationalism, whose basic attitude towards land as a place – a homeland belonging to the nationals – made the thinking often blur the distinction between sovereignty and ownership.[45]

The idea of a connection between ownership and sovereignty is not, however, new—there has indeed for a long time in Western thought been posed a connection between ownership and freedom through sovereignty. Arendt has written about property in land and its connection to power and freedom in the Greek world. "Man," she writes, "could liberate himself from necessity only through power over other men, and he

[42]Reeve (1986), p. 82.

[43]According to Reeve, this is a point made at least as early as Adam Smith: Reeve (1986), p. 82.

[44]For two good analyses of the development of the modern state see Poggi, Gianfranco, *The Development of the Modern State: A Sociological Introduction*, Hutchinson, London (1978); and Rokkan, Stein, *Stat, Nasjon, Klasse: essays I politisk sosiologi*, Universitetsforlaget, Oslo (1987), pp. 268–381.

[45]Engerman, Stanley, and Jacob Metzer (eds.), *Land Rights, Ethno-nationality, and Sovereignty in History*, Routledge, London (2004), p. 10.

could be free only if he owned a place, a home in the world."[46] This may be oversimplified and is probably not applicable to dominant thought on property and freedom today, but it does point to the general connection between ownership of landed property and power/sovereignty. Indeed, Reeve similarly notes that there are three power relations connected to property rights in general: economical power, dominion over others and various forms of authority.[47] Historically, all these aspects have been present in the ownership of landed property. Therefore landed property and political power (sovereignty) historically have gone hand in hand, from Greek and Roman democracy, to European feudalism, to the early, modern, Western property-based national democracies. In short, there is both an historical and a conceptual connection between nationalism and private property rights through the concept of territorial sovereignty. There is also though, as we have seen, both an historical connection going back to antiquity and a conceptual connection between private property and individual freedom.

Due to these connections, landed property came to be seen as indispensable to individual freedom and the constitution of sovereignty. The national identity of Americans and Norwegians was to be propertied men,[48] and thus free men (they were indeed primarily men). It might be useful to invoke Isaiah Berlin's two forms of liberty here to say what this freedom meant.[49] The members of the national movement in my cases were concerned both with negative and with positive freedom. The right to property, because it is an exclusive right, immediately brings in the concept of negative freedom, but it is important to understand that this was seen as a precondition for positive freedom. It was seen as crucial in the national ideology that no one could, without consent, interfere in the exclusive sphere of the individual granted by the right to property. When this right was secured, the right to property was seen as conferring

[46] Reeve (1986), p. 81.

[47] Reeve (1986), p. 80.

[48] This view assumes that national identity as such is not really important, essential or fixed, rather what matters is the ideological imperatives in nationalism, and the incentives and meanings it creates. This view of nationalism was elaborated and asserted in Malesevic, Sinisa, "The chimera of national identity," *Nations and Nationalism*, Vol. 17, No. 2 (2011).

[49] Berlin, Isaiah, "Two concepts of liberty," in Henry Hardy (ed.), *Liberty*, Oxford University Press, Oxford (2002).

on individuals a positive freedom to act in the world, to realize one's own will. We might say that the freedom derived from property was an ontological freedom, it was essential and it was what made someone a full and whole individual. To have property was, as it were, an essential property of being. If one did not have property, then one was not fully a human being—one *was* not,[50] because one had no material means to realize oneself and to be independent. I do not wish to exaggerate this aspect or elevate this to a mystical, metaphysical level, but I do want to accentuate that the right to property became fundamental in the understanding of what it meant to be a national citizen, which was seen to be, above anything else, a free, propertied man. It must be stressed that this vision was in large part produced by the fact of widespread ownership of land in the US and Norway—this was a reality in which it made sense to speak of property as a fundamental right of all men.

Liberal and Marxian Paradoxes

At this point it is appropriate to explain how the book came to focus on property rights, and to seek the origins of nationalism and its relationship to private property in the property assumptions of the late–eighteenth and early–nineteenth century agrarian societies of the US and Norway. The questions that led this book to these societies in this time period were informed by the period of industrialization and democratization in the late nineteenth and early twentieth century. The book starts from two paradoxes, one in liberal theory and one in Marxist theory.

Liberal Paradox: Property and Democracy

From a liberal standpoint, there is a paradox in the way in which the ideological and conceptual relationship between property and popular sovereignty changed from the nineteenth to the twentieth century within

[50]We might relate this to the idea of "social death." Not to have property was to be sub-human, a slave, to be socially dead. See Patterson, Orlando, *Slavery and Social Death: A Comparative Study*, Harvard University Press, Cambridge (1982). This is also the basis for C.B. Macpherson's theory of possessive individualism. Macpherson writes: "the individual in possessive market society *is* human in his capacity as proprietor of his own person; his humanity does depend on his freedom from any but self-interested contractual relations with others." See Macpherson (1962), pp. 271–272. This idea will become more evident throughout the book, as propertied freedom was consistently contrasted with slavery and understood in different ways.

the nation-states of the West. Norway and the US exemplify this. The political constitutions of the US and Norway, in the agrarian phase under which they first became nation-states, makes them clear examples of states where private property and popular participation in government were seen to be in tension, and where the preservation of landed property was one of the most central goals of politics. These assumptions took the form of a landed property-based democracy where landless individuals were largely excluded from political power—here, landless people represented a danger to the stability of private property and had to be excluded from power. When, however, the US and Norway became industrializing societies, the relationship between property and popular sovereignty became reversed: universal suffrage (at the time understood as male suffrage) and private property came to be seen as interdependent. This paradox was identified by Gøran Therborn as one between property and democracy:

> In the nineteenth and early twentieth centuries, as both political practice and constitutional debate clearly demonstrate, prevailing bourgeois opinion held that democracy and capitalism (or private property) were incompatible ... In modern times, however, since at least the outbreak of the Cold War, bourgeois ideologists have maintained that only capitalism is compatible with democracy.[51]

I would like to invoke a quote from Walter Benjamin (from the 1930s) which inspired much of my initial thinking on this. Benjamin asserted in the age of fascism that:

> Fascism attempts to organize the newly created proletarian masses without affecting the property structure which the masses strive to eliminate. Fascism sees its salvation in giving these masses not their right, but instead a chance to express themselves.[52]

Although this quote concerns nationalism in its interwar fascist form specifically, it made me wonder if there was a connection between nationalism in general and the perseverance of private property. Was it the case

[51] Therborn, Gøran, "The rule of capital and the rise of democracy," *New Left Review*, Vol. 1, No. 103 (May/June, 1977).

[52] Benjamin, Walter, "The work of art in the age of mechanical reproduction" (1936). https://www.marxists.org/reference/subject/philosophy/works/ge/benjamin.htm (accessed 17.06.2015).

that nationalism gave the masses only an ideological semblance of power while keeping wealth concentrated in a few hands by private property holdings?

Marxian Paradox: The Nation-State and "The Rights of Man"

There is also a Marxian paradox connected to the existence of private property and the nation-state. According to classical Marxist theory, the nation-state and private property should not have the enduring legitimacy that they have[53]; on the contrary, class antagonism in capitalism should bring about a proletarian world revolution that would grant freedom to all and abolish nations and private property. History has shown, however, that the masses have not strived to eliminate the national property structure as, for example, Benjamin thought—instead the masses have accepted, as it were, the offer to "express themselves" (in Benjamin's term) through the nation, even without the spell of fascism. It has been through the nation-state with a private property regime and liberal democracy that the individual has seen his or her freedom and rights fulfilled and guarded. Hannah Arendt observed that in the world of nation-states, "Man, it turns out, can lose all the so-called Rights of Man without losing his essential quality as a man, his human dignity. Only the loss of a polity itself expels him from humanity."[54] This points to something fundamental about the legitimacy of the nation form and its formation throughout history: it has been established as practically the only real guarantor of rights and freedoms of the individual, and, at least in the Western world, these rights have come to be seen as inseparable from the right to private property. So, if it is true, as Harold Laski once put it (and as Benjamin hinted at), that there is an "antithesis between property rights and the fulfillment of the democratic idea," because "political power is the handmaid of economic power" and that "a mere ballot box democracy is, as a consequence, utterly unreal in the presence of large inequalities of property,"[55] then one can wonder why

[53]Greenfeld, Liah, "Trancending the nation's worth," *Daedalus*, Vol. 122. No. 3 (1993) offers an interesting discussion of this issue.

[54]Arendt, Hannah, *The Origins of Totalitarianism*, Meridian Books, Cleveland and New York (1958), p. 197.

[55]Quoted in Townshend, Jules, *C.B Macpherson and the Problem of Liberal Democracy*, Edinburgh University Press, Edinburgh (2000), pp. 8–9.

such states are so widely accepted. Indeed as Thomas Piketty has recently shown, contemporary, Western nation-states are marked by increasing inequalities in distribution of wealth based on ownership of private property.[56] It is true that there have been other alternatives to the liberal nation form, especially in the twentieth century with its fascist and communist states; and still today there exist totalitarian states both religious and secular in form. Yet, there is some truth to Francis Fukuyama's infamous "end of history" thesis, in that the bourgeois liberal nation-state with a private property regime is today the most prevalent political form on the globe.[57]

Why Nationalism?

It seemed to me that an investigation into the relationship between nationalism and private property rights could provide useful insights into the above-described paradoxes, and, indeed, it led me to assert a new theory of nationalism. Admittedly, there arises a question of what to call the beast, so to speak. I have said that what this book investigates and explicates is nationalism. One could ask: why not call it republicanism, or liberalism... why is this nationalism? It will become evident to the reader who knows these two traditions of thought (republicanism and liberalism) that what is put forward in the following pages has resemblances to both. Indeed, one might also say, with a considerable amount of strength, that nationalism is something else entirely than what is described in the following pages. To these accusations I answer that this book proposes a new concept of nationalism. The book goes back to what I see as nationalism's origins and follows an aspect of its development previously neglected. This is why what is described in these pages may not sound like nationalism as traditionally described, and it is also why what is described has similarities to republicanism and liberalism—because this book sees the origins of nationalism as a fusion of aspects of these traditions with specific material realities in a specific historical moment.

[56] Piketty, Thomas, *Capital in the Twenty-First Century*, Belknap Press, Cambridge, MA and London (2014).

[57] Fukuyama, Francis, *The End of History and the Last Man*, Free Press, New York (1992).

Nationalism is understood in this book as an historical, unfolding concept, to be found in a range of actions, thoughts and discourses formed at specific times, as well as manifest in institutions and traditions. We can invoke Max Weber's understanding of capitalism in *The Protestant Ethic and the Spirit of Capitalism*. Here, Weber understood capitalism as a "complex of elements associated in historical reality which we unite into a conceptual whole."[58] Such an historical concept:

> Must be gradually put together out of the individual parts which are taken from historical reality to make it up. Thus the final and definitive concept cannot stand at the beginning of the investigation, but must come at the end.[59]

Applied in this book, this means that I look at various parts (specifically property and sovereignty, and concepts derived from or connected to these) that make up nationalism over time, and trying to see certain trends or defining principles. It follows from this that I see nationalism primarily as ideology, in a similar vein as the nationalism scholar Sinisa Malesevic, as a:

> social process through which human actors articulate their actions and beliefs … human beings rely on existing ideological maps and concepts to decipher the meaningful interpretations of these events and facts … ideological narratives impose structure and provide coherence to what otherwise would be incoherent and utterly contingent images, events and acts. So ideology is a process that incorporates thinking and action whereby our behaviour is dependent on (but not determined by) ideologically articulated cognitive maps.[60]

Viewed historically, this means to see nationalism as an emergent phenomena. In the words of Liah Greenfeld—nationalism as:

> "An emergent phenomenon", that is, a phenomenon whose nature – as well as the possibilities of its development and the possibilities of the developments of which [it] is composed – is determined not by the character

[58] Weber (1992), p. 13.

[59] Weber (1992), p. 13.

[60] Malesevic, Sinisa, "The chimera of national identity," *Nations and Nationalism*, Vol. 17, No. 2 (2011), p. 283.

> of any of its elements, but by a certain organizing principle which makes these elements into a unity and imparts them a special significance.[61]

Furthermore:

> In the case of emergent social phenomena, which are structurally parallel to the phenomena of life, we can answer the question of what brings elements together, and why, and discover the unifying principle, if we choose to do so.[62]

In the course of the investigations that led up to this book, I came to hold private property and its connection to popular sovereignty and individual freedom as the "organizing principle" of national ideology.

In the quest for the organizing principle of nationalism, this book applies the method of discourse analysis of key historical documents, setting them in their historical context.[63] It is appropriate here to note the limitations of such an approach—the focus of this book is on the formation of an ideology as read from sources and interpreted against the background of the material reality in which they were written; what this book does not so much take into account is the possible influence on the emergence of the ideology from political and military events—although such events do serve as a frame for the analysis. This book has chosen a narrower focus. My primary interest has been in the ideology of nationalism itself, its anatomy, and its genealogy, so to speak. Therefore, the focus has been mostly on the content of the ideology and the aspects of the historical context most immediately relating to it. It has been my intention to understand nationalism from a sociological viewpoint, pointing to how interactions between individuals—and between individuals and their material context—form specific patterns of ideas and intuitions. As explained by Ellen Meiksins Wood:

> Human beings enter into relations with each other and with nature to guarantee their own survival and social reproduction. To understand the

[61] Greenfeld, Liah, *Nationalism: Five Roads to Modernity*, Harvard University Press, Cambridge (1993), p. 7.

[62] Greenfeld (1993), notes to pp. 7–13, particularly note 4.

[63] For a good example of this method see Skinner, Quentin, "Meaning and understanding in the history of ideas," *History and Theory*, Vol. 8, No. 1 (1969), p. 53.

> social practices and cultural products of any time and place, we need to know something about those conditions of survival and social reproduction, something about the specific ways in which people gain access to the material conditions of life, about how some people gain access to the labour of others, about relations between people who produce and those who appropriate what others produce, about the forms of property that emerge from these social relations, and about how these relations are expressed in political domination, as well as in resistance and struggle.[64]

In trying to explore nationalism and private property, I have focussed on these relations within the US and Norway, and not so much on the political, diplomatic, and military events surrounding this. I have found such a non-political/non-military approach most useful in trying to present nationalism as a property rights ideology. This focus also leaves out ethnic and cultural elements, because such elements were simply not part of the property rights discourse (although such elements were certainly part of the broader ideology). Nationalism, as presented here, might thus look different from standard political (and cultural) understandings of it, but it *is* nationalism; or at least that is what this book shall try to convince the reader of in the course of the following chapters. It is, however, of course, the reader who ultimately has to judge if this endeavor has been successful or not.

Literature

Anderson, Benedict, *Imagined Communities: Reflections on the Origins and Spread of Nationalism*, Verso, London (2006) [1983].

Anthony, *National Identity*, Penguin, London (1991).

Arendt, Hannah, *The Origins of Totalitarianism*, Meridian Books, Cleveland and New York (1958).

Arendt, Hannah, *On Revolution*, Penguin Books, London (1990) [1963].

Armstrong, John, *Nations Before Nationalism*, University of North Carolina Press, Chapel Hill (1982).

Aston, T.H., and C.H.E. Philpin, *The Brenner Debate: Agrarian Class Structure and Economic Development in Pre-industrial Europe*, Cambridge University Press, Cambridge (1985).

[64]Wood, Ellen Meiksins, *Citizens to Lords: A Social History of Western Political Thought from Antiquity to the Late Middle Ages*, Verso, London (2008), p. 12.

Benjamin, Walter, "The work of art in the age of mechanical reproduction" (1936). https://www.marxists.org/reference/subject/philosophy/works/ge/benjamin.htm (accessed 17.06.2015).

Berlin, Isaiah, "Two concepts of liberty," in Henry Hardy (ed.), *Liberty*, Oxford University Press, Oxford (2002).

Buck-Morss, Susan, "Hegel and Haiti," *Critical Inquiry*, Vol. 26, No. 4 (Summer, 2000).

Breuilly, John, *Nationalism and the State*, Manchester University Press, Manchester (1993).

Deutsch, Karl, *Nationalism and Social Communication: An Inquiry into the Foundations of Nationality*, MIT Press, New York (1953).

Ellickson, Robert C., and Charles Thorland, "Ancient Land Law, Mesopotamia, Egypt, Israel," *Yale Law School Legal Scholarship Repository* (01.01.1995).

Engerman, Stanley, and Jacob Metzer (eds.), *Land Rights, Ethno-nationality, and Sovereignty in History*, Routledge, London (2004).

Fukuyama, Francis, *The End of History and the Last Man*, Free Press, New York (1992).

Gellner, Ernest, *Nations and Nationalism*, Blackwell, Oxford (2006) [1983].

Gellner, Ernest, *Plow, Sword and Book: The Structure of Human History*, Paladin, London (1988).

Gellner, Ernest, "The coming of nationalism and its interpretation: The myths of nation and class," in Gopal Balakrishnan (ed.), *Mapping the Nation*, Verso, London (1999) [1996].

Gorski, Philip S., "The mosaic moment: An early modernist critique of modernist theories of nationalism," *American Journal of Sociology*, Vol. 150, No. 5 (March, 2000).

Greenfeld, Liah, "Transcending the nation's worth," *Daedalus*, Vol. 122, No. 3 (1993).

Greenfeld, Liah, *Nationalism: Five Roads to Modernity*, Harvard University Press, Cambridge (1993).

Grosby, Steven, *Biblical Ideas of Nationality: Ancient and Modern*, Eisenbrauns, Winona Lake (2002).

Hallowell, Irving, *Culture and Experience*, University of Pennsylvania Press (1955).

Hastings, Adrian, *The Construction of Nationhood: Ethnicity, Religion and Nationhood*, Cambridge University Press, Cambridge (1997).

Hroch, Miroslav, *Social Preconditions of National Revival in Europe: A Comparative Analysis of the Social Composition of Patriotic Groups in the Smaller European Nations*, Cambridge University Press, Cambridge (1985).

Hearn, Jonathan, *Rethinking Nationalism: A Critical Introduction*, Palgrave Macmillan, Basingstoke (2006).

Hearn, Jonathan, "The origins of modern nationalism in the North Atlantic interaction sphere," *Sociological Review Online*, Vol. 14, No. 5 (2009).

Hobsbawm, Eric, *The Age of Revolution: Europe 1789–1848*, Weidenfeld & Nicolson, London (1962).

Hobsbawm, Eric, *Nations and Nationalism Since 1780: Program, Myth, Reality*, Cambridge University Press, Cambridge (1992).

Hobsbawm, Eric, and Terrence Ranger, *The Invention of Tradition*, Cambridge University Press, Cambridge (1983).

Kohn, Hans, *The Idea of Nationalism: A Study in Its Origins and Background*, Transaction Publishers, New Brunswick (2005) [1944].

Macpherson, C.B., *The Political Theory of Possessive Individualism: Hobbes to Locke*, Clarendon Press, Oxford (1962).

Macpherson, C.B., *Property: Mainstream and Critical Positions*, Blackwell, Oxford (1978).

Malesevic, Sinisa, "The chimera of national identity," *Nations and Nationalism*, Vol. 17, No. 2 (2011).

Mann, Michael, *The Sources of Social Power, Vol. 2: The Rise of Classes and Nation States 1760–1914*, Cambridge University Press, Cambridge (1993).

Marx, Anthony, *Faith in Nation: Exclusionary Origins of Nationalism*, Oxford University Press, Oxford (2003).

Marx, Karl, and Frederick Engels, *Manifesto of the Communist Party*, New York Labour News, New York (1908) [1848].

Marx, Karl, and Frederick Engels, *The German Ideology*, Lawrence & Wishart, London (1970) [1846–1847].

Merriman, John, *A History of Modern Europe: From the Renaissance to the Present*, W. W. Norton & Co., New York and London (1996).

Mukund, Kanakalatha, "Indian textile industry in 17th and 18th centuries: Structure, organisation and responses," *Economic and Political Weekly*, Vol. 22, No. 38 (1992).

Nietzsche, Frederick, *The Antichrist*, Project Gutenberg EBook (2006), p. 8. http://archive.org/stream/theantichrist19322gut/19322.txt (accessed 06.03.2015).

Palmer, R.R., *The Age of Democratic Revolution: A Political History of Europe and America*, Vol. 1, Princeton University Press, Princeton and London (1959).

Palmer, R.R., *The Age of Democratic Revolution: A Political History of Europe and America*, Vol. 2, Princeton University Press, Princeton and London (1964).

Patterson, Orlando, *Slavery and Social Death: A Comparative Study*, Harvard University Press, Cambridge (1982).

Paul, Ellen Frankel, Fred D. Miller Jr., and Jeffery Paul, *Property Rights*, Cambridge University Press, Cambridge (1994).

Piketty, Thomas, *Capital in the Twenty-First Century*, Belknap Press, Cambridge, MA and London (2014).
Poggi, Gianfranco, *The Development of the Modern State: A Sociological Introduction*, Hutchinson, London (1978).
Polanyi, Karl, *The Great Transformation*, Beacon Press, Boston (1957) [1944].
Reeve, Andrew, *Property*, Macmillan, London (1986).
Rokkan, Stein, *Stat, Nasjon, Klasse: essays I politisk sosiologi*, Universitetsforlaget, Oslo (1987).
Skocpol, Theda, and Margaret Somers, "The use of comparative history in macro social inquiry," *Comparative Studies in Society and History*, Vol. 22 (1980).
Sejersted, Francis, *Demokrati og rettsstat*, Pax Forlag, Oslo (2002).
Skard, Sigmund, *USA i Norsk historie, 1000–1776–1976*, Det Norske Samlaget, Oslo (1976).
Skinner, Quentin, "Meaning and understanding in the history of ideas," *History and Theory*, Vol. 8, No. 1 (1969).
Skinner, Quentin, and Peter Garnsey, *Thinking About Property: From Antiquity to the Age of Revolution*, Cambridge University Press, Cambridge (2007).
Therborn, Gøran, "The rule of capital and the rise of democracy," *New Left Review*, Vol. 1, No. 103 (May/June, 1977).
Townshend, Jules, *C.B. Macpherson and the Problem of Liberal Democracy*, Edinburgh University Press, Edinburgh (2000).
Tilly, Charles, *Big Structures, Large Processes, Huge Comparisons*, Russell Sage Foundation, New York (1984).
Wallerstein, Immanuel, *The Modern World-System: Capitalist Agriculture and the Origins of the European World-Economy*, Academic Press, New York (1974).
Wallerstein, Immanuel, *The Modern World-System: Mercantilism and the Consolidation of the European World-Economy*, Academic Press, New York (1980).
Weber, Max, *The Protestant Ethic and the Spirit of Capitalism*, Routledge, London (2001) [1930].
Wolf, Eric, *Europe and the People Without History*, University of California Press, Berkeley (1982).
Wood, Ellen Meiksins, *The Pristine Culture of Capitalism: A Historical Essay on Old Regimes and Modern States*, Verso, London and New York (1991).
Wood, Ellen Meiksins, *Citizens to Lords: A Social History of Western Political Thought from Antiquity to the Late Middle Ages*, Verso, London (2008).
Wood, Ellen Meiksins, *Liberty and Property: A Social History of Western Political Thought from the Renaissance to the Present* (2012).

PART I

Agrarian Moment: Land and Freedom

The first part of the book deals with the agrarian moment of this history of nationalism in the US and Norway. The time period covered is roughly the years between 1760 and 1815. Within this time period both the elite of the American colonies and in the Kingdom of Norway declared independence from the empires to which they had belonged for centuries. This was based on an ideology of nationalism, which was, at the time, a novelty. In the course of this part of the book, I seek to show how the new ideology of nationalism emerged as a powerful political force in the landed, agrarian societies of colonial America and Oldenburg Norway. The main focus of Part I will be on demonstrating how landed property relations in the two societies were important for how the national ideology formed.

After a short general introduction to theagrarian world of the late eighteenth and early nineteenth century, Chapter 2 starts by looking at the American colonies. The peculiar property relations of colonial America that was marked by widespread ownership of land will be noted, and then the discussion moves on to the imperial crisis between the colonies and the imperial capital of London. There will be a focus on how key public figures asserted the property rights of colonial Americans, and how they came to connect this to the idea of popular sovereignty and, finally, to national independence. Main events covered will be the Declaration of Independence and the Constitutional Convention.

Next, Chapter 3 moves east across the Atlantic to Norway. As with the American colonies, the chapter on Norway starts by establishing the relatively widespread ownership of land in Norway. Then the text moves on to discuss the relationship between the Kingdom of Norway and the Oldenburg/Danish Empire to which the Kingdom of Norway belonged, and from which the country was ruled. The chapter then moves on to discuss how events in the Napoleonic war spawned the Norwegian movement for independence. There will be a discussion of key public figures, and a discussion on how they, like in America, asserted special Norwegian rights to property and connected this to popular sovereignty and to national independence. The main events covered will be Prince Christian Frederik's campaign for an independence movement and a constitutional assembly.

The key point here will be to emphasize how similar the developments in these two societies were. Such a similarity allows us to come up with a theory of the nature and emergence of nationalism as an agrarian, landed phenomenon.

The Agrarian Context for the Emergence of Nationalism in the American Colonies and Norway

Nationalism in the US and Norway formed during the eighteenth and nineteenth century. It is important to remember, as Eric Hobsbawm pointed out long before the study of nationalism became fashionable, that this time period was an age of agriculture. It was a world where the vast majority of wealth came from agricultural production, and where agriculture constituted the livelihood of more than 90% of the people of Europe and America. The major form of property was thus land, and therefore "what happened to land determined the life and death of human beings."[1] There were in this time period various ways in which landed property was organized: from the viewpoint of agrarian property relations, writes Hobsbawm, it makes sense to divide the Western Hemisphere in this time period into three large segments.[2] There were the European colonies which were, with the exception of the northern part of the British North American colonies, primarily slave driven. Eastern Europe (and parts of Spain and Italy) might be classified as a

[1] Hobsbawm, Eric, *The age of Revolution: Europe 1789–1848*, Wiendfeld and Nicholson, London (1962), p. 149.

[2] Hobsbawm (1962), pp. 13–18.

second segment where agriculture was done by serfs who were politically and economically unfree. While the distinction in dignity and wealth was not as great as that between slave and master, the difference in power and wealth was still enormous between landlords/aristocrats on one side and cultivators of the soil on the other. The unfree cultivators constituted the bulk of the population in this segment, while a small majority owned the bulk of the land—and ownership of land gave titles, privileges and rank which formed the basis of a social reality of great distinctions. This was similar to the third segment, which covered Western Europe, but here the cultivators of the land had relatively more economical freedom, although landlords were a pervasive feature. In this segment, property in land had gradually emerged as an individual economic right, often decupled from aristocratic privilege and power.[3] It was in this segment that private landed property first became cemented as an economic right, thus also separating it from political, extra-economic powers, such as legal sovereignty. Ellen Meiksins Wood suggested that one of the most distinguished and decisive features of Western development since antiquity is a strong distinction between two sources of power: the state and private property. I will quote at some length from Wood to elaborate on this:

> developments in what would be Western Europe, with roots in Greco-Roman antiquity and especially the Western Roman Empire, gave property, as a distinct locus of power, an unusual degree of autonomy from the state ... [Rome] achieved imperial expansion without a strong state, governed instead by amateurs, an oligarchy of landed aristocrats, in a small city-state with minimal government. While peasants were part of the civic community, they remained subordinate to the propertied classes ... The Roman Empire represents the first known example of a strong imperial state combined with strong private property. This powerful, if sometimes uneasy, partnership is expressed in the Roman concepts of ***imperium*** and ***dominium*** The Roman concept of ***dominium***, when applied to private property, articulates with exceptional clarity the idea of private, exclusive and individual ownership, with all the powers it entails, while the ***imperium*** defines

[3]The issue of land and class relations in western Europe is complex, for a slightly more in depth and detailed overview than that of Hobsbawm, see Aston, T.H and Philipin C.H.E., The Brenner debate: agrarian class structure and Economic Development in Pre-industrial Europe, Cambridge University Press, Cambridge (1985).

> the right of command attached to certain civil magistrates, and eventually the emperor himself.[4]

In short, the uniqueness of Rome was that there existed a clear distinction between *imperium* and *dominium*, where *imperium* gave those possessing it strong exclusive rights and powers over things and people vis-à-vis the emperor.

One can trace the relationship between *dominium* and *imperium* in the West all the way up until the modern era. After the fall of the Western Roman Empire in the fifth century, the application of these concepts resulted in what Perry Anderson has called the parcellization of sovereignty in much of Western Europe. This was a situation where political power became fragmented and tied to a complicated chain of dependencies, rights, and dues. A central state with any power of *imperium* on the scale of the Roman Empire had long not existed in Europe, and political power was exercised by local landlords through *dominium* from ownership of landed property, which also gave the owner economic power over landless peasants. The parcellization of sovereignty thus invested property with public powers, and this gave property both political (*imperium*) and private economical (*dominium*) functions. Property also became less exclusive as many people could have overlapping rights to the same land.[5] Thus the distinction between *imperium* and *dominium* also became blurred. This is what was normally called feudalism, and it is precisely this parcellization of sovereignty and the infusion of political rights ("extra economic cohesion" in the terms of Anderson[6]) into landed property that defines feudalism.

During the sixteenth and seventeenth centuries the distinction between *imperium* and *dominium* became stronger again as absolutist states emerged in Western Europe. A depoliticization of property happened, making it strictly an economic right.[7] At the outset of the

[4]Wood, Ellen Meiksins, Liberty and Property: A social history of western political though from the renaissance to the present, Verso, London (2012), pp. 6–7.

[5]Anderson, Perry, Passages from antiquity to Feudalism, New Left Books, London (1974), pp. 147–197. Wood, Ellen Meiksins, Citizens to lords, a social history of western political though from antiquity to the late medieval ages, Verso, London (2008), pp. 164–176.

[6]Anderson (1974), p. 147.

[7]Anderson, Perry, Lineages of the Absolutist State, Verso, London (1974), pp. 15–42.

modern era we have, instead of *imperium* and *dominium,* the concepts of *sovereignty* and *property.* The most fundamental difference between *imperium* and *dominium*, on one side, and sovereignty and property, on other, is that the latter two were universalistic concepts. The nature of *imperium* and *dominium*, with its legacy continued from the Roman world into the Middle Period, had been particularistic and hierarchically organized. Even the *imperium* of the Roman Empire was not universal and abstract (so that it encompassed all domains within the Empire). The *imperium* of the Empire was precisely that—it was concerned with political issues and the military power of the empire, but was also specifically connected to the institution or the person of the emperor, not to any abstract idea of "the state" that constituted an all-encompassing sphere of its own. Hence, the *dominium* that landlords had was relatively autonomous from the *imperium* of the emperor, and there was an important distinction between public and private law. At the same time, *dominium* was not for all: Roman law distinguished between *homo* and *civis*, the latter term describing an unfree slave—a person who could have no *dominium* under the civil law. Others, however, could have *dominium* over them. This notion was the same for slavery and the feudal bonds of subordination,[8] and *dominium* was a force in opposition to *imperium.* With the emergence of modern sovereignty in the age of absolutism this started to change. The sovereignty of the monarch became, at least in theory, absolute, and it encompassed all spheres and aspects of society: sovereignty became the state, and everybody became subject to the same laws. As Blandine Krigel writes, it was seen to be:

> The antithesis of feudal power, in the sense that it was neither *imperium* nor *dominium.* It was not an *imperium* because it was not based on military power; and it was not *dominium,* because it did not institute a relation of subjection, in the manner of the relation between master and slave.[9]

This kind of sovereignty is different from *imperium* because it is primarily about administrative authority of the whole state:

[8] Krigel, Blandine, "The rule of the State and natural Law" in Hunter, Ian and David Saunders, Natural Law and Civil Sovereignty: Moral Right and State Authority in Early Modern Political Thought , Palgrave Macmillam, New York (2002), p. 19.

[9] Krigel, in Hunter and Saunders (2002), p. 15.

> Sovereignty is first and foremost the absolute autonomy of the state … the sovereign state increasingly affirms the priority of domestic politic over foreign policy … the first duty of the state becomes good administration. The delivery of good justice across the whole "square field" or "pre carre."[10]

This dismantles ***dominium*** because it disconnects property from political/public powers: "Arbitration of conflicts through law directly undermines the pre-eminence of the ***dominium***; it leads to complete severance of the link between power and property."[11]

These developments prepared important ground for the emergence of nationalism and nation-states. In fact, this book suggests they were a precondition for these developments. Thus, nationalism and nation-states emerged early on in this Western European segment of agrarian relations. The very first nation-state to emerge however—the United States—was not strictly speaking placed within this geographical segment, although it was placed in a sociological and political extension of that segment, and with a very peculiar landed property structure of relatively widespread individual ownership. The last part, widespread ownership of land, became one of the most important formative factors of pristine agrarian nationalism, and it was also a determining factor for the very emergence of nationalism. Chapter 2 will now look at the peculiarities of colonial American society, and the property structure upon which it was erected. Then it will look at the structure of American nationalism as an ideology. Afterwards, in Chapter 3 we shall see that despite some differences similar conditions were also to be found in Norway and provided fertile ground for the growth of nationalism, similar in form to that of America.

Literature

Anderson, Perry, *Passages from Antiquity to Feudalism*, New Left Books, London (1974).

Anderson, Perry, *Lineages of the Absolutist State*, Verso, London (1974).

Aston, T.H. and C.H.E. Philpin, *The Brenner Debate: Agrarian Class Structure and Economic Development in Pre-industrial Europe*, Cambridge University Press, Cambridge (1985).

[10] Krigel, in Hunter and Saunders (2002), p. 15.

[11] Krigel, in Hunter and Saunders (2002), p. 17.

Hobsbawm, Eric, *The Age of Revolution: Europe 1789–1848*, Weidenfeld & Nicolson, London (1962).

Krigel, Blandine, "The rule of the state and natural law" in Ian Hunter and David Saunders (eds.), *Natural Law and Civil Sovereignty: Moral Right and State Authority in Early Modern Political Thought*, Palgrave Macmillan, New York (2002).

Wood, Ellen Meiksins, *Citizens to Lords: A Social History of Western Political Thought from Antiquity to the Late Middle Ages*, Verso, London (2008).

Wood, Ellen Meiksins, *Liberty and Property: A Social History of Western Political Thought from the Renaissance to the Present*, Verso, London (2012).

CHAPTER 2

America: "Destined to Let Freedom Grow"

The character and origins of American society has, ever since Columbus "discovered" the continent in 1492, captured the minds of thinkers on both sides of the Atlantic. For the historical sociologist, perhaps the most fascinating thing about American society is what Liah Greenfeld has pointed out:

> In America, to begin with, there was almost no social reality, other than the one the settlers brought with them in their own minds. (One could say that here were no structural constraints apart from the constraints of the symbolic structure).[1]

What is important here is that when the settlers first came to America there was no existing social structure.[2] For my argument the most important factor is the absence of an established feudal property structure in the colonies. Already by the 1830s, Alexis de Tocqueville, in his *Democracy in America* (1835), said that one of the fundamental bases

[1] Greenfeld, Liah, *Nationalism: Five Roads to Modernity*, Harvard University Press, Cambridge, MA (1993), p. 402.

[2] I am of course aware of the fact that there existed populations of Native Americans in America when the European settlers came—and in no way do I wish to undermine this or legitimize how the setters treated them. The point is that the settlers treated the New World very much as if these people and their social reality did not exist.

E. M. Fuglestad, *Private Property and the Origins of Nationalism in the United States and Norway*,
https://doi.org/10.1007/978-3-319-89950-3_2

for American democracy was the equality in condition that existed in America. "The ground, once cleared, was by no means fertile enough to make both a landlord and a tenant rich," wrote Tocqueville, and "the land was naturally broken up into little slots." Because of this the American colonies seemed destined, according to Tocqueville, to "let freedom grow, not the aristocratic freedom of the motherland, but a middle-class and democratic freedom of which the world's history had not previously provided a complete example."[3] Similarly, Louis Hartz wrote, "the outstanding thing about the American effort of 1776 was bound to be, not the freedom to which it led, but the established feudal structure it did not need to destroy."[4] Nothing in history is ever destined, of course, but more than anything else perhaps it was the availability of land and wide ownerships of it by British settlers that formed American nationalism, which was above anything else concerned with propertied freedom.

The Socio-economic Situation in the Colonies at the Eve of the Revolution

Widespread private ownership had not always or everywhere been a feature of colonial America. In the first colonies, Virginia and Plymouth, land was at first owned by colonial promoters, and the colonists worked the land collectively, for which they received food, shelter and clothing, while the surplus went to the owning company. This scheme was not successful in the long run, however. Individual ownership of land was introduced in the late 1620s, and all colonies established after 1629 immediately introduced private landholding.[5] The granting of land rights was based on the idea that the British king had sovereignty over all newly found land in the colonies, and that he could thus grant land to joint stock companies or proprietors. Property rights granted from the king gave the companies and proprietors the right to appoint

[3]Tocqueville, Alexis, *Democracy in America* (edited by J.P. Mayer and Max Lerner), Harper & Row, New York and London (1988) [1840], pp. 27–28.

[4]Hartz, Louis, *The Liberal Tradition in America: An Interpretation of American Political Thought Since the Revolution*, Harcourt, Brace & Co., New York (1955), p. 35.

[5]Nettles, Curtis P., *The Roots of American Civilization: A History of American Colonial Life*, Meredith Publishing, New York (1963) [1938], pp. 222–229.

judges, to tax and form governments—these were rights that were associated with sovereignty. Manorial systems emerged in some places, such as in the Hudson Valley and Maryland; and, during the seventeenth century, companies and proprietors in Virginia devised a system that gave land to middling immigrants who could finance their own journey, and granted them more land for each servant, slave, or other person brought with them. Some men could thus acquire large properties of land. This was known as the headright system. The headright system was gradually abandoned, however, and by the late seventeenth century direct land sales to individuals had become the norm in all the colonies. The system of direct sales resulted in efficient and widespread allocation of land, so that by the end of the seventeenth century almost all householders owned land. In Salem, Massachusetts, only 4 of the 238 first inhabitants were landless. Half of the men in New England owned land by the age of 30, and 95% of men owned land by the age of 36. In 1690 six sevenths of all farmers in Connecticut owned land, in 1704 two thirds of the households in Surry County, Virginia, owned land, and in Pennsylvania landownership was almost universal during the 1690s.[6]

Individual landownership remained high during the eighteenth century. Nearly two thirds of farmers in eastern New England, Long Island and Tidewater, Virginia, owned land—only one sixth of farm workers remained tenants all their lives. In Essex County, Massachusetts, 84% of men between the age of thirty-seven and sixty owned land. Two thirds of taxpayers in Deadham owned land both in 1735 and in 1771, and seven tenths of the taxpayers in Concord owned land in 1749, while the number rose to four fifths in 1771. Tenancy remained low, and seven tenths of small village and town householders in Massachusetts owned land in 1771. Connecticut, New Hampshire, and East New Jersey also had a high degree of self-ownership. In revolutionary era New Jersey, for example, two thirds of taxed men owned land, but four fifths of men over twenty-seven—which constituted almost all the households—owned land.[7]

[6]This paragraph follows closely the description in Kulikoff, Allan, *From British Peasants to Colonial American Farmers*, University of North Carolina Press, Chapel Hill and London (2000), pp. 106–118.

[7]This paragraph follows closely the description in Kulikoff (2000), pp. 127–131.

Population, Economy and Social Hierarchy in the Colonies

The American colonies received a steady flow of immigrants during the century leading up to the revolution. The southern colonies received most immigrants and had the highest population growth amongst the colonies. By the 1770s, 47% of the population lived in the southern states. The most distinguishing feature of these states was the existence and pervasiveness of chattel slavery—in fact, African slaves were the largest group of people coming to the colonies as a whole during the eighteenth century. Hence, slaves constituted a significant proportion of the total population in the colonies; on the eve of the revolution, one out of every five people living in the colonies were slaves—that is, human beings defined by law and custom as property, a commodity to be bought and sold. Slavery was largely accepted in the colonies before the revolution, and so was the notion and fact that society was a hierarchical and paternalistic one. At the top of the social hierarchy was a small group of people (around 5% of the population) who consisted mainly of merchants and large plantation owners. Just below this small group of people was a slightly larger group of men who were educated and had professions, such as lawyers, schoolmasters and doctors. It was these two groups that provided most of the members to the national movement. Below this group was a large group of farmers, the occupation of one out of every four free males. The majority (70% as referred to above) of these farmers owned their own land; hence, to own land was a relatively reasonable and realistic expectation for a large proportion of the rural population. This, along with the fact that titles and privileges were not prevalent, made social mobility relatively high. Social mobility and economic advancement was, of course, more real for some than for others. This was especially so in urban areas, where there was an increasing concentration of capital and wealth in few hands and increasing groups of labourers who had little chance of economic and social advancement. There were also regional differences in wealth; in the south the average wealth per free wealth holder was £394, whereas in New England it was £161. This was largely because the slaves in the south had no, or almost no, wealth at all. Wealth increased considerably in the colonies during the eighteenth century as the economy was growing steadily, making the colonies an important component of the British imperial economy. The slave trade and the export of staple crops made up the bulk of the transatlantic trade in which the southern colonies played a particularly central role.[8]

The Property Regime of the British Empire

On the eve of the American Revolution, there were thirteen British colonies on the northern Atlantic coast of the American continent, with just over three million inhabitants in total. It was a population that was growing fast, mainly because of immigration (but also helped by high birth rates), so that by the turn of the nineteenth century there were more than five million inhabitants in the thirteen colonies. These inhabitants were subjects in an empire whose general political and economic development, at least since the signing of the Magna Carta, was following a trajectory very different from that of most Western states. By the seventeenth century Britain's unique trajectory was particularly striking. While the monarchs of many European states had by the late seventeenth century centralized and increased their power, resulting in the creation of absolutist states, the British Crown had during that time lost many of its powers becoming in practice subject to parliament—or, rather, to the power of the landed aristocracy.

Perhaps the most fascinating and unique thing about the British state after the Glorious Revolution (1688) was highlighted by Ellen Meiksins Wood: the British propertied class taxed itself in order to increase the power of the state which they themselves were in control of, thus transferring to the state the wealth that they had appropriated from the propertyless.[9] One essential point is that there was amongst the elite a

[8]The account of class structure in the preceding paragraph draws on Cogliano, Francis D., *Revolutionary America 1763–1815: A Political History*, Routledge, London (1999), pp. 5–26. In addition I have relied on: Henretta, James A., "Wealth and social structure," in Jack Greene and J.R. Pole (eds.), *Colonial British America*, Johns Hopkins University Press, Baltimore and London (1984); Jones, Alice Hanson, *Wealth of a Nation to Be: The American Colonies at the Eve of the Revolution*, Colombia University Press, New York (1980); and Main, Jackson Turner, *The Social Structure of Revolutionary America*, Princeton University Press, Princeton (1965).

[9]Wood, Ellen Meiksins, *Liberty and Property: A Social History of Western Political Thought from the Renaissance to the Present*, Verso, London (2012), p. 282.

common definition and agreement over property. Woods writes in reference to the eighteenth-century British debates about property:

> It seems perverse to define political discourse in eighteenth century England in the terms of a dispute amongst propertied classes whose agreements on the existing property regime far outweighed their disagreements; or to magnify ill-tempered disputes among gentlemen into conflicts of revolutionary moment.[10]

Assumptions as to shared property were capitalistic with property being understood as a private, individual, exclusive right. It was common in British law by the early eighteenth century to define property as an absolute exclusive right. It was said about the proprietor that: "An absolute proprietor hath an absolute Power to dispose of his Estate as he pleases, subject only to the Laws of the Land."[11] By 1729 Giles Jacob's law dictionary says about property:

> Every Man (if he hath not forfeited it) hath a Property and Right allowed him by the Law, to defend his Life, Liberty, and Estate; and if either be violated, it gives an Action to redress the Injury, and punish the Wrongdoer.[12]

Americans inherited such definitions of property. A private property regime became practically uncontested in revolutionary America. In the words of John R. Nelson:

> A private property system and its political, economic, and social implications pervaded the thought and actions of the early national leaders (in America). Their concept of freedom and independence were inextricably bound up with individual ownership of productive property … slavery or contract might be challenged by a "radical", but never the systems as a whole.[13]

This kind of private property system became the foundation for the national ideology in America.

[10] Wood (2012), p. 283.

[11] Alymer, G.E., "The meaning and definition of 'property' in seventeenth century England," *Past and Present*, No. 86 (February, 1980), p. 95.

[12] Quoted in Alymer (1980), p. 95.

[13] Nelson, John R., *Liberty and Property: Political Economy and Policymaking in the New Nation 1789–1812*, Johns Hopkins University Press, Baltimore (1987), p. 164.

Different Property Structures

The property assumptions of Britain and the colonies were the same, but the actual relations of property were different. In Britain at the time of the American Revolution the ratio between freemen (i.e., self-owners) was the reverse of what it was in the American colonies; whereas 70% of the land in America was owned by freeholding families, in England only 30% owned their own land. The whole situation of landownership was very different; England was densely populated, made up of a plethora of small villages where landlords owned most of the land. From the sixteenth century onwards, enclosing landlords created private property at the expense of commons, and substituted traditional rights to revenue with short-term leases. Thus, a form of agrarian capitalism based upon tenancy for the many and ownership by the few was created.[14]

Many colonial Americans looked with pity on the social conditions of Britain, and contrasted their own situation with it. Benjamin Franklin's thoughts on this are telling:

> I have lately made a tour through Ireland and Scotland. In those countries, a small part of the society are landlords, great noblemen, and gentlemen, extremely opulent, living in the highest affluence and magnificence. The bulk of the people are tenants, extremely poor, living in the most sordid wretchedness, in dirty hovels of mud and straw, and clothed only in rags.[15]

In America, though, the situation was different: Franklin wrote, "I thought often of the happiness of New England, where every man is a freeholder, has a vote in public affairs."[16] That every man in New England was a freeholder was of course an exaggeration, but there were more than in Britain, and their situation was more free. This difference

[14] Kulikoff (2000), pp. 8–27. The classic study by Barrington Moore is also illuminating on this subject. See Moore, Barrington, *Social Origins of Dictatorship and Democracy: Lord and Peasant in the Making of the Modern World*, Beacon Press, Boston (1966).

[15] Benjamin Franklin to Joshua Babcock, January 13, 1772 in Bigelow, John, *The Works of Benjamin Franklin, Including the Private as Well as the Official and Scientific Correspondence, Together with the Unmutilated and Correct Version of the Autobiography*, G. P. Putnam's Sons, New York (1904), Vol. V (Letters and Misc. Writings 1768–1772), p. 278. http://oll.libertyfund.org/titles/2459#Franklin_1438-05_878 (accessed 29.01.2015).

[16] Bigelow (1904), p. 278.

was reflected through law. In Britain, writes Edward White, "It seems fair to say that by 1750 English law of trusts and estates served to protect the interests of wealthy landed families."[17] English law was also colonial law.[18] Yet it soon became apparent that there was a mismatch between the assumptions and prerogatives of these laws and the American reality. If English law made it relatively difficult for the majority of people to own and transfer land, it was made comparatively easier in the colonies. Colonial property law was still mostly English property law (and by the property of being so, it provided powerful protection of landed property interests), but it was moderated, softened and made more democratic in the sense that it was easier for most people to obtain it: entail and primogeniture was less common and regarded with skepticism by many; in courts it was easier to challenge titles to land; and there was a system of land acquisition—the recording system—more in tune with the American reality of vast amounts of uncultivated land. There was no general treatise produced on American law until 1826, when James Kent's *Commentaries on American Law* was published.[19] However, when it comes to property rights specifically, we can refer to "the father of the constitution," James Madison, who produced his now famous *Essay on Property* (1792). In the essay, property is defined, as in English law, as an exclusive right to the individual: "Property," writes Madison, "is that dominion which one man claims and exercises over the external things of the world, in exclusion of every other individual."[20] Madison had a wide conception of property. In a larger sense, he wrote:

[17]White, Edward, *Law in American History, Vol. 1: From the Colonial Years through the Civil War*, Oxford University Press, Oxford and New York (2012), p. 69.

[18]Hoffer, Peter Charles, *Law and People in Colonial America*, Johns Hopkins University Press, Baltimore and London (1998), p. 100. For a comprehensive survey of the influence of English common law on American law see Thomas, David A., *History of American Land Law, Vol. 2: Land Law in the American States*, Vandeplas Publishing, Lake Mary (2013), pp. 800–1147.

[19]Alexander, George S., *Commodity and Property: Competing Visions of Property in American Legal Thought*, University of Chicago Press, Chicago and London (1997), p. 21.

[20]Hunt, Gaillard, *The Writings of James Madison, Comprising His Public Papers and His Private Correspondence, Including His Numerous Letters and Documents Now for the First Time Printed*, Vol. 6, G. P. Putnam's Sons, New York (1900), p. 102. http://oll.libertyfund.org/titles/1941#Madison_1356-06_466 (accessed 02.12.2015).

> It embraces everything to which a man may attach value and have a right; and which leaves to everyone else the like advantage. In the former sense, a man´s land or merchandize, or money, is called his property. In the latter sense, a man has property in his opinion and his free communication of them ... He has property very dear to him in the safety and the liberty of his person ... In a word, as a man is said to have a right to property, he may be equally said to have a property in his rights.[21]

We can also look to public documents and statutes to get an idea of how property was understood. The North West Ordinance (1787), for instance, stated that the inhabitants of the territories it covered had the right to private property:

> No man shall be deprived of his liberty of property but by the judgement of his peers, or the law of the land, and should the public exigencies make it necessary, for the common preservation, to take any persons property, or to demand his particular services, full compensation shall be made for the same.[22]

This passage demonstrates the way in which property was relatively democratic in America: all men have the right to it, and nobody can be deprived from it other than by judgment of his or her peers.

Prelude to Nationalism in America

The Right to Property of British Subjects

Colonial Americans in the eighteenth century were imbedded in a wider Western political tradition that posed strong links between ownership of property and freedom, and this tradition stood particularly strong in the Anglo-Saxon tradition to which the colonists belonged.[23] It was particularly land that was seen to be important, and this must be understood in the agrarian context of relative widespread landownership in which

[21] Hunt (1900), p. 102.

[22] Thomas (2013), p. 1033.

[23] Some of the classics here are: Wood, Gordon, *The Creation of the American Republic*, W. W. Norton, New York (1969); Bailyn, Bernard, *The Ideological Origins of the American Revolution*, Harvard University Press, Cambridge, MA (1992) [1967]; and Pocock, J.G.A., *The Machiavellian Moment*, Princeton University Press, Princeton and Oxford (1975).

the colonists lived. Although landed property, however, was central, the property right to the land itself was partly based on the assertion that the labor one engaged in, and the fruits that it produced, was exclusive to the individual—it was his property—which was properly his or her own.[24] To have property in this way was a necessary condition for individual freedom to exist. John Dickinson wrote in the late 1760s in response to measures from the British Parliament:

> Let these truths be indelibly impressed on our minds – that we cannot be happy, without being free – that we cannot be free, without being secure in our property – that we cannot be secure in our property, if, without our consent, others may, as by right, take it away.[25]

John Dickinson (born 1732 in Delaware) has been dubbed the penman of the revolution. Dickinson was a plantation owner and lawyer who became a contributor to the emergent national ideology in the late 1760s as a result of the implementation of the Townshend Acts. In 1767/1768 he anonymously published an attack on the act signed "A farmer," which became known as *Letters from a Farmer in Pennsylvania*. The same year Dickinson wrote "The Liberty Song" which was also an assertion of American property rights. Later Dickinson became a delegate both to the Continental Congress and the Federal Convention. Dickinson, however, refused to sign the Declaration of Independence, believing in a reconciliation with Britain.[26] This was because he held the widespread view that the property rights of the colonists were inseparable from their belonging to Britain. He wrote in his *Letters from a Farmer* that, although the British government was sometimes unjust, Britain and the British Constitution was also the origin and protector of the liberty of the colonists:

[24]This was similar to how John Locke had defined property. J.G.A. Pocock reminds us that the English word property comes from what is properly one's own. See Pocock, J.G.A., *Virtue, Commerce and History: Essays on Political Thought and History, Chiefly in the Eighteenth Century*, Cambridge University Press, Cambridge (1985), p. 56.

[25]John Dickinson, February 15, 1768 in McDonald, Forrest (ed.), *Empire and Nation: Letters from a Farmer in Pennsylvania (John Dickinson) and Letters from the Federal Farmer (Richard Henry Lee)*, Liberty Fund, Indianapolis (1999), p. 81. http://oll.libertyfund.org/titles/690#Mcdonald_0010_289 (accessed 29.01.2015).

[26]Carnes, C. Mark, and John A. Garraty (eds.), *American National Biography*, Vol. 6, Oxford University Press, New York and Oxford (1999), pp. 566–569.

> What have these colonies to ask, while they continue free? Or what have they to dread, but insidious attempts to subvert their freedom? Their prosperity does not depend on ministerial favors doled to particular provinces. They form one political body, of which each colony is a member. Their happiness is founded on their constitution; and is to be promoted, by preserving that constitution in unabated vigor, throughout every part. A spot, a peak of decay, however small the limb on which it appears, and however remote it may seem from the vitals, should be alarming. We have all the rights requisite for our prosperity. The legal authority of Great Britain may indeed lay hard restrictions upon us; but like the spear of Telephus it will cure as well as wound.[27]

The colonies formed "one political body" with Britain, and "their happiness [was] founded on their constitution." Dickinson wrote to his fellow colonists that the point was to respect both oneself and the Crown, and know what was theirs and what belonged to the Crown:

> You will support the character of freemen, without losing that of faithful subjects—a good character in any government—one of the best under a British government. You will prove, that Americans have that true magnanimity of soul, that can resent injuries, without falling into rage; and that tho' your devotion to Great Britain is the most affectionate, yet you can make PROPER DISTINCTIONS, and know what you owe to yourselves, as well as to her.[28]

This distinction between what belonged to the individual and what belonged to the Crown should of course, wrote Dickinson, also be respected by the Crown. Nobody deserved to be deprived of what "can be properly called our own," because this was the most fundamental right of any free man:

> As long as the products of our labor, and the rewards of our care, can properly be called our own, so long it will be worth our while to be industrious and frugal. But if when we plow—sow—reap—gather—and thresh—we find, that we plow—sow—reap—gather—and thresh for others, whose PLEASURE is to be the SOLE LIMITATION how much they shall take, and how much they shall leave, WHY should we repeat the

[27] John Dickinson, February 15, 1768 in McDonald (1999), p. 81.

[28] John Dickinson, February 15, 1768 in McDonald (1999), p. 85.

> unprofitable toil? Horses and oxen are content with that portion of the fruits of their work, which their owners assign them, in order to keep them strong enough to raise successive crops; but even these beasts will not submit to draw for their masters, until they are subdued by whips and goads. Let us take care of our rights, and we therein take care of our prosperity. "SLAVERY IS EVER PRECEDED BY SLEEP."[29]

This quote demonstrates again the centrality of property ownership to the colonists' concept of freedom: property was what made men free, and not "slaves" or like "beasts subdued by whips and goads." We can also clearly see here the agrarian frame of reference in which Dickinson writes, referring to plowing, sowing and reaping. Property had the potential of creating independence for the individual because, by utilizing and shaping the earth through one's labor and having exclusive (property) right to it, one created the means to act freely in the world. Property was thus understood as a natural and unrestricted right as long as it did not interfere with another's right to do the same. In a letter that Thomas Jefferson wrote to a friend thirty years after the American Revolution, he also expressed the importance of private property if an individual was to be free:

> A right to property is founded on our natural wants, in the means in which we are endowed to satisfy those wants, and the right to what we require by these means without violating the similar rights of other sensible beings.[30]

Owning landed property could satisfy the wants and needs of an individual, this made him or her free. For this reason, there was also posed a link between it and political power (sovereignty). French immigrant and intellectual J. Hector St. John de Crevecoeur expressed this clearly in his *Letters from an American Farmer* (1782):

> The instant I enter on own land, the bright idea of property, of exclusive right, of independence exalt my mind. Precious soil ... What should we American farmers be without the distinct possession of that soil? It feeds, it clothes us ...This formerly rude soil has been converted by my father

[29] John Dickinson, February 15, 1768 in McDonald (1999), p. 81.

[30] Thomas Jefferson, quoted in Kantz, Stanley, "Thomas Jefferson and the right to property in revolutionary America," *Journal of Law and Economics*, No. 19 (1976), p. 475.

> into a pleasant farm, and in return it has established all our rights; on it is founded our rank, our freedom, our power as citizens.[31]

Again we see the agrarian frame in which property was understood—it is possession of the soil that makes an American and gives him his rights and powers.

Before 1776 colonial Americans in general saw the right to property and their "power as citizens" as protected by the British Crown. After 1776 this changed. Due in large part to new British policies in the colonies from the early 1760s, many Americans became convinced by 1776 that, as John Adams put it in 1765, "There seems to be a direct and formal design on foot, to enslave all America."[32] Slavery was the opposite of having the right to property, and Adams was led to argue Americans were being enslaved by the British government's interference with the colonists' right to property through its taxation. Many agreed with him. Dickinson put this expressly: "We are taxed without our own consent, expressed by ourselves or our representatives. We are therefore – slaves."[33] And he continued:

> If they have any right to tax us—then, whether our own money shall continue in our own pockets or not, depends no longer on us, but on them. "There is nothing which" we "can call our own; or, to use the words of Mr. Locke—WHAT PROPERTY HAVE WE IN THAT, WHICH ANOTHER MAY, BY RIGHT, TAKE, WHEN HE PLEASES, TO HIMSELF?"[34]

[31] de Crevecour, J. Hector St. John, *Letters from an American Farmer*, Everyman's Library, London (1971) [1782], p. 24.

[32] John Adams, October 21, 1765 in Taylor, Robert J. (ed.), *Papers of John Adams*, Vol. 1, Belknap Press, Cambridge, MA (1977), p. 127. Adams was born in 1735 and was educated to become a lawyer. His main contributions to national ideology started after the introduction of the Stamp Act in 1765. One of his responses to this was his writing of "A dissertation on the canon and feudal law" (1765), which demonstrates very well the historical and propertied nature of nationalism. Another representative piece on the national ideology was written nine years later, known as the *Novanglus Essays* (1774). See Carnes, C. Mark, and John A. Garraty (eds.), *American National Biography*, Vol. 1, Oxford University Press, New York and Oxford (1999), pp. 100–111.

[33] John Dickinson, January 11, 1768 in McDonald (1999), p. 45.

[34] John Dickinson, January 11, 1768 in McDonald (1999), p. 45.

Subjection to British parliamentary laws became increasingly seen as distorting the freedom of the colonists. Adams asked in 1775 about accepting British parliamentary legislature:

> Would not such an unlimited subjection of three millions of people to that parliament, at three thousand miles distance, be real slavery? There are but two sorts of men in the world, freemen and slaves. The very definition of a freeman is one who is bound by no law to which he has not consented. Americans would have no way of giving or withholding their consent to the acts of this parliament, therefore they would not be freemen.[35]

To sustain their position as "freemen" with the right to property, the members of the American national movement found a new source of sovereignty—the American landed property structure and the people that were part of it. This idea was both latent and present in America in the decades leading up to the revolution. However, before 1776 nationalism was only a potentiality, a spirit not yet materialized and which had not yet found its way into the world. From the 1760s onwards, however, conflicts with the center of the Empire, ultimately caused by the property structure in the American colonies,[36] created an opening for the spirit to enter. It is to the realization of political ideology of *the amalgamation of people, property and sovereignty* that we now turn.

Enter the Spirit: The Triggering Factors

Imperial politics from the 1760s onwards brought some complex issues about sovereignty to the surface. As Jack P. Green once put it, at the end of the Seven Years War (known as the French and Indian War in America), "the only certainty about constitutional arrangements within the large extended polity that constituted the early modern British

[35] John Adams, January 30, 1775 in Thompson, Bradly, *The Revolutionary Writings of John Adams*, Liberty Fund, Indianapolis (2000), p. 164. http://oll.libertyfund.org/titles/592#Adams_0284_458 (accessed 29.01.2015).

[36] On the imperial power structure see Greene, Jack P., *Peripheries and Center: Constitutional Development in the Extended Polities of the British Empire and the United States, 1607–1788*, University of Georgia Press, Athens and London (1986). For the uniting factor of the property structure see White (2012), pp. 102–107; and Appleby, Joyce, *Capitalism and a New Social Order: The Republican Vision of the 1790s*, New York University Press, New York and London (1984), pp. 39–46.

Empire was their uncertainty."[37] When suddenly and glaringly brought to the surface, these issues created feelings of deep dissatisfaction in the colonies. The end of the Seven Years War was a major event causing issues over sovereignty to be displayed. Britain's victory in this war eliminated the French threat in the north, creating a state of political security for the colonists not seen before. This also opened up vast amounts of new land for potential settlement, but the British government responded by creating the Proclamation Line, which basically restricted the colonists from settling the new land. These were probably some of the immediate factors contributing to independence. Indeed, the Proclamation Line can be seen as the first of many parliamentary restrictions on the colonists' real or perceived rights. There came many more restrictions, for the Seven Years War like all wars cost money. British politicians only thought it fair that the colonists contributed to payment of this war—after all, the war had been fought largely to protect them. Thus, in 1764 the Sugar Act and the Currency Act were passed, the former levying new duties on textiles, wines, coffee and sugar shipped to the colonies, the latter forbidding the colonists from using their own paper money for payment of debts. Then came the Stamp Act in 1765, creating revenue on stamps required on most printed commodities. The Quartering Act of the same year stated that the colonists were to house and feed British troops stationed there. In 1767 the Townshend Act was initiated, increasing duties on a range of imported commodities, creating a Board of Customs Commissioners in Boston and more vice-admiralty courts. These measures were greeted with provocation by the colonists, and the presence of British troops made the situation more tense. On 5 March 1770 the tension resulted in the "Boston Massacre," where five civilians were killed when a British soldier fired into a crowd after being assaulted. After this the British Parliament repealed many of its previous acts. When the Tea Act of 1773 was enacted, though, unrest broke out again with the Boston Tea Party. After this, parliament passed the Coercive Acts (or the Intolerable Acts) in 1774, which stated parliament's absolute and final legislative authority over the colonies. It also closed the Port of Boston and replaced the Massachusetts Assembly with a body appointed by the colonial governor. It was these measures against the colonists that created an opening through which the spirit of nationalism could enter,

[37] Greene (1986), p. 79.

and it was the American property structure of relatively widespread landownership that provided a worldly form for the spirit—without it, the spirit would have remained an apparition only. Widespread landownership and protection of the right to hold land in such a situation spawned an ideology in which popular sovereignty and landed property became interconnected.

Nationalism Unleashed

Sage of Nationalism: Thomas Jefferson

The members of the national movement started asserting their right to property against the British Crown and Parliament based on their perceived historical rights to land. The past was invoked to justify current and future freedoms. Thomas Jefferson, the slave-owning freeman of Virginia, provides us with a most clear and systematic expression of the historical vision. Jefferson hangs as a looming spectre over revolutionary America. As principal author of the *Declaration of Independence*, he inevitably becomes a key figure when exploring revolutionary discourse. Jefferson was born in Virginia in 1743, and it was in this colony that he also settled as a young adult as a plantation owner and slaveholder. Jefferson also practised as a lawyer and was a local representative of the House of Burgess in the early 1770s. Jefferson's contributions to a national ideology started after the passing of the Intolerable Acts with his writing "A summary view of the rights of British America" (1774), which is a clear example of the historical and propertied nature of the national ideology. Then, one year later, when the Continental Congress was constituted, Jefferson became a representative from Virginia, and it was in this role that he drafted the *Declaration of Independence* (1776). After the revolution Jefferson occupied various political positions, including Minister to France (1785–1789) and Secretary of State (1790–1793), but most importantly, perhaps, as President from 1801–1809, during which he practised his own vision of nationalism.[38]

History became a way of defining the proper relationship between property and society for Jefferson. George S. Alexander has suggested that this vision might be summed up in Jefferson's famous statement

[38] Carnes, C. Mark, and John A. Garraty (eds.), *American National Biography*, Vol. 11, Oxford University Press, New York and Oxford (1999), pp. 909–917.

that "the earth belongs to the living." Alexander writes: "That the earth belongs to the living, then, represents an attempt to create public meaning of property in the new republic in terms of time."[39] In Jefferson's vision, individuals were supposed to be free not only from present arbitrary power, but also from feudal and aristocratic bondage which could be inherited from the past. Thus Jefferson started "A Summary View of the Rights of British America"—a tract written before the first continental congress in 1774 which set down a list of grievances against the British king and parliament—by invoking the first settlers, America's ancient ancestors: "Our ancestors, before their emigration to America, were the free inhabitants of the British dominions in Europe …",[40] from which he continues:

> America was conquered, and her settlements made, and firmly established, at the expence of individuals, and not of the British public. Their own blood was spilt in acquiring lands for their settlement, their own fortunes expended in making that settlement effectual; for themselves they fought, for themselves they conquered, and for themselves alone they have right to hold.[41]

Nevertheless, the colonial ancestors, according to Jefferson, choose to adopt British laws:

> Under which they had hitherto lived in the mother country, and to continue their union with her by submitting themselves to the same common sovereign, who was thereby made the central link connecting the several parts of the empire thus newly multiplied.[42]

This did not mean, however, that the British Parliament had any right to interfere with the property of the colonists. Jefferson writes:

> Shall these governments be dissolved [the colonial governments], their property annihilated, and their people reduced to a state of nature, at the

[39] Alexander, George S., *Commodity and Property: Competing Visions of Property in American Legal Thought*, University of Chicago Press, Chicago and London (1997), p. 27.

[40] Thomas Jefferson, July 4, 1774 in Boyd, Julian (ed.), *The Papers of Thomas Jefferson*, Vol. 1, Princeton University Press, Princeton, NJ (1950), p. 121.

[41] Thomas Jefferson, July 4, 1774 in Boyd (1950), Vol. 1, p. 122.

[42] Thomas Jefferson, July 4, 1774 in Boyd (1950), Vol. 1, p. 122.

> imperious breath of a body of men, whom they never saw, in whom they never confided, and over whom they have no powers of punishment or removal, let their crimes against the American public be ever so great? … Were this to be admitted, instead of being a free people, as we have hitherto supposed, and mean to continue ourselves, we should suddenly be found … slaves.[43]

The colonists were not slaves however; they were freemen because of the nature of their landholdings, which they had inherited from their ancestors:

> Our Saxon ancestors held their lands, as they did their personal property, in absolute dominion, disencumbered with any superior, answering nearly to the nature of those possessions which the feudalists term allodial. William, the Norman, first introduced that system generally … America was not conquered by William the Norman, nor its lands surrendered to him, or any of his successors. Possessions there are undoubtedly of the allodial nature. Our ancestors, however, who migrated hither, were farmers, not lawyers. The fictitious principle that all lands belong originally to the king, they were early persuaded to believe real.[44]

The colonial ancestors may not have been lawyers, only freeholders. Jefferson, however, was both a lawyer and a freeholder—he could not be fooled by the "fictitious principle." Indeed, he knew and held that "our properties within our own territories shall [not] be taxed or regulated by any power on earth but our own."[45] Americans constituted a distinct people of free, landed individuals, and according to Jefferson, they thus had the right to form their own government in order to preserve their property, as it is declared in the *Declaration of Independence*:

> It becomes necessary for one people to dissolve the political bands which have connected them with another, and to assume among the powers of the earth, the separate and equal station to which the Laws of Nature and of Nature's God entitle them.[46]

[43]Thomas Jefferson, July 4, 1774 in Boyd (1950), Vol. 1, p. 126.

[44]Thomas Jefferson, July 4, 1774 in Boyd (1950), Vol. 1, p. 132.

[45]Thomas Jefferson, July 4, 1774 in Boyd (1950), Vol. 1, p. 133.

[46]Thomas Jefferson, July 4, 1776 in Boyd (1950), Vol. 1, p. 429.

Brian Steele has suggested that only after independence, in retrospect, can "A Summary View" be seen as a part of a national history of legitimization. Furthermore, Steele suggests that Jefferson was more radical than anyone else in his assertions, because he claimed that historically, not only had parliament never held any rights over the colonies, but neither had the king.[47] I do not think this is as important as is the fact that Jefferson claims the colonists' rights on account of an American history in "A Summary View"—and that property is integral to his argument. It is in fact this that is being done in the *Declaration of Independence* as well: the claims of universal natural rights made therein may be seen as an expression of the American national character that, as Steel himself put it, "legitimizes the statehood of the entity that will have the charge ... of securing those rights."[48] It was property that was the most fundamental of these rights and the main reason for declaring independence. It was around landed property that the national history and the new nation-state were built. In a draft to an act that became part of the Sessions Act of May 1779, Jefferson stated this quite directly: before separation from the British Empire, Jefferson wrote that the colonists had, "all the rights of natural born subjects in the other [parts of the Empire], & so might lawfully take & hold real property." However,

> When by the tyrannies of that [the British] prince, & the open hostilities committed by his armies & subjects inhabitants of the other parts of his dominions on the good people of the sd United States they are obliged to wage war in defense of their rights & finally to separate themselves from the rest of the British Empire.[49]

The Common Sense of Thomas Paine

By the summer of 1776 the American property rights and freedoms were understood by most members of the national movement

[47] Steele, Brian, *Thomas Jefferson and American Nationhood*, Cambridge University Press, Cambridge (2012), p. 24.

[48] Steele (2012), p. 40.

[49] Thomas Jefferson, June 4, 1779 in Boyd, Julian (ed.), *The Papers of Thomas Jefferson*, Vol. 2, Princeton University Press, Princeton, NJ (1950).

as self-sustained, self-evident rights that were no longer dependent on Britain.[50] This was now, we could say, *Common Sense*, which was the title of Thomas Paine's extremely popular pamphlet, concluding as early as January 1776 that "Tis time to part!"[51] [with Britain]. Paine was a recent English immigrant to America—he had gotten there only in 1774 after Benjamin Franklin had given him a letter of recommendation. Paine's life in England had been turbulent. He lived in London in the winter of 1757–1758 where he became acquainted with Newtonian rationalism, something that probably greatly influenced his politics of natural law. Paine later held positions as a teacher and revenue officer but in 1774 when he was fired from the latter job, his belongings were sold and his wife divorced him. It was then that a friend introduced him to Franklin and he came to America.[52] That Paine, an Englishman, started so forcefully to advocate for the rights of the Americans might be another indicator of the Englishness of the rights that the colonists

[50] Many others expressed the national vision in the same manner as Jefferson. John Adams in 1765 agreed with Jefferson that the colonists had freedom on account of being American. "We have a right," he wrote in his *Dissertation on the Canon and Feudal Law*, "derived from our maker." But "if we had not, *our fathers have earned and bought it for us*, at the expense of their estates, their pleasures, and their blood." The colonists, when they arrived, had "formed their plan, both of ecclesial and civil government, in direct opposition to the cannon and the feudal systems." See John Adams, September 30, 1765 in Taylor (1977), Vol. 1, pp. 120–121. Feudalism, for Adams, represented "the most impertinent and fantastical ideas that ever got into a human pericranum." He said later in his *Novanglus Essays*. See John Adams, March 13, 1775 in Taylor, Robert J., *Papers of John Adams*, Vol. 2, Belknap Press, Cambridge, MA (1977), p. 331. Moreover, everyone who had written on the subject, said Adams, knew that "to have any right to life or property or freedom more than the beasts of the field, and who was not hired or enlisted under arbitrary, lawless power, has been always willing to admit the feudal system to be inconsistent with liberty and the rights of mankind." See John Adams, August 19, 1765 in Taylor (1977), Vol. 1, p. 117.

[51] The whole quote reads: "Everything that is right or reasonable pleads for separation. The blood of the slain, the weeping voice of nature cries; TIS TIME TO PART!" See Thomas Paine, January 10, 1776 in Conway, Moncure Daniel, *The Writings of Thomas Paine*, G. P. Putnam's Sons, New York (1894), Vol. 1, p. 90. http://oll.libertyfund.org/titles/343#Paine_0548-01_160 (accessed 19.01.2015).

[52] Carnes, C. Mark, and John A. Garraty (eds.), *American National Biography*, Vol. 16, Oxford University Press, New York and Oxford (1999), pp. 925–928.

were advocating.[53] These rights were increasingly understood, at least in America, as universal rights. In *Common Sense*, Paine explained that separation from Britain was on the grounds of natural universal rights:

> The cause of America is in a great measure the cause of all mankind. Many circumstances have, and will arise, which are not local, but universal, and through which the principles of all lovers of mankind are affected, and in the event of which their affections are interested. The laying a country desolate with fire and sword, declaring war against the natural rights of all mankind, and extirpating the defenders thereof from the face of the earth, is the concern of every man to whom nature hath given the power of feeling.[54]

Freedom was now seen to be antithetical to the British Constitution, and it was the monarchical and aristocratic elements of it that made it unfit for proper freedom, and which had made it necessary to part, wrote Paine. It was the character of the people that made nations free. Only if they themselves governed and made laws could independency exist. Paine wrote:

> Independency means no more, than, whether we [the people] shall make our own laws, or whether the king, the greatest enemy this continent hath, or can have, shall tell us "THERE SHALL BE NO LAWS BUT SUCH AS I LIKE."[55]

The king's sovereignty is here refuted in favor of that of "the people". To base sovereignty on the people, however, meant in actuality to base sovereignty on the right to landed property. The idea of popular sovereignty was interconnected with the assertion of the centrality of individual property ownership in establishing freedom for the individual. These two ideas have been married at least since the writing of the *Declaration of Independence*. I shall demonstrate this in the following section by looking at debates during and around the Federal Constitutional Convention.

[53] As Greenfeld put it: "the main reason why the colonists so strongly asserted their freedom and wanted a break with England was 'because their national identity was English'." See Greenfeld (1993), p. 412.

[54] Thomas Paine, January 10, 1776 in Conway (1894), Vol. 1, p. 68.

[55] Thomas Paine, January 10, 1776 in Conway (1894), Vol. 1, p. 95.

Nationalism and the Federal Constitution: Amalgamating People, Property and Sovereignty

Origins of the Constitution

In the midst of the Revolutionary War, in 1781, the thirteen colonies signed the Articles of Confederation, which established a loose union between the states. This was to ensure the rule of the people, but a government by the people proved difficult to organize: the Revolutionary War had left the various colonies and the Continental Congress with huge debts that proved difficult to pay, especially since the Articles of Confederation did not vest the central government with the power of taxation. Serious financial issues created much unrest and debate amongst various factions, groups and classes. An infamous example of this was the 1786/1787 insurrection in Massachusetts, known as Shay's Rebellion, against federal taxes in which local farmers arose in armed revolt against the central authorities. John Jay's complaint here about "the insecurity of property"[56] may sum up the general concern at the time in the national movement and the primary principle of nationalism. By the fall of 1787, as Edmund Randolph (1753–1813) of Virginia put it, it had became clear to many, if not most, "that the confederation fulfilled *none* of the objects for which it was framed"[57]—for example, the protection of the property rights and freedoms of Americans. Thus, the colonists started work on a new constitution that created a stronger federal government, which was ratified in 1789.

The constitution, propagated by people who came to be known as Federalists, was ratified under much debate, and it was not so obvious

[56]John Jay, quoted in Larkin, Pascal, *Property in the Eighteenth Century: With Special Reference to England and Locke*, Cork University Press, Dublin and Cork (1930), p. 153. Thomas Jefferson of course famously proclaimed in the wake of this rebellion that "a little rebellion now and then is a good thing, and as necessary in the political world as storms in the physical ... it prevents the degeneracy of government." See Thomas Jefferson to James Madison, January 30, 1787 in Boyd, Julian, *The Papers of Thomas Jefferson*, Vol. 10, Princeton University Press, Princeton, NJ (1955), p. 93. However, the security of property was as essential to Jefferson as to Jay, although the two men had different ideas of how this was to be done.

[57]Edmund Randolph, May 29, 1787 in Farrand, Max (ed.), *The Records of the Federal Convention of 1787*, Yale University Press, New Haven (1911), Vol. 1, p. 25. http://oll.libertyfund.org/titles/1057#Farrand_0544-01_209 (accessed 19.01.2015).

to everyone that a stronger government in the manner in which the new constitution suggested was the safest bulwark against "the insecurity of property." George Mason reflected on this in a letter to his son sent from the Federal Convention, which sums up the general ambiguous position on the subject. Mason reflected:

> The revolt from Great Britain and the formations of our new governments at that time, were nothing compared to the great business now before us; there was then a certain degree of enthusiasm, which inspired and supported the mind; but to view, through the calm, sedate medium of reason the influence which the establishment now proposed may have upon the happiness or misery of millions yet unborn, is an object of such magnitude, as absorbs, and in a manner suspends the operations of the human understanding....[58]

At the time of the Federal Convention the "enthusiasm" from the revolution had transformed in many minds into a form of discouragement in front of the serious and difficult task that lay ahead, into "such magnitude ... that suspends the operations of the human understanding." How were liberty and property actually to be secured? As George Washington put it in a letter to a friend the people were practically screaming for an answer:

> The pressure of the public voice was so loud, I could not resist the call to a convention of the States which is to determine whether we are to have a Government of respectability under which life – liberty, and property will be secured to us, or are to submit to one which may be the result of chance or the moment, springing perhaps from anarchy and Confusion...[59]

"The whole Community" was anxious with this question. "And there can be no doubt but that the result will in some way or other have a powerful effect on our destiny," wrote James Madison to Thomas Jefferson, who at the time was in France serving as Minister for the Confederation.[60]

[58] George Mason to George Mason Jr., June 1, 1787 in Farrand (1911), Vol. 3, p. 33.
[59] George Washington to La Fayette, June 6, 1787 in Farrand (1911), Vol. 3, p. 34.
[60] James Madison to Thomas Jefferson, June 6, 1787 in Farrand (1911), Vol. 3, p. 36.

Popular Landownership, Popular Sovereignty

The debates over the constitution were in the broadest sense about centralization of sovereignty. Adopting a national constitution would mean a reduction of the sovereignty of the individual states as had been established with the Articles of Confederation, and the critics of the constitution (the Anti-federalists) claimed that this would put the rights and liberties of the people in danger.[61] The debates over the issue of centralization of sovereignty actually show, however, the cementation of a broader, overreaching view of the connection between property and popular sovereignty. This idea transcended the differences between the Federalists and the Anti-federalists—there was a common underlying vision. It should be no surprise that this was the case, and that this vision was similar to, for example, Jefferson's ideas about property and sovereignty. The people who drafted the constitution were, after all, elite land and plantation owners like Jefferson—and wealthy merchants and thirty-four were lawyers like Jefferson.[62] The Anti-federalists tended to be less wealthy, but even these men were primarily men of landed property, generally small farmers.[63] It must be significant also that all these men had as a common reference the myth and reality of America, where landownership was relatively widespread and where new land was available. Because of this the freedom derived from landholding became coupled

[61]The critics of the constitution became known as the Anti-federalists, but they had the same property assumptions. For some works on the Anti-federalists see Cornell, Saul, *The Other Founders: Anti-federalism and the Dissenting Tradition in America*, University of North Carolina Press, Chapel Hill (1999); and Main, Jackson Turner, *The Anti-federalists: Critics of the Constitution, 1781–1787*, University of North Carolina Press, Chapel Hill (1962). There is also an interesting comment on the federal convention that sums up the anti-federalists' views on the matter in Wills, Garry, *Inventing America; Jefferson's Declaration of Independence*, Doubleday, New York (1978). Wills writes: "The convention that drew up the constitution went far beyond their mandate; in effect, smuggled a new nation in upon the continent rather than bringing it forth by intellectual impregnation. The founding legend begins to look more like a case of Sabine rape than virginal conception." See Wills (1978), p. xvii.

[62]The classic account of the class composition of the constitutional conventions is Beard, Charles, *An Economic Interpretation of the Constitution of the United States*, Free Press, New York (1941). For a modern engagement with the book and the constitution see MacDonald, Forrest, *We the People: The Economic Origins of the Constitution*, Transaction Publishers, New Brunswick (1992). Cogliano (1999), pp. 115–125 also has a clear and substantial overview on which I have relied.

[63]Main (1962), pp. 1–21.

with popular sovereignty. The mixing of popular sovereignty with individual landholding was a direct result of the relative widespread ownership of landed property in the US. Sovereignty was popular because property was popular. Noah Webster[64] pointed this out quite directly:

> *A general and tolerably equal distribution of landed property is the whole basis of national freedom*: The system of the great Montesquieu will ever be erroneous, till the words *property or lands in fee simple* are substituted for *virtue*, throughout his *Spirit of Laws*.[65]

Moreover, Webster continued:

> Virtue, patriotism or love of country never was and never will be, till men's natures are changed, a fixed, permanent principle and support of government. But in an agricultural country a general possession of land in fee simple may be rendered perpetual.[66]

Charles Pinckney (1757–1824) of South Carolina, delegate to the constitutional convention, made a similar statement at the convention:

> The people of the U. States are perhaps the most singular of any we are acquainted with. Among them there are fewer distinctions of fortune & less of rank, than among the inhabitants of any other nation. Every freeman has a right to the same protection & security; and a very moderate share of property entitles them to the possession of all the honors and privileges the public can bestow: hence arises a greater equality, than is to be found among the people of any other country, and an equality which is

[64] Noah Webster is probably best known for his 1828 publication, *An American Dictionary of the English Language*. However, he was also a firm supporter of Federalist nationalism. Webster was born in 1758 the son of a Connecticut farmer and went on to study languages and law at Yale College. During the 1780s he worked as a teacher, but in 1793 he became editor of a Federalist newspaper in New York. Webster had, since the Federal Convention, been a strong supporter of Federalist ideas. See Carnes, C. Mark, and John A. Garraty (eds.), *American National Biography*, Vol. 22, Oxford University Press, New York and Oxford (1999), pp. 874–875.

[65] Noah Webster, October 17, 1787 in Sheehan, Colleen A., and Gary L. McDowell (eds.), *Friends of the Constitution: Writings of the "Other" Federalists, 1787–1788*, Liberty Fund, Indianapolis (1998), p. 400. http://oll.libertyfund.org/titles/2069#lfSheehan_1174 (accessed 29.01.2015).

[66] Noah Webster, October 17, 1787 in Sheehan and MacDowell (1998), p. 400.

> more likely to continue – I say this equality is likely to continue, because in a new Country, possessing immense tracts of uncultivated lands, where every temptation is offered to emigration & where industry must be rewarded with competency, there will be few poor, and few dependent … the whole community will enjoy in the fullest sense that kind of political liberty which consists in the power the members of the State reserve to themselves, of arriving at the public offices, or at least, of having votes in the nomination of those who fill them.[67]

It was for this reason that the people (because they had property) could be sovereign, and it was for this reason that the people could also be the protector of the right to property. "He that is wise," reflected Thomas Paine, will see that "the safest asylum … is, the love of the people. All property is safe under their protection."[68] In a later pamphlet, *Agrarian Justice* (1797), Paine also gives the people, led on by revolutionary principles, a key role in securing landed property, and in handing out justice to those who do not have property.[69]

Propertied Individuals as Sovereign People

During the federal convention, George Mason observed that:

> A new set of ideas seems to have crept in since the articles of confederation were established. Conventions of the people, or with power derived expressly from the people, were not then thought of.[70]

The sovereignty of the people had indeed become a pervasive principle in America by the time the constitution was written. Noah Webster wrote in his "An examination into the leading principles of the federal

[67]Charles Pinckney, June 25, 1787 in Farrand (1911), Vol. 1, p. 399.

[68]Thomas Paine, April 8, 1776 in Conway (1894), Vol. 1, p. 159.

[69]In the pamphlet Paine claims that landed property is a product of civilization, and that at first all the earth was the common property of all men. Therefore property was unjust. Because property did create inequality, society should mend this by creating a national fund which every year should give a certain amount of money to all the members of the nation. This, however, "could not be brought forward afterwards till heaven had opened the way by a revolution in the system of government." See Thomas Paine, January, 1797 in Conway (1894), Vol. 3, p. 331. In other words, a government by the people will protect property.

[70]George Mason, July 23, 1787 in Farrand (1911), Vol. 2, p. 92.

constitution" (1787) that "the source of power is in the people of this country, and cannot for ages, and probably never will be, removed." However, Webster also asked rhetorically in the same text: "in what ... does real power consist?" and answered thus, "the answer is short and plain – in property."[71] The two principles to which Madison and Webster refer show that the sovereignty of the people was based on the sovereignty of every individual, and that the sovereignty of the individual was based on his or her right to (landed) property. There was no contradiction between Webster's two assertions (power in the people, and real power in property); and the "new set of ideas" that Mason felt had "crept in" were not that new. Popular sovereignty was constituted by consenting propertied individuals—it was derived from the freedom and powers that the colonists, as we saw, attributed to ownership of property. Alexander Hamilton wrote in *The Federalist* No. 81, "it is inherent in the nature of sovereignty, not to be amenable to the suit of an individual without its consent."[72] Yet, George Washington said, "to secure all rights of independent sovereignty to each, and yet provide for the interest and safety of all"[73] it was essential that "individuals entering into society, must give up a share of liberty to preserve the rest." Hamilton and Washington were talking of consolidating a federal union here, but in doing so they demonstrated the general principle of American nationalism. John Jay (1745–1829) also pointed to this. Jay was born to a wealthy merchant family in New York and became a legal practitioner in 1768. In 1774 he was elected as a member of the First Continental Congress. He was not a member of the Federal Convention, but became a strong advocate of the federal constitution, co-writing *The Federalist Papers* with James Madison and Alexander Hamilton.[74] In *Federalist* No. 2, he wrote about government:

> Nothing is more certain than the indispensable necessity of government; and it is equally undeniable, that whenever and however it is instituted, the

[71] Noah Webster, October 17, 1787 in Sheehan and McDowell (1998), p. 398.

[72] Alexander Hamilton, May 28, 1788 in Cooke, Jacob E. (ed.), *The Federalist*, Wesleyan University Press, Middletown, CT (1961), pp. 548–549.

[73] George Washington, September 17, 1787, in Carey, George W., and James McClellan, *The Federalist (The Gideon Edition)*, Liberty Fund, Indianapolis (2001), p. 423. http://oll.libertyfund.org/titles/788#Hamilton_0084_1322 (accessed 19.09.2014).

[74] Carnes, C. Mark, and John A. Garraty (eds.), *American National Biography*, Vol. 11, Oxford University Press, New York and Oxford (1999), pp. 891–894.

> people must cede to it some of their natural rights, in order to vest it with requisite powers.[75]

This was an argument for the centralization of powers in the federal government from the states. But the principle is the same: the interest that the individual has in property (his or her freedom) becomes transferred to society as a whole. The thoughts of Gouverneur Morris (1752–1816) of Pennsylvania, a delegate to the Federal Convention, are telling on this at an individual level. As the Convention records state, Morris reflected on representation to the federal government and:

> He thought property ought to be taken into the estimate as well as the number of inhabitants. Life and liberty were generally said to be of more value, than property. An accurate view of the matter would nevertheless prove that property was the main object of Society. The savage State was more favorable to liberty than the Civilized; and sufficiently so to life. It was preferred by all men who had not acquired a taste for property; it was only renounced for the sake of property which could only be secured by the restraints of regular Government.[76]

A propertied community was created in which individuals alienated some of their liberty (based on their ownership of land) in order to maintain their right to property. Thomas Paine seems to have agreed with Morris. He explained in *Common Sense* that: "Society in every state is a blessing, but government, even in its best state is but a necessary evil." However, to protect his property, man:

> Finds it necessary to surrender up a part of his property to furnish means for the protection of the rest; and this he is induced to do by the same prudence which in every other case advises him, out of two evils to choose the least. Wherefore, security being the true design and end of government, it unanswerably follows that whatever form thereof appears most likely to ensure it to us, with the least expense and greatest benefit, is preferable to all others.[77]

Government was supposed to be instituted to protect the rights of property for all, and based on the right to property of all. In *Agrarian Justice*,

[75]John Jay, October 31, 1787 in Cooke (1961), p. 8.

[76]Gouverneur Morris, July 5, 1787 in Farrand (1911), Vol. 1, p. 534.

[77]Thomas Paine, January 10, 1776 in Conway (1894), Vol. 1, p. 69.

Paine said that private property was the product of civilization, but that in reality all men had the earth in common, and thus all men had a property right to it. Private property was therefore in one sense unjust. One could not, however, abolish private property—that would be unjust to the present owners—but with a government of the people, one could make it just and secure some property for all.[78] Federalist Alexander Hamilton was also clear on the point in deciding to enter into government: it was "the additional security which its adoption will afford to republican government, to liberty, and to property."[79] Or, as Webster put it:

> an equality of property, with necessity of alienation, constantly operating to destroy combinations of powerful families, is the very soul of a republic – while this continues, the people will inevitably possess both power and freedom.[80]

The Rule of Law

The way in which the people protected property was through legislative power—the rule of law. As we saw, Thomas Paine had as early as 1776 stated this as fundamental to "independency." Jefferson agreed, and wrote in a letter to a friend nearly forty years after the revolution:

> Everyone, by his property, or his satisfactory situation, is interested in the support of law and order. And such men may safely and advantageously reserve to themselves a wholesome control over their public affairs.[81]

[78] Paine wrote that "It is a position not to be controverted that the earth, in its natural uncultivated state was, and ever would have continued to be, *the common property of the human race*. In that state every man would have been born to property." Private property was thus unjust. "The fault, however, is not in the present possessors. No complaint is tended, or ought to be alleged against them, unless they adopt the crime by opposing justice. The fault is in the system … But the fault can be made to reform itself by successive generations; and without diminishing or deranging the property of any of the present possessors, the operation of the fund can yet commence, and be in full activity, the first year of its establishment, or soon after, as I shall show." See Thomas Paine, January, 1797, in Conway (1894), Vol. 3, pp. 329–332.

[79] Alexander Hamilton, October 27, 1787 in Carey and McClellan (2001), p. 4.

[80] Noah Webster, October 17, 1787 in Sheehan and McDowell (1998), p. 402.

[81] Thomas Jefferson to John Adams, October 28, 1813 in Looney, J. Jefferson, *The Papers of Thomas Jefferson: Retirement Series*, Vol. 6, Princeton University Press, Princeton and Oxford (2009), p. 566.

Moreover, again we can see how the rule of law, or popular sovereignty, is dependent on widespread ownership of land. "Here [in America]," said Jefferson, "Everyone may have land and labor for himself."[82] This was a new form of government, very different from the "aristocratic" type found before ("A government adopted to such men would be one thing; but a very different one that for the men of these states"[83]). It was because property was widespread in America that the people could be sovereign, assume power of government, as lawmakers. Similar to Jefferson, smallholding farmer William Manning wrote that it was "asserted by the many that government is founded on property," and that the protection of this right was "the sole end of government."[84] To achieve such a government, one had:

> To be governed by known laws in which the whole nation had a voice in making by full and fair representation, and in which all the officers in every department are (or ought to be) servants and not masters.[85]

Manning was born in rural Massachusetts in 1747 and stayed there as a farmer all his life. In 1775 he participated in some of the first acts of violence during the American Revolution, which he later saw as an important moment in his political awakening. "I saw almost the first blood that was shed," Manning reflected, "and scores of men dead, dying and wounded in the cause of Liberty."[86] This, he claimed, awoke his political interest. During the 1790s he became a member of the Democratic-Republican Party, and he drafted political pamphlets. None of his writings were published during his lifetime, however, and only in 1922 was his main work *Key of Liberty* published.[87] That Manning the smallholder and Jefferson the slave holding plantation owner held similar ideas about property and sovereignty might once again accentuate the common national vision in this time period—to be found also amongst

[82] Thomas Jefferson to John Adams, October 28, 1813 in Looney (2009), p. 566.

[83] Thomas Jefferson to John Adams, October 28, 1813 in Looney (2009), p. 566.

[84] William Manning, 1798 in Merrill, Michael, and Sean Wilentz, *The Key of Liberty: Life and Democratic Writings of William Manning "A Laborer", 1747–1814*, Harvard University Press, Cambridge, MA (1993) [1922], pp. 131 and 135.

[85] William Manning, 1798 in Merrill and Wilentz (1993), p. 130.

[86] William Manning, 1798 in Merrill and Wilentz (1993), p. 16.

[87] I have relied on the information in Merrill and Wilentz (1993), Preface and pp. 14–21.

the Federalists. We might end this topic by once more going back to Federalist Noah Webster's text quoted at the beginning of this section. Webster wrote that it was the majority of the people that were to make laws in a free society. Through a strong executive based on widespread ownership of land, one could ensure a society "where laws govern, and not men ... The laws are the sole guardians of right ..."[88] When power was based on widespread ownership of land, as Webster had asserted, then one had popular sovereignty, the rule of law.

The First Form of the Nation: A Nation of Freeholders

Jefferson's Nation of Small Farmers

The rule of law was conducted through a propertied democracy—that is to say, a democracy where enfranchisement was confined primarily to those owning a certain amount of landed or real property, and where the right to property was secured through the rule of law made by these people. This already had its origin in the colonial era when a £40 freehold was the most widely used property qualification for participation in local government. This was connected to taxation and could in some states be fulfilled by owning personal property. As paper money became increasingly more common around and after the revolution, acres of land became a common deciding factor.[89] At the time the national constitution was written, property qualifications made 90% of adult white males eligible to vote in New Jersey, Pennsylvania, Georgia, North Carolina and South Carolina, and New Hampshire, and most towns in Massachusetts. In Virginia 70–90% were eligible, in Maryland 70% and in New York 60%.[90] This highlights the importance of propertied preconditions for popular sovereignty.

Thomas Jefferson is the person par excellence who exemplifies the idea of a nation of free farmers, and a national sovereignty seen to be derived from the landed property of its members. Indeed, Jefferson took

[88] Noah Webster, October 17, 1787 in Sheehan and McDowell (1998), p. 380.

[89] Collier, Christopher, "The American people as Christian white men of property: Suffrage and elections in early national America," in Donald W. Rogers (ed.), *Voting and the Spirit of American Democracy: Essays on the History of Voting and Voting Rights in America*, University of Illinois Press, Urbana and Chicago (1992), p. 23.

[90] Collier in Rogers (1992), p. 26.

the idea of rule by men of landed property so seriously, and saw it as so fundamental to a healthy republic, that he even suggested once to give the amount of land required for individual independence to all those in Virginia not possessing it.[91] Jefferson believed that:

> We have an immensity of land courting the industry of the husbandman. Is it best then that all our citizens should be employed in its improvement, or that one half should be called off from that to exercise manufactures and handicraft arts for the other? Those who labour in the earth are the chosen people of God, if ever he had a chosen people, whose breasts he has made his peculiar deposit for substantial and genuine virtue. It is the focus in which he keeps alive that sacred fire, which otherwise might escape from the face of the earth."[92]

To maintain the "sacred fire" of freedom, America was to be a governed by "those who labour in the earth" because:

> The mobs of great cities add just so much to the support of pure government, as sores do to the strength of the human body. It is the manners and spirit of a people which preserve a republic in vigour. A degeneracy in these is a cancer which soon eats to the heart of its laws and constitution.[93]

When Jefferson became president, his "empire of liberty" was to be one ruled by propertied men, and it was one that would persist and expand into the future. Jefferson first used the term "empire of liberty" during the Revolutionary War in a letter to one of the generals, talking about expansion of the confederacy. Here Jefferson envisioned the future "empire of liberty" an "extensive and fertile country."[94] This expansion of the US into fertile land was integrated into Jefferson's political vision.

[91] Wood, Gordon (1993), p. 179.

[92] Jefferson, Thomas, *Notes on the State of Virginia*, Harper & Row, New York (1964) [1785], p. 157.

[93] Jefferson (1964), p. 158.

[94] Thomas Jefferson to George Rogers Clark, December 25, 1780 in Boyd, Julian (ed.), *The Papers of Thomas Jefferson*, Vol. 4, Princeton University Press, Princeton, NJ (1951), p. 237.

One important principle of Jefferson's political vision was "the encouragement of agriculture, and of commerce as its handmaid."[95] Agriculture was central to a free republic; commerce and manufacture were only to be the "handmaid" of agriculture. With the Louisiana Purchase in 1803, Jefferson acquired a territory in which to realize this vision of an agrarian, "extensive and fertile empire of liberty." Louisiana, he said, was "an ample provision for our posterity, and a wide-spread field for the blessings of freedom and equal laws."[96] With this territory, his vision from *Notes of the State of Virginia* could be realized:

> Let us never wish to see our citizens occupied at a work bench, or twirling a distaff. Carpenters masons, smiths, are wanting in husbandry; but, for the general operations of manufacture, let our workshops remain in Europe.[97]

Since landed property was the kind of property that conferred freedom and virtue on individuals in Jefferson's vision, wage laborers could not be properly free or vitreous. American liberty was therefore best secured by men of landed property. Jefferson elaborated on this in a paragraph from *Notes* in a letter that he wrote during his presidency, explaining that the situation in America, at the present, was unique and especially favorable to good government:

> I had under my eye when writing [*Notes*], the manufactures of the great cities in the old countries, at the present time, with whom the want of food and clothing necessary to sustain life, has begotten a depravity of morals, a dependence and corruption, which renders them an undesirable accession to a country whose morals are sound. My expressions look forward to the time when our own great cities would get into the same state. But they have been quoted as if meant for the present time here. As yet our manufactures are as much at their ease, as independent and moral as our agricultural habits, and they will continue so as long as there are vacant

[95] Thomas Jefferson, March 4, 1801 in Oberg, Barbara B. (ed.), *The Papers of Thomas Jefferson*, Vol. 33, Princeton University Press, Princeton and Oxford (2006), p. 151.

[96] Thomas Jefferson, October 17, 1803 in Oberg, Barbara B. (ed.), *The Papers of Thomas Jefferson*, Vol. 41, Princeton University Press, Princeton and Oxford (2014), p. 535.

[97] Jefferson (1964), p. 157.

> lands for them to resort to; because whenever it shall be attempted by the other classes to reduce them to the minimum of subsistence, they will quit their trades and go to laboring the earth.[98]

We see here the consistency of Jefferson's vision from the 1780s to the early 1800s; the belief in America as unique and inherited with the possibility of freedom and independence due to its property relations—that Americans always had the possibility to "quit their trades and go to laboring in the earth."

Locke and Labour in America

Jefferson's contemporary Crevecoeur is another famous proclaimer of the uniqueness of America and the importance of smallholding farms. He proclaimed in his famous *Letters from an American Farmer*, written towards the end of the Revolutionary War, that, "We have no princes, for whom we toil, starve and bleed: we are the most perfect society now existing in the world. Here man is free as he ought to be."[99] The American was free because he had gone "from being the slave of some despotic prince, to become a free man, invested with lands." Indeed, wrote Crevecoeur: "The American is a new man … From involuntary idleness, servile dependence, penury, and useless labour, he has passed to toils of a very different nature, rewarded by ample subsistence."[100] These are all strong assertions of the importance of landed property and again demonstrate the propertied basis for popular sovereignty, but as much as these passages point to the importance of landed property, there are also other important topics to note. The words labour, dependence, and slavery are frequently invoked. As we saw, Jefferson wrote about independence when he elaborated on his passage in *Notes*, that labourers, if reduced to "minimum subsistence," could "quit their trades and go to laboring in the earth." It is central that Jefferson here writes "labouring in the earth" and not own land. The same idea we see with Crevecoeur when he wrote that the American, as opposed to the "slave of some despotic prince," was "passed to toils" which rewarded him with "ample subsistence." This points us to one underlying assumption of property

[98] Thomas Jefferson, January 4, 1805 in Leicester Ford (1904–5), Vol. 4, p. 87.

[99] Crevecoeur (1971), p. 41.

[100] Crevecoeur (1971), p. 44.

and freedom in the national ideology—a point that had been expressed by John Locke in his *Two Treatises on Government*:

> Every man has a *property* in his own *person:* this nobody has any right to but himself. The *labour* of his body, and the work of his hands, we may say, is properly his. Whatsoever then he removes out of the state that nature hath provided, and had mixed his *labour* with, and joined to it something that is his own, and thereby makes it his *property*.[101]

Landed property had special significance in the American national ideology, but it was derived in part from the more general idea that "every man has property in his own person" and that putting labour into the earth he "makes it his property." Owning landed property was by many seen to be a particularly secure way of insuring the right to one's labour. This had to do with the landed agrarian context in which American nationalism emerged, and the American context of widespread individual landownership was important in cementing the idea of private exclusive ownership. Widespread ownership of land, however, and the relative ease by which one could acquire property by investing one's labour in unused land also contributed to understanding the right to property as based on investment labour. In the future, land came to lose its importance in favor of abstract wealth, which was secured to the individual by his labour. This was a *transvaluation of property*, or a shift from land to labour, and it happened with the coming of industrial society, as we shall see in Part II of this book. In the agrarian phase it was land that remained important. This was also similar in Norway, to which we shall now move.

Summary

This chapter has covered the period between 1760 and 1790. The first part of the analysis dealt with the period from about 1762 to 1776: the prelude to nationalism. I invoked primarily the writings of Thomas Jefferson, John Dickinson, and Thomas Paine to demonstrate the importance of private property to the concept of freedom, and to show how this went from being understood as a British right to an American right.

[101] Locke, John, *Two Treatises of Government*, London (1764) [1690], pp. 216–217. http://oll.libertyfund.org/titles/222 (accessed 28.01.2015).

The second part of the analysis revolved around the Federal Constitutional Convention (1787) and its aftermath. The focus was on how individuals' right to property became connected to the idea of rule by the people. We might call this the amalgamation of nationalism. The chapter relied primarily on records of the Constitutional Convention, *The Federalist Papers* (1788) and Noah Webster's "An examination into the leading principles of the Federal Constitution" (1791). Finally, the chapter discussed *the first form of the nation*—how *the amalgamation of property, people and sovereignty* was understood in a way so that the sovereignty of the people and property were seen to be secure through a propertied democracy based on men of landed property. This was very much based on a discussion on Thomas Jefferson's ideas about American smallholding farmers.

Literature

Alexander, George S., *Commodity and Property: Competing Visions of Property in American Legal Thought*, University of Chicago Press, Chicago and London (1997).

Alymer, G.E, "The meaning and definition of 'property' in seventeenth century England," *Past and Present*, No. 86 (February, 1980).

Appleby, Joyce, *Capitalism and a New Social Order: The Republican Vision of the 1790s*, New York University Press, New York and London (1984).

Bailyn, Bernard, *The Ideological Origins of the American Revolution*, Harvard University Press, Cambridge, MA (1992) [1967].

Beard, Charles, *An Economic Interpretation of the Constitution of the United States*, Free Press, New York (1941).

Bigelow, John, *The Works of Benjamin Franklin, Including the Private as Well as the Official and Scientific Correspondence, Together with the Unmutilated and Correct Version of the Autobiography*, G. P. Putnam's Sons, New York (1904), Vol. V (Letters and Misc. Writings 1768–1772), p. 278. http://oll.libertyfund.org/titles/2459#Franklin_1438-05_878 (accessed 29.01.2015).

Boyd, Julian (ed.), *The Papers of Thomas Jefferson*, Vol. 1, Princeton University Press, Princeton, NJ (1950).

Boyd, Julian (ed.), *The Papers of Thomas Jefferson*, Vol. 2, Princeton University Press, Princeton, NJ (1950).

Boyd, Julian (ed.), *The Papers of Thomas Jefferson*, Vol. 4, Princeton University Press, Princeton, NJ (1951).

Boyd, Julian (ed.), *The Papers of Thomas Jefferson*, Vol. 10, Princeton University Press, Princeton, NJ (1955).

Carey, George W., and James McClellan, *The Federalist (The Gideon Edition)*, Liberty Fund, Indianapolis (2001).

Carnes, C. Mark, and John A. Garraty (eds.), *American National Biography*, Vol. 1, Oxford University Press, New York and Oxford (1999).

Carnes, C. Mark, and John A. Garraty (eds.), *American National Biography*, Vol. 6, Oxford University Press, New York and Oxford (1999).

Carnes, C. Mark, and John A. Garraty (eds.), *American National Biography*, Vol. 11, Oxford University Press, New York and Oxford (1999).

Carnes, C. Mark, and John A. Garraty (eds.), *American National Biography*, Vol. 16, Oxford University Press, New York and Oxford (1999).

Carnes, C. Mark, and John A. Garraty (eds.), *American National Biography*, Vol. 22, Oxford University Press, New York and Oxford (1999).

Cogliano, Francis D., *Revolutionary America 1763–1815: A Political History*, Routledge, London (1999).

Collier, Christopher, "The American people as Christian white men of property: Suffrage and elections in early national America," in Donald W. Rogers (ed.), *Voting and the Spirit of American Democracy: Essays on the History of Voting and Voting Rights in America*, University of Illinois Press, Urbana and Chicago (1992).

Conway, Moncure Daniel, *The Writings of Thomas Paine*, G. P. Putnam's Sons, New York (1894), Vol. 1, p. 90. http://oll.libertyfund.org/titles/343#Paine_0548-01_160 (accessed 19.01.2015).

Cooke, Jacob E. (ed.), *The Federalist*, Wesleyan University Press, Middletown, CT (1961).

Cornell, Saul, *The Other Founders: Anti-federalism and the Dissenting Tradition in America*, University of North Carolina Press, Chapel Hill (1999).

Farrand, Max (ed.), *The Records of the Federal Convention of 1787*, Yale University Press, New Haven (1911), Vol. 1. http://oll.libertyfund.org/titles/1057#Farrand_0544-01_209 (accessed 19.01.2015).

Greene, Jack P., *Peripheries and Center: Constitutional Development in the Extended Polities of the British Empire and the United States, 1607–1788*, University of Georgia Press, Athens and London (1986).

Greenfeld, Liah, *Nationalism; Five Roads to Modernity*, Harvard University Press, Cambridge, MA (1993).

Henretta, James A., "Wealth and social structure," in Jack Greene and J.R. Pole (eds.), *Colonial British America*, Johns Hopkins University Press, Baltimore and London (1984).

Hoffer, Peter Charles, *Law and People in Colonial America*, Johns Hopkins University Press, Baltimore and London (1998).

Hunt, Gaillard, *The Writings of James Madison, Comprising His Public Papers and His Private Correspondence, Including His Numerous Letters and Documents Now for the First Time Printed*, G. P. Putnam's Sons, New York (1900),

Vol. 6, p. 102. http://oll.libertyfund.org/titles/1941#Madison_1356-06_466 (accessed 02.12.2015).

Jefferson, Thomas, *Notes on the State of Virginia*, Harper & Row, New York, (1964) [1785].

Jones, Alice Hanson, *Wealth of a Nation to Be: The American Colonies at the Eve of the Revolution*, Columbia University Press, New York (1980).

Hartz, Louis, *The Liberal Tradition in America: An Interpretation of American Political Thought Since the Revolution*, Harcourt, Brace & Co., New York (1955).

Kantz, Stanley, "Thomas Jefferson and the right to property in revolutionary America," *Journal of Law and Economics*, No. 19 (1976).

Kulikoff, Allan, *From British Peasants to Colonial American Farmers*, University of North Carolina Press, Chapel Hill and London (2000).

Larkin, Pascal, *Property in the Eighteenth Century: With Special Reference to England and Locke*, Cork University Press, Dublin and Cork (1930).

Locke, John, *Two Treatises of Government*, London (1764) [1690]. http://oll.libertyfund.org/titles/222 (accessed 28.01.2015).

Looney, J. Jefferson, *The Papers of Thomas Jefferson: Retirement Series*, Vol. 6, Princeton University Press, Princeton and Oxford (2009).

Main, Jackson Turner, *The Anti-federalists: Critics of the Constitution, 1781–1787*, University of North Carolina Press, Chapel Hill (1962).

Main, Jackson Turner, *The Social Structure of Revolutionary America*, Princeton University Press, Princeton (1965).

McDonald, Forrest, *We the People: The Economic Origins of the Constitution*, Transaction Publishers, New Brunswick (1992).

McDonald, Forrest (ed.), *Empire and Nation: Letters from a Farmer in Pennsylvania (John Dickinson) and Letters from the Federal Farmer (Richard Henry Lee)*, Liberty Fund, Indianapolis (1999), p. 81. http://oll.libertyfund.org/titles/690#Mcdonald_0010_289 (accessed 29.01.2015).

Merrill, Michael, and Sean Wilentz, *The Key of Liberty: Life and Democratic Writings of William Manning "A Laborer", 1747–1814*, Harvard University Press, Cambridge, MA (1993) [1922].

Moore, Barrington, *Social Origins of Dictatorship and Democracy: Lord and Peasant in the Making of the Modern World*, Beacon Press, Boston (1966).

Nelson, John R., *Liberty and Property: Political Economy and Policymaking in the New Nation 1789–1812*, Johns Hopkins University Press, Baltimore (1987).

Nettles, Curtis P., *The Roots of American Civilization: A History of American Colonial Life*, Meredith Publishing, New York (1963) [1938].

Oberg, Barbara B. (ed.), *The Papers of Thomas Jefferson*, Vol. 33, Princeton University Press, Princeton and Oxford (2006).

Oberg, Barbara B. (ed.), *The Papers of Thomas Jefferson*, Vol. 41, Princeton University Press, Princeton and Oxford (2014).

Pocock, J.G.A., *The Machiavellian Moment*, Princeton University Press, Princeton and Oxford (1975).

Pocock, J.G.A., *Virtue, Commerce and History: Essays on Political Thought and History, Chiefly in the Eighteenth Century*, Cambridge University Press, Cambridge (1985).

Sheehan, Colleen A., and Gary L. McDowell (eds.), *Friends of the Constitution: Writings of the "Other" Federalists, 1787–1788*, Liberty Fund, Indianapolis (1998), p. 400. http://oll.libertyfund.org/titles/2069#lfSheehan_1174 (accessed 29.01.2015).

Steele, Brian, *Thomas Jefferson and American Nationhood*, Cambridge University Press, Cambridge (2012).

Taylor, Robert J. (ed.), *Papers of John Adams*, Vol. 1, Belknap Press, Cambridge, MA (1977).

Taylor, Robert J. (ed.), *Papers of John Adams*, Vol. 2, Belknap Press, Cambridge, MA (1977).

Thomas, David A., *History of American Land Law, Vol. 2: Land Law in the American States*, Vandeplas Publishing, Lake Mary (2013).

Tocqueville, Alexis, *Democracy in America* (edited by J.P Mayer and Max Lerner), Harper & Row, New York and London (1988) [1840].

White, Edward, *Law in American History, Vol. 1: From the Colonial Years Through the Civil War*, Oxford University Press, Oxford and New York (2012).

Wills, Garry, *Inventing America; Jefferson's Declaration of Independence*, Doubleday, New York (1978).

Wood, Ellen Meiksins, *Liberty and Property: A Social History of Western Political Thought from the Renaissance to the Present*, Verso, London (2012).

Wood, Gordon, *The Creation of the American Republic*, W. W. Norton, New York (1969).

CHAPTER 3

Norway: "A Free Constitution … Was Centuries in the Making"

Since the eleventh century, there had been a comparatively well-organized state apparatus covering the area that would later constitute the Norwegian nation, and since the 1660s this kingdom was an integral part of one of the most consequential absolutist states in Europe, the Danish Oldenburg state. Despite this difference in historical conditions from the British North American colonies, landed property relations in Norway had become, by the time of its own national revolution, surprisingly similar to those in the American colonies. In a way, this difference in historical conditions constitutes a similarity to the American case. If, in America, the foundation for the national ideology was the lack of historically imbedded social structures, in Norway it was precisely because the social structure was so historically imbedded that an ideology of nationalism was prone to emerge. Like in America, the Norwegian property structure had resulted in widespread ownership of real property.

Norwegian historians of all convictions have always noted the peculiar property structure and its effect on the development and formation of the Norwegian nation and its separation in 1814 from the imperial

This is the first of two chapters on Norway. There are several quotes from historical documents in both chapters. The quotes were originally written in Danish or Norwegian, but for the purpose of this book the quotes have been translated into English by me.

E. M. Fuglestad, *Private Property and the Origins of Nationalism in the United States and Norway*,
https://doi.org/10.1007/978-3-319-89950-3_3

Danish state of which it had been part since 1537. The writings of Ernest Sars, written in the last quarter of the nineteenth century, are normally taken to constitute the beginning of the modern historiographical debate. Sars held, and vigorously advocated, the opinion that the Norwegian national movement had indeed been prepared over centuries of inner development owing to its peculiar property structure. Sars wrote that "a free constitution … was centuries in the making" and it was "the ancient personal freedom and property rights" of the Norwegian farmer—the *odelsbonde*[1]—that was the most important precondition and cause for the creation of a nation-state.[2] A generation later, Marxist historian Halvdan Koht continued this same line of argument.[3] Since then the importance of the role of the *odelsbonde* and the peculiar property structure to the preparation of the national movement has largely been downplayed or even dismissed completely.[4] In recent years, historians and sociologists have tended to give a more balanced account of the matter emphasizing both the importance of the property structure and other factors.[5] There has also been a renewed focus on the special Norwegian allodial right to land—the *odelsrett*—from a cultural constructivist perspective in recent years.[6] This chapter adds a more materialist dimension to these arguments, thus being similar to Kåre Lunden's approach from the early 1990s.[7] Lunden's views, and the leftist tradition

[1]This term is explained below.

[2]Sars, Ernst, *Historisk indledning til Grundloven*, Folkeskriftsselskabet, Kristiania (1887), p. 3.

[3]Koth, Halvdan, *Norsk bondereising: fyrebuing til bondepolitikken*, H. Aschehoug & Co., Oslo (1926).

[4]Steen, Sverre, *1814*, J.W. Cappelen Forlag AS, Oslo (1989). See also Mykkland, Knut, *Kampen om Norge*, Cappelen, Oslo (1958); and Seip, Jens Arup, *Utsikt over Norges historie*, Gyldendal Norsk Forlag (1974).

[5]Sejersted, Francis, *Demokrati og rettstat*, Pax Forlag AS, Oslo (2001); and Sejersted, Francis, *Demokratisk Kapitalisme*, Pax Forlag, Oslo (2000) are good examples of this.

[6]Sørensen, Øystein, *Kampen om norges sjel: norsk idehistorie bind II*, Aschehoug, Oslo (2001). See also Glenthøj, Rasmus, *Skilsmissen: dansk og norsk identitet før og efter 1814*, Syddansk Universitetsforlag, Odense (2012); Storsveen, Odd Arild, *Norsk patriotisme før 1814*, KULT's skriftserie nr 88, Oslo (1997); and Hommerstad, Marthe, "Allodial rights and the Norwegian Constitution: Christian Magnus Falsen and the idea of the Norwegian farmer," *Nordic Historical Review*, No. 10 (2010), pp. 83–94.

[7]Lunden, Kåre, *Norsk Grålysning: Norsk nasjonalisme, 1770–1814 på allmenn grunn*, Det Norske Samlaget, Gjøvik (1992). See also Lunden, Kåre, *Nasjon eller union: Refleksjonar og røynsler*, Det Norske Samlaget, Oslo (1993).

they represent, are the ones most congruent with my own in its emphasis on the propertied precondition for the national revival. I do not believe, as Sars did, in the heroic and unique attributes of the Norwegian farmer, but his right to property "centuries in the making" was decisive.[8]

The Socio-economic Situation on the Eve of the Norwegian Declaration of Independence

Early in the history of Norway, in the eighth and ninth century, most farmers living in the Norwegian area probably owned their own land (although there is no certain data on this)[9] and ownership of land conferred powers of sovereignty on the farmer: all landowners could meet at the legislative assembly and decide the laws and taxes that were to be imposed.[10] As the medieval period progressed into the twelfth and thirteenth centuries, fewer farmers were owners of their land as the king and the Church acquired rights to large areas of land—by 1300, the Church, the king and the aristocracy owned 63% of the land in Norway.[11] This land, however, never became centralized into manors, which made it possible for farmers to maintain a relatively independent position.

In 1661 the Norwegian kingdom officially became an absolutist state as part of the Danish Oldenburg state. Absolutism was instituted by the Danish king with help from the class of city burghers and merchants. This class supported the king in what was actually a *coup d'état*, depriving the aristocracy of their privileged political powers. Thus, the city burghers came to have a larger influence in the running of the state, and, amongst other things, they initiated sales of Crown and church land. This involved the gradual dissolution of a peculiar Norwegian landowning system that had developed in the late medieval period

[8] Recently, Nils Rune Langeland put forward an argument about the Norwegian Constitution that also places more emphasis on the property rights of the Norwegian farmer. See Langeland, Nils Rune, "Røysteretten som mål på politisk kompetanse," in Langeland (ed.), *Politisk kompetanse: grunnlovas borgar, 1814–2014*, Pax Forlag AS, Oslo (2014), pp. 27–59.

[9] Siggurdson, Jon Vidar, *Det Norrønne samfunnet: Vikingen, Kongen, Erkebiskopen og Bonden*, Pax Forlag, Oslo (2008), pp. 191–194.

[10] Krag, Claus, *Norges historie fram til 1319*, Universitetsforlaget, Oslo (2000), pp. 35–37.

[11] Krag (2000), p. 152.

(*skyldsystemet*),[12] where the worth of a farm was measured in a certain value of goods. This meant that, similar to a shareholding company,[13] different people could own parts of the value of a farm without actually having the right to the land itself. Thus, it was often the case that the Church or the elite had the right to appropriate a certain amount of the value of a farm. During the eighteenth century this system gradually dissolved. In the first instance, Crown land was bought in large chunks by wealthy individuals, but was often later sold to Norwegian farmers. These sales of Crown land contributed to creating an ownership structure where one third of farmers owned their own land in 1720. In the northeastern valleys of eastern Norway the percentage of self-ownership was as high as 60–70%, while the southwest had a self-ownership percentage between 15 and 30%. In the farm areas around Trondheim (Trøndelag), self-ownership varied in areas from 5 to 20%. Self-ownership gradually increased during the eighteenth century, largely because of further public sales of land to private persons: there was one wave of land sales during the 1720s and one during the 1750s. By 1800 the percentage of self-ownership was as high as 80% in some areas in the eastern parts of Norway, while the percentage had risen to about 60% in the southwest and to 50% in Trøndelag. For the country as a whole, almost 60% of farmers owned their own land in 1801.[14]

Economy and Population in Norway and Denmark

On the eve of the national revolution in Norway the population had reached 884,000 people. Almost all of these were Lutheran and almost all were ethnically Norwegian. Some 90% of the population lived in rural areas and 80% of the working population was employed in farming, fishing or forestry. Only 6% of the population was engaged in manufacturing

[12] It was Andreas Holmsen who coined this term and carried out many important seminal studies on the issue. See, for example, Holmsen, Andreas, *Gård og Gods I Noreg I Eldre tid*, Universitetsforlaget, Oslo (1980).

[13] I borrow this metaphor from Knut Dørum. See Dørum, Knut, "Det Norske Skyldssystemet – et særnorsk fenomen?" *Historisk Tidsskrift*, Vol. 101, No. 2 (2001), p. 291.

[14] This paragraph relies heavily on Moseng, Ole Georg, et al., *Norsk Historie II: 1537–1814*, Universitetsforlaget, Oslo (2003), pp. 207–211, 221–222 and 265–270.

or industry, whereas 15% of the population was engaged in commerce or transport. Export of raw materials—of which fish and lumber were the most important—constituted the bulk of Norwegian exports. Lumber went mainly to the British Isles and the Netherlands, whereas fish was exported to Southern Europe. There were also exports from mining and salt production which went mainly to Copenhagen due to the mercantile policies of the Oldenburg absolutist state. Exports went by sea, and by the early nineteenth century a small Norwegian merchant class owned one of the most considerable trading fleets in Europe. It was, however, farming and work related to the farm that dominated the relations of ownership and appropriation: about 260,000 heads of household were listed as being employed in agriculture in 1801. There were 78,000 independent or semi-independent farmers at this time, 60% of whom were self-owners. The remaining 40% were tenants (*leiglendinger*). They were given land that they farmed as their own and had free status with no obligations. There was also a group of crofters (*husmenn*) who can be divided into two main groups: 39,000 who not only had been granted some land of their own on a main farm, but also had labour obligations on the main farm; and some who were landless (about 40,000 people). In addition to these, there was also a large group of household servants consisting of more than 100,000 people. It is worth noting that there was practically no landed/feudal aristocracy in Norway. There existed literally only two units in the whole country that came close to resembling a manor.[15] Since the Norwegian Kingdom was part of the absolutist Oldenburg state, there existed formal aristocratic titles or privileges given by the king, but which were not connected to the ownership of manors. Hence, there was no landed aristocracy. The ruling class of Norway instead included clergymen and state officials, and many of these became central members of the national movement. Although these were not primarily landed aristocrats, they often owned significant properties and were relatively wealthy. This was a small group and, indeed, only a small portion of the population of Norway became members of the national

[15]One was the Barony of Rosendal (established 1678) in the southwest of Norway. See Bratberg, Terje, "Baroniet Rosendal," *Store Norske Leksikon* (2010). https://snl.no/Baroniet_Rosendal (accessed 10.02.2016). The other was the County of Jarlsberg (established 1684). See Bratberg, Terje, "Jarlsberg," *Store Norske Leksiko* (2010) https://snl.no/Jarlsberg (accessed 10.02.2016).

movement that instigated the revolution in 1814.[16] The movement consisted mainly of a small group of state officials, which constituted no more than 1% of the population, and a small group of merchants, but there were also freeholding farmers amongst its members. It was the elite who led the movement, nevertheless it managed to secure the support also of the freeholding farmers and integrated them into the movement. The basis for their common interest was the securing of private landed property.

The State

The Norwegian national movement grew within the framework of a strong absolutist state. It may be useful to define the state to which the Norwegian Kingdom belonged after the Reformation as *den Oldenborgske heilstaten* ("the dynastic Oldenburg state"). This sets our focus on the fact that it was the Oldenburg dynasty which ruled over the Norwegian Kingdom (and others), and that it was a state that ruled over several different linguistic and cultural areas where political power was legitimized and exercised by monarchical lineage. It was a state where sovereignty was theoretically vested solely in the Oldenburg monarch, thus making landed property in theory disconnected from political rights. In fact, yet, even though the Norwegian kingdom was subject to the Oldenburg Crown—a province[17]—it was still in some ways seen as a separate kingdom. The monarch often stressed his right to the kingdoms of Norway and Denmark, and Norwegian medieval law was kept intact.[18] Nevertheless, despite this formal division of the two kingdoms, the Oldenburg state became, after 1660, one of the most consolidated and centralized monarchies in Europe.[19] The state was highly patriarchal, and absolute loyalty and love was demanded of its subjects. There were

[16]Pryser, Tore, *Norsk Historie 1814–1860: Frå Standssamfunn mot klassesamfunn*, Det Norske Samlaget, Oslo (1999), pp. 30–36, 59–74 and 164–168.

[17]When the kingdoms merged, it was declared that Norway was to be "a province of Denmark till the end of time."

[18]Ersland, Geir Atle and Hilde Sandvik, *Norsk historie, 1300–1625: eit rike tek form*, Det Norske Samlaget, Oslo (1999), pp. 162–163.

[19]This monarchy was, for instance, the only absolutist monarchy that had a written absolutist constitution. See Glenthøj, Rasmus, "Enevælde under afvikling. Schlegel og tidens

systems of local rule and government in which the population participated, but in theory there were almost no political, civic or economic freedoms within the absolutist state. The monarch was, according to the law, "the first and highest authority on earth and over all human law."[20] On the other hand, during the eighteenth century, the king was increasingly seen to have duties on behalf of his subjects, amongst other things to secure justice and bourgeoisie liberties[21] (and in fact, also the bulk of the population, the farmers, saw the Oldenburg king as a protector of their rights against local officials[22]), and by the late eighteenth century the absolutist monarchy was held in general high esteem; both in Norway and in Denmark, he was generally seen by the elite and the farmers as protecting liberties and their rights.[23] There had developed a notion of loyalty and belonging to the monarchy as an entity with rituals and mythologies feeding of both Norwegian and Danish history and myth.[24] There was also a pervasive intellectual environment inspired by the enlightenment that focussed on freedoms and rights of the citizens within this state. This environment laid some important foundations for the national movement that emerged in Norway in 1814.

skiftende oppfatelse av kongemakt og konstitution," in Mestad Ola (ed.), *Frihetens forskole: Professor Schlegel og Eidsvollsmennenes læretid i København*, Pax Forlag AS, Oslo (2013), p. 68.

[20]Quoted in Kvestad, Lars, "Frå undersaater til Norske borgere: Utviklinga av eit statsrettsleg frå eineveldet fram mot konstitusjonelt demokrati i 1814," in Langeland (2014), p. 61.

[21]Glenthøj in Ola Mestad (ed.) (2013). See also Holm, Edvard, *Den offentlige mening og Statsmagten i den dansk-norske stat i Slutningen av det 18de Aarhundrede 1784–1799*, København (1888); and Seip, Jens Arup, *Teorien om det opinionsstyrte eneveldet*, Universitetsforlaget, Oslo (1958).

[22]Koth (1926). See also Østerud, Øyvind, *Agrarian Structure and Peasant Politics in Scandinavia: A Comparative Study of Rural Response to Economic Change*, Universitetsforlaget, Oslo (1978). Østerud writes: "to the peasant mind the king often seems to have been perceived as a guarantor of legal rights against injustice from local power groups – including the provincial officialdom," p. 227.

[23]In fact, one can find expressions of feelings of freedom and pride of belonging to the Oldenburg monarchy, very similar to those expressed by colonial Americans in the decades leading up to the revolution: it was felt that the Oldenburg monarchy secured bourgeoisie freedoms more perfectly than any other state. See Olsen, Brian Kjær, "Frækhed er frihedens grænse. J.F.W. Schlegel og den republikanske udfordring," in Ola Mestad (ed.) (2013).

[24]Glenthøj in Ola Mestad (ed.) (2013). I shall elaborate on this below.

Norwegian Prelude

The Odelsbonde and Nordic Freedom Under Danish Rule

Like the American colonists in the late eighteenth century, the Norwegian elite of the early nineteenth century was also imbedded in a tradition of political thought where the connection between property and freedom was central.[25] Authors in both the Norwegian and the Danish part of the Oldenburg Empire had, since the early eighteenth century, developed and investigated theories of natural rights,[26] and by the late eighteenth century this was a major intellectual trend at the University of Copenhagen, the only university in the empire at the time (a university was established in the Norwegian capital of Christiania in Norway in 1811). Like in the British colonies, though, these ideas became adapted to local circumstances and applied to a specific Norwegian tradition of rights related to the property structure. In the agrarian society of Norway, with relative widespread ownership of land, landed property became particularly important, similar to what happened in the American colonies.

The Norwegian medieval state and the way in which farmers participated in government through the *ting* based on their special right to land—the *odelsrett*—was a pervasive element in the Norwegian strand of thought. The *odelsrett* was a familial right of preemption and redemption regarding landed property. It kept the landed property in the hands of the family that was farming the property and secured the owner exclusive rights of use. In this latter sense the *odelsrett* was what is called an allodial right to land, which can be contrasted to feudal land where rights of use are not exclusive, where the person using the property pays homage to a landlord and has limited rights regarding disposition of

[25] The American Revolution had been made public in Copenhagen in September 1776, whereas the fall of the Bastille in 1789 had been announced only 17 days after it happened, and the Declaration of the Rights of Man was announced in September that year. See Mestad, Ola, "Innledning - Eneveldehovudstad, politikk og studiar," in Ola Mestad (ed.) (2013).

[26] Jakobsen, Rolv Nøtvik, "Holberg etter Puffndorf, Guberus etter Darjes, Shlegel før 1814: Om autoritetar og fridom i dansk norsk natur – og folkerett på 1700 talet," in Ola Mestad (ed.) (2013). See also Bregnsbo, Michael, "Det politisk intellektuelle offentlige miljø for de kommende grunnlovsfedre. Overgang frå enevælde til forfattining – idemessigemellemregninger," in Ola Mestad (ed.) (2013).

the property. The *ting* was connected to this right, and an early medieval form of government where the men with *odelsrett* met every year to form the laws of the country.[27] This right to form laws through property rights implied in the *odelsrett* was, in the late eighteenth century, seen by many as the foundation of Nordic freedom. The *odelsrett* made men free because it was an exclusive right to land which made the individual sovereign a lawgiver. This vision of freedom tended to project upon the Norwegian self-owning farmer (referred to as the *odelsbonde*) of the present the idealized image of the free Norwegian medieval farmer. Due to land sales that had been carried out in the eighteenth century there was some truth to the idea that many Norwegian farmers were in control of their own land. One can also trace a trend of increasing institutionalization and standardization in relation to land sales from the seventeenth century onwards, ordering land sales and property relations in strict economic forms.[28]

One of the most famous advocates for the idea of Norwegian freedom in the late eighteenth century was the historian Gerhard Schøning (1722–1780). Educated in ancient Norse history and modern philosophy, he began working as a scholar in Trondheim where he started writing a history of Norway.[29] Here he emphasized the *odelsrett* and the *ting* as the ancient foundation of Norwegian freedom. The rule of King Håkon den gode (Håkon the Good, 918–961) especially was idealised by Schøning. He wrote about King Håkon: "He had the most sincere concern for his subjects' wellbeing, for their peace and their security."[30] This he did by making "laws and duties for the wellbeing of the people,

[27]For more on the *odelsrett* see, Skeie, John, *Odels og Aasetesretten*, Gyldendal Norsk forlag, Oslo (1950); and Gjerdåker, Brynjulv, *Til odel og eie: odels og åsetesretten gjennom eit millenium, med vekt på dei 250 siste åra*, Norsk Institutt for Landbruksforskning, Oslo (2001).

[28]Nygard, Mons Sandnes, *Eigedomsavhending i norsk rettshistorie*, Universitetsforlaget, Oslo (1977), pp. 127–159 and 271–282.

[29]My account on Schøning builds mostly on Grankvist, Rolf, "Gerhard Schøning," *Norsk Biografisk Leksikon*. http://nbl.snl.no/Gerhard_Sch%C3%B8ning (last edited 13.02.2009, accessed 18.07.2014). My account also builds on Christensen, Olav, "En nasjonal identitet tar form," in Øystein Sørensen (ed.), *Jakten på det Norske: perspektiver på utviklingen av en Norsk nasjonal identitet på 1800 talet*, Gyldendal Norsk Forlag, Oslo (2001).

[30]Schøning, Gerhard, *Om Norges Riiges historie: første del, rigets ældste historie frå det begyndelse til Harald Haarfagres tider*, Kiøbenhavn (1771), p. 289.

building a framework for their life and for their future that was both just and good."[31] Håkon the Good granted these laws based on the *ting*, and it was this that made them good, because they were sanctioned by the free-propertied people of Norway. Such laws, asserted Schøning, were in fact the foundation of all the free states that had existed in Europe:

> The oldest and mightiest states of Europe are founded by people from the north; the laws, customs and statutes of these people are the foundation of the European constitutions; and the Nordic flame, freedom and courage liberated the southern nations from enslavement.[32]

Thus, Norwegian history should be seen not only as that of "a kingdom, but as an integral part of universal history."[33] Some wondered whether the ancient Nordic freedom was in too deep a sleep in Norway at the time. One of Schøning's contemporaries, the priest Nordahl Brun (1745–1816), asked, borrowing a quote from the sixteenth-century priest Peder Absalon Byer, "perhaps Norway could one day awaken from its sleep?"[34] The language here is a classic example of nationalist revival ideology, and Brun connected this very much to the idea of the *odelsrett*. In his pamphlet "Tanker om Norges Odels-ret" (1788), he compared the *odelsrett* to the rights of the aristocracies in other countries, but this was not to say that he had much sympathy for the institution of an aristocracy—as such, he wrote: "This noble blood that supposedly flows through the veins of some men, I do not much care for." Rather, it was because the *odelsrett* gave the Norwegian farmer a right to landed property, and thus "the possibility to become a great man."[35] In Norway, precisely because of the *odelsrett*, there was no landed aristocracy, said Brun, and it was precisely therefore that the bulk of the population could be elevated to the position of aristocracy (i.e., to have material security and freedom—a right to property in land).[36] The *odelsbonde* was

[31] Schøning, Gerhard (1771), p. 299.

[32] Schøning (1771), Preface.

[33] Schøning (1771), Preface.

[34] Quoted in Sørensen (2001), p. 59.

[35] Brun, Johan Nordahl, *Tanker om Norges Odels-ret* (1788), p. 23.

[36] One of the most prominent intellectuals that the Oldenburg empire produced, the Norwegian playwright and philosopher Ludvig Holberg, had written, similar to Brun,

thus free and noble: "Odelsmenn of old! Men of honor, you love freedom, and rights you have!"[37] Freedom was here inseparably bound with landed property. This freedom was not aristocratic in nature, however, it was natural and just: "The odelsrett, seems to me, equally natural as any other civic right," wrote Brun, and it was connected to the kind of state in which Brun understood himself to be living in: "equality, independence and fraternity are the treasures of nature, but the only just enforcer of any right is the civic state."[38] The "civic state" that Brun refers to is the Oldenburg absolutist state. This might seem odd, but Brun points to the interconnectedness of these specific freedoms of property and the absolutist Oldenburg monarch. The *odelsbonde* was sometimes held and contrasted with the Danish farmer, who in this case was seen to be unfree.[39] Though Norwegian freedom was seldom during this phase contrasted with the absolutist monarchy as such. Shøning, for example, dedicated the first volume of his history of Norway to the Oldenburg monarch, and he was central in organizing the jubilee for the Oldenburg monarch in 1760. His dedication to the king reads:

> It is not because I have such high thoughts of my work that I dedicate it to your highness, but because of a sincere feeling of duty and gratefulness, on behalf of the people whose history I have written. You, your highness have, on so many occasions shown mercifulness and love towards this nation.[40]

The reason why one could emphasize the peculiar Norwegian national character and at the same time be sincere in one's dedication to the absolutist monarch was perhaps partly because a prevailing notion was, as Brun famously said, that in the Oldenburg state, one had two

that the Norwegian farmer was a "nobleman in miniature". Quoted in Hommerstad (2010), p. 85.

[37] Brun (1788), p. 31.

[38] Brun (1788), pp. 10–11.

[39] There had for centuries existed a semi-feudal system of manorial farming in Denmark alien to Norway where such systems never existed. For some literature on the Danish farming system, see Olsen, Gunnar, *Hovedgård og bondegård, studier over stordriftens udvikling I Danmark i tiden 1525–1774*, Kiøbenhavn (1957); Skrubbletrang, Fridlev, *Det Danskelandbosamfund 1500–1800*, Odense (1978); and Rasmussen, Carsten Porskrog, *Det Danske godssystem. Udvikling og afvikling 1519–1919*, Århus (1987).

[40] Schøning (1773), Preface.

homelands: one natural, and one civic, and there was no antagonism between them.[41] In fact, Norwegians and Danes were bound together by the Oldenburg monarch, and the people were, said Brun, the children of the monarch, "never his slaves"[42]—they were free. That the subjects could be free and yet be "children" of the monarch was not a contradiction because the freedom of Norwegians was seen as protected by the absolutist king. Although the *odelsrett* was originally Norwegian, Brun believed that the Danish Oldenburg king had since protected it. Brun wrote:

> The odelsrett was the right of Norway before Denmark and Norway, by the marriage of their respective royal families, became united. It has since been preserved by the Danish kings, and are by his laws now protected.[43]

The Norwegian farmer was seen as free under already-existing social and political conditions. Another contemporary writer, the priest Jens Zetlitz (1761–1821), also praised the freedom of the Norwegian farmer within the kingdom. The Norwegian farmer, he wrote, had "from time immemorial been held in high esteem, because from time immemorial he has been free," and he was freer than any common man anywhere else. However, the fact that they were now being ruled by the Oldenburg monarch was seen to be no problem at all; in fact, he was "the mildest monarch in all Europe." It was precisely because he was free that the farmer was loyal: "the large degree of freedom, that the farmer here enjoys, is, if not the only, then surely the strongest source of his patriotic love and his loyalty."[44] Industrialist and landowner Jacob Aall (1773–1844), member of the national movement of 1814, wrote in his history of the period almost half a century later about what he perceived as the free nature of Oldenburg rule in Norway at the time:

> Norway's relation to Denmark had been of a peculiar nature; despotic laws had placed the country solely at the mercy of the king, yet, they were mildly carried out in Norway, and they took into account local

[41] Brun, Nordahl, *Til Nordmænd: om troskab mod kongen og kiærlighed til fædrelandet* (1773).

[42] Brun (1773), p. 6.

[43] Brun (1788), p.10.

[44] Zetlitz, Jens, *Sange til den norske bondestand* (1795), Preface.

> circumstances. The internal laws were made in accordance with the simplicity of nature, and with the natural rights of men.[45]

This praise of the current monarchical situation as protector of unique liberties is, as we might remember, very similar to how Americans saw their liberties protected by the British king before 1776.

As in America the change of discourse in Norway was brought forth largely by external factors. It was not till a crisis suddenly materialized—when the Napoleonic Wars cut the tie between the Norwegian people and its sovereign in 1814—that the idea of Norwegian freedom became connected to a nationalist ideology. Aall explained in his history how, due to the war, as early as 1809: "The rock-solid tie to the old order, and the loyal affection to the old royal family that ruled over Norway, started, in the beginning of this decade, if not to waver, at least it started to be tested."[46] The actual break that came in 1814 was actually regrettable and unfortunate, wrote Aall. The Napoleonic Wars forced a new Swedish government (I explain this below) on the Norwegians, and Norwegians were thus forced to:

> Protest ... against a form of government, where it could not be guaranteed that the local circumstances of the country would be taken into account, as had been the case with the old government.[47]

It was the Treaty of Kiel, signed January 14, 1814 as part of the settlement of the Napoleonic Wars, that caused a national movement to emerge in Norway when the throne of Norway was taken from the Oldenburg monarch and given to the king of Sweden by decree of the victor of the war. As in the British north American colonies, nationalism existed before this in Norway but only as a potential ideology: it took the flames of the Napoleonic Wars to give the idea form in the world, and the nation became erected upon the Norwegian property structure of widespread landholding.

[45] Aall, Jacob, *Erindringer som bidrag til Norges historie frå 1800–1815*, Cappelen, Christiania (1844), pp. 359–360.

[46] Aall (1844), p. 3. According to Aall, people started to consider a break with Denmark, but when it happened many including Aall considered it a "catastrophe." See Aall (1844), p. 6. He was not the only one, as we shall see below.

[47] Aall (1844), p. 360.

Triggering Factor: The Napoleonic Wars and the Treaty of Kiel

The Oldenburg state became involved in the Napoleonic Wars in August 1807 when the British fleet hijacked the Oldenburg imperial armada anchored in Copenhagen and bombarded the city. This practically forced the Oldenburg state into an alliance with Napoleon. When the Oldenburg state thus became officially allied with revolutionary France, the British mustered a naval blockade that effectively cut off the Norwegian part of the empire from the Danish part for the next seven years. For the Norwegian part of the empire, this had disastrous consequences as Norwegians were dependent on imported corn from Denmark. Thus, famine soon broke out in the Norwegian part of the empire. The consequences for the city merchants were also bad, as most of their trade had been directed towards Britain or the Netherlands. Furthermore, involvement in the Napoleonic Wars brought battle to the eastern Norwegian borders (1808–1809) as Napoleon, for strategic reasons, demanded an attack on Sweden. This war stirred patriotic feelings in many people. Much of this patriotic sentiment was tied to Prince Christian August who led the southern division of the Norwegian army in successful raids against the Swedish. Christian August was the prince of the Oldenburg southern province of Schlesvig-Holstein. As he grew into adulthood he became a skilled military commander, learning many of his skills in the Austrian army where he had a position during the late 1790s. In 1803 he was sent to Norway as commander in chief of the southern army division, and when the war broke out he was appointed leader of the provisional government in Norway by the Oldenburg king. The Swedish elite, however, also had an eye on him, and after unrest and revolution in Sweden in 1809 he was appointed and accepted the Swedish throne in 1810.[48] When the prince departed from Norway, a great party was held for him, and at this party the initiative was taken to establish *Det kongelige selsgab for Norges vel* (The Royal Society for the Wellbeing of Norway), which became the first countrywide civil society organization. The society became a platform for advancing Norwegian interests vis-à-vis the Oldenburg monarch during the war.

One of the founders of *Det kongelige selsgab for Norges vel* was Count Herman Wedel Jarlsberg. Born in 1779 to a Danish/Norwegian

[48] Mykland, Knut, "Christian August," *Norsk Biografisk Leksikon*. https://nbl.snl.no/Christian_August (last edited 13.03.2009, accessed 26.01.2015).

diplomat and count, Wedel Jarlsberg was one of the very few real aristocrats in Norway at the time. He spent most of his youth in continental Europe, visiting his barony with his family primarily during the summers. In 1801 he received a university degree in law at the University of Copenhagen, and spent the next years in the financial committee of the Oldenburg government. In 1806 he moved to Norway and became an administrator of a county in the southeast. When the Oldenburg state became involved in the Napoleonic Wars, Wedel was appointed by the government commission in Norway to provide corn. During the war years, Wedel became more and more discontent with Oldenburg rule, and saw it as incompatible with the existence of national freedom. Securing civic liberties was essential to Wedel, and they could not, he thought, be safe under Oldenburg absolutism. In 1809, when Swedish revolutionaries had started contemplating the idea of promoting Christian August as Swedish king, Wedel saw an opportunity to realize an old dream of his that involved uniting Norway with Sweden under a liberal constitution. It was especially after the war of 1809 that Wedel gathered support for this plan, particularly amongst industrialist and merchants in the southeast of the country, whose loyalty to the Oldenburg monarchy, as Aall has written, had "started to be tested." Christian August, however, was reluctant to do this, and the plans stalled completely when he died unexpectedly of heart failure in the summer of 1810.[49] Other than this attempt by Wedel and the group of merchants supporting him, there was little direct nationalist opposition to Oldenburg rule before the spring of 1814. The Treaty of Kiel, signed that winter, thus marked a decisive shift in the course of the national movement. The treaty in effect transferred the throne of Norway to Swedish King Karl Johan. However, Karl Johan was not able to claim the throne until August (the time it took to move his armies to the Norwegian border). It was in this vacuum, where the Kingdom of Norway was left without any sovereign, that the heir to the Oldenburg throne, Prince Christian Frederik (1786–1848), animated the

[49] Wedel spearheaded a group of merchants advocating a breakup with Denmark and a union with Sweden. For more on this and Wedel's life and politics, see Nielsen, Yngvar, *Grev Herman Wedel Jarlsberg og hans samtid, 1779–1840*, Alb. Cammermeyer og P.T. Mallings boghandel, Kristiania (1888) and Storsveen, Odd Arvid, "Grev Herman Wedel Jarlsberg," *Norsk Biografisk Leksikon*. http://nbl.snl.no/Herman_Wedel_Jarlsberg (last edited 13.02.2009, accessed 18.07.2014).

Norwegian national movement.[50] In 1813, at the age of 26, disguised as a deckhand on a fishing boat, Prince Christian Frederik had sailed from Denmark to Norway, navigating through enemy British warships, on a mission to preserve the integrity of the Oldenburg state. When the Treaty of Kiel was signed, the prince took action to prevent Norway from falling into the hands of Swedish King Karl Johan—actions which resulted in the Norwegian declaration of independence.

Prince Christian Frederik: King by the Will of the People

There is an endless and ongoing discussion about the true motives of Christian Frederik: were his actions in 1814 motivated by an underlying wish to later reunite Norway with Denmark? Did he actually believe in the sovereignty of the people? Is he to be hailed as a hero or judged as a traitor?[51] I think that it is beyond any doubt that the prince was

[50]The background for the signing of this treaty was the following: Sweden, under its new king, Karl Johan (king from August 1810) had joined Great Britain in the effort to defeat Napoleon and his allies. This was very much the work of Karl Johan. His name of birth was Jean Baptiste-Bernadotte, and he was a French nobleman who had served as general under Napoleon during several important and successful battles. In 1810, after the death of Christian August, he was approached by a Swedish agent in Paris who asked him to be candidate for the election of a new Swedish king. Bernadotte agreed, and was elected king August 21, 1810, taking the name of Karl Johan. The previous year Sweden had lost Finland to Russia, and as new king of Sweden, Karl Johan wanted to restore the pride and might of Sweden. His solution to this became, in the end, to join the allies against Napoleon in exchange for the promise that by the defeat of Napoleon and his allies (which still included the Oldenburg state), Norway would become part of the crown of Sweden. As the Napoleonic Wars approached its finale in 1813, Karl Johan led the Swedish troops at the Battle of Leipzig and defeated his former emperor Napoleon who fled towards Paris. Karl Johan did not join the allies in pursuit towards Paris, but moved his army instead north to Denmark. Not trusting the promise of Britain to give him Norway, he took matters in his own hands. By January 1814, his huge and well-trained Swedish force stood ready to capture the Oldenburg capital of Copenhagen, forcing the Oldenburg king to bestow on Karl Johan the throne of Norway. See Bjørnskau, Erik, "Karl 3 Johan," *Norsk Biografisk Leksikon*. https://nbl.snl.no/Karl_3_Johan (last edited 13.02.2009, accessed 26.01.2015).

[51]Georg Sverdrup, prominent, member of the national movement, for example accused the Prince of cowardice after the Prince had declared an armistice with Sweden when Karl Johan had invaded with his army. The Prince expressed his regrets to Sverdrup that so

crucial in leading the national movement and making the writing of the constitution and the declaration of independence possible. In this way, the prince must surely be held as a key figure in securing Norwegian independence. Although his underlying motives for this can perhaps never be known, it is nevertheless a fact that he did agree to become King of Norway by consent of the people: he accepted that the people were vested with ultimate legislative power, that they should exercise this sovereignty through their representatives, and that he himself was vested only with executive powers and was in fact not a king that ruled over subjects but one that ruled on behalf of citizens. One can of course wonder if he really wanted this, and one can point to the fact that when he later became King of Denmark, he long refused to give to the Danish people what he seemingly so ardently fought to give the Norwegians. In the case of Norway, he seems to really have believed in the freedom of the Norwegian people and its connection to the propertied freedom of the farmers.[52] Reading the entries in his notebook from 1814, one gets the impression of a man passionately caring for the freedom and right of the people, a man who is fighting for the natural right of a people to live in freedom and not under enslavement. He said he would "Rather die with weapon in hand than to be slaves of the Swedish."[53] He hoped in the long term to make the Norwegian people happy, telling himself:

much blood had been spilt on his account, but Sverdrup answered that the problem was rather that *not enough* blood had been spilt. The people of Norway, thought Sverdrup, had been betrayed by their leader for not being willing to lead them in a fight for freedom whatever the costs. This was the beginning of a long tradition of distrust and discredit of Christian Fredrik. This anecdote can be found in Langeland (2014), footnote 1, p. 346.

[52]The worldviews of the prince seems to have been deeply founded on a Christian humanism taught to him by a childhood teacher. Clearly, he was familiar with the French revolution, and thinkers like Rousseau and Voltaire. See Langslet, Lars Roar, *Christian Frederik, Konge av Norge (1814, Konge av Danmark (1839–48)*, J.W. Cappelens Forlag, Gjøvik (1998), pp. 25–31. The Prince formed early in his life a close friendship with Norwegian merchant Carsten Anker, who later became a central member of the national movement. Anker was a man of the world but developed strong patriotic sentiments towards Norway. Several times during the war years he implored Christian Frederik to come to Norway to save its freedom.

[53]Alnæs, Jan Jørgen, *Christian Fredriks dagbok frå 1814*, Gyldendal Norsk Forlag, Oslo (1954), p. 28.

> God knows that my highest wish is to see this people happy. If only the power was bestowed upon me to grant this people all the happiness that I aim to give them, the happiness that they deserve.[54]

The prince's enthusiasm was at least partly based on his belief in the special characteristics of the Norwegian people, the propertied farmers. During a journey to Trondheim in the winter of 1814 the prince met many local farmers, and he took note of "their awesome national sentiment." The prince reflected: "one does not know such a people if one thinks that one can take away their freedom with the stroke of a pen."[55] It was also on the initiative of the prince that it was decided that at least one of the representatives to the later constitutional assembly from each county should be a farmer.[56] The prince, according to his diary, believed in the freedom-loving spirit of these people: "the nation … will do everything for its freedom and independence, it would rather die than have a life in slavery." Seeing this, he told himself: "there cannot be any doubt about what I have to do." The answer was to fight for the cause of the Norwegians: "Even if all of Europe is against us, there is always the option to fight till the last man standing."[57] One interpretation of this is seeing a man acting out of a powerful moral conviction of what he sees as naturally right, even at the risk of great personal costs.[58] The prince was not, however, at first, prepared to accept the throne of Norway by the grace of a sovereign people: during the first weeks after the signing of the Treaty of Kiel, the prince assumed sovereignty in Norway on account of the hereditary rights he had as heir of the Oldenburg monarch. In February 1814, he changed his mind and decided to legitimize his right to rule Norway by the will of the people. According to his own diary, he decided to do this after a meeting at Eidsvoll on February 16, 1814, when Professor Georg Sverdrup (1770–1850) pointed out to him that since sovereignty was ultimately vested in the people, the professor himself had a claim to the throne

[54] Alnæs (1954), pp. 120–121.

[55] Alnæs (1954), p. 110.

[56] Hommerstad (2010), p. 84.

[57] Alnæs (1954), p. 78.

[58] Indeed, the actions of the prince could be seen to be directly traitorous towards the Oldenburg state, and the king even directly told the prince in a letter that he would withdraw his hereditary right to the Oldenburg throne if he carried his plans to conclusion.

equally just and legitimate as that of the prince's claim. Sverdrup had studied in Copenhagen and in Göttingen where he had been acquainted with German romanticism, and became one of the first professors of the University of Christiania (present day Oslo) (established 1811). He was an acquaintance of Christian Frederik, and thus became involved in the Eidsvoll meeting where he told Christian Frederik that he could only be a legitimate king if he appealed to the sovereignty of the people.[59] Sverdrup's influence on Christian Frederik's decision is arguable, but the prince does mention this in his diary, and again in a way that makes him sound earnest in his belief:

> This is a day that I will never forget. I have listened to the speech that professor Sverdrup held for me with a joy that only one possessing a pure mind knows. He said that the rights that Fredrik 6 (King of the Oldenborg state) have given away will fall back to the hand of the people, and that it is from the hand of the people that I shall receive my crown.[60]

Regardless of the motivation and cause of this decision, it was crucial to how the realization of nationality happened in Norway, as it marks the moment that opened up the possibility for that peculiar *amalgamation of people, property and sovereignty* which characterizes nationalism as described in this book. Because of this decision, the prince was obliged to post an "Open letter from the regent of Norway" throughout the kingdom. The letter proclaimed that elections for a national assembly to write a constitution were to take place at Eidsvoll as a reaction to Karl Johan's plan to incorporate the kingdom into Sweden.[61]

Impending Chaos and the Chains of Slavery

When the prince sent his open letter across the country, most of the answers he got back expressed regret of the break with the Oldenburg

[59] Storsveen, Odd Arvid, "Georg Sverdrup," *Norsk Biografisk Leksikon*. https://nbl.snl.no/Georg_Sverdrup_-_1 (last edited 13.02.2009, accessed 26.04.2015).

[60] Alnæs (1954), pp. 44–45.

[61] I am not saying that the prince did this purely for idealistic reasons. No doubt there were pragmatic considerations of power involved as well. The point is that the fact that the prince chose this option made it possible for the national movement to emerge in the way in which it did. This is not to say that a national movement of a similar nature would never have emerged without the actions of the prince.

state and hostility towards Sweden. It was with "the deepest of sorrows" read one letter, that "we recognize that the bond which for so long have tied our two kingdoms together is now broken."[62] Indeed, stated another letter, "we feel as children bereft of our loving father … with anger we see that the ancient throne of Harald [Norwegian Viking king] now falls in the hand of the Swedish."[63] Another letter proclaimed that, "We would never be slaves of the Swedish."[64] There was little doubt that with the Treaty of Kiel, the people had been "doomed to slavery"[65] under the Swedish. This may indicate that loyalty to the prince and the monarchy was still prevalent in much of the population,[66] and it was perhaps precisely because the prince represented the Oldenburg monarchy that so many came to support him in the endeavour to create an independent Norwegian state in opposition to the decision of the great powers and Sweden. The prince represented the principle to which people were loyal, and the institution which represented stability and freedom, the Oldenburg monarchy. There was a pervasive underlying assumption at the Eidsvoll assembly that the Norwegian kingdom was on the brink of chaos. The state of which Norwegians had been a part for over 400 years had been dissolved, and imperial sovereignty had disappeared—had fallen back to the people. It was up to the people now to secure balance and freedom. This freedom and security one had to fight for, however: "every thinking man in the state will realize," it was claimed, that independence could not be achieved, "without the most grave sacrifices and great struggle by all our

[62]Christopher H. Storm, March 18, 1814 in Olafsen, Arnet, *Riksforsamlingens forhandlinger, 2den del: Adresser og fuldmagter*, Grøndhal og søns Boktrykkeri, Kristiania (1914), p. 197.

[63]Jacob Nauman, February 25, 1814 in Olafsen (1914), Vol. 2, p. 7.

[64]P. Knudsen, March 18, 1814 in Olafsen (1914), Vol. 2, p. 386.

[65]Christopher H. Storm, March 18, 1814 in Olafsen (1914), Vol. 2, p. 387.

[66]It is of course difficult to know how earnest this was, too. The letters that the prince received were public letters sent by the local authorities across the country, and it is difficult to imagine that such letters would be anything other than positive towards the prince. On the other hand, there had been a series of wars between Norway and Sweden in the seventeenth and eighteenth century. Sweden had thus been a long-time rival. However, there is serious doubt as to how much the locals who signed the letters really cared whether their king was Danish or Swedish. Nevertheless, the letters do provide interesting insights into the political discourse of the time and might at least indicate the loyalty amongst the elite to the Oldenburg monarchy, and shed interesting light on the idea of slavery.

citizens."[67] Another member of the convention said: "either the nation will have to bend its back under foreign yoke, or with ancient Nordic power, uphold its freedom."[68] The members of the national movement knew very well that they were in the midst of the Napoleonic Wars and the dire state in which it had left Norwegian society and economy, and they knew that an invasion by Sweden was immanent. Prince Christian Frederik was by many given—and, as we saw above, gave himself—the role as saviour from both slavery and anarchy. The prince was seen by some as "the only one who could save the state from anarchy."[69] Hence, Christian Frederik was to be elected king of the New Norwegian state, but "neither in form nor in action will he be a despot."[70]

Christian Frederik became an elected constitutional monarch as he himself had promised; he was king only by the will of the people and with restricted powers. It was felt that it was a decision of a sovereign people: in seeking to avoid "the misfortunes of anarchy," said one member of the Eidsvoll Convention, the best men of the nation had been called together "on behalf of the people to create a constitution that secures civic liberty and earthly happiness in the land of Norway."[71] It was for these causes and on such a foundation that Christian Frederik became king—chosen by the members of the Eidsvoll Assembly who represented the will of the people. He was himself absent from the main negotiations of the constitutional assembly, but before the proceedings started the prince emphasized the national character of his rule. He knew that the people of Norway had a longing for freedom within them, he said, and he knew that "no longing could be as strong as that to liberty." Indeed, a people who would willingly give up its liberty was worth "nothing but the chains of slavery." The prince promised to help the Norwegians establish the wisest and best form of government, that which "secures civic liberties and makes the law sacred."[72] Law was a central aspect of Norwegian nationalism; integrated into the conceptions of sovereignty of the people and security of property—and ultimately to

[67] A.C. Møller, May 7, 1814 in Olafsen, Arnet, *Riksforsamlingens forhandlinger, 1ste del: Protokoller med bilag og tillæg*, Grøndhal (1914), p. 196.

[68] D. Hegerman, May 12, 1814 in Olafsen (1914), Vol. 1, p. 350.

[69] Christian Magnus Falsen, May 17, 1814 in Olafsen (1914), Vol. 1, p. 67.

[70] Christian Frederik, May 19, 1814 in Olafsen (1914), Vol. 1, p. 113.

[71] H.J. Stabel, April 5, 1814 in Olafsen (1914), Vol. 1, pp. 123–124.

[72] Christian Frederik, April 11, 1814 in Olafsen (1914), Vol. 1, p. 2.

national and individual freedom. Rule of law meant rule by the people, and rule by the people secured freedom—that is, the right to property for the individual. This was to a large extent based on the widespread ownership of landed property in Norway. To elaborate on this, I shall first invoke one of the most influential constitutional drafts that were presented at the Eidsvoll Convention. This draft was written by Johan Gunder Adler and Christian Magnus Falsen.

The Eidsvoll Assembly: Amalgamation of People, Property and Sovereignty

The Adler–Falsen Constitutional Draft

It is unclear who was the principal author of the Adler–Falsen constitutional draft. During the first century and a half after 1814, Falsen was given credit for writing most of it, but doubt was raised in the late 1940s, and Johan Gunder Adler became held as the main author of the draft. I invoke the draft here mainly as an example of Falsen's thought because Falsen became one of the most prominent members of the national movement in 1814 and after. Indeed, Falsen's thought stands out as an ideal type for the national ideology in Norway.

Christian Magnus Falsen (1782–1830) came from a long tradition of state officials serving in Norway for the Oldenburg monarchs. He grew up in Norway and studied in Copenhagen, where he became interested in history, especially history of democracy and the ancient Norwegian past. After his studies he got a position as a magistrate in Norway and he bought a farm that he also ran. Falsen was for a long time loyal to the Oldenburg monarchy and a personal friend of Prince Christian Frederik. As late as 1813 he was a firm supporter of the monarchy and even agreed to spy on Wedel Jarlsberg and his plans for a Norwegian union with Sweden. After Christian Frederik declared that he would be king of an independent Norwegian state based on the sovereignty of the people, Falsen became one of his most firm supporters. He was an active debater at the Eidsvoll proceedings and, together with Johan Gunder Adler, he put forth a constitutional draft which strongly influenced the final constitution. Falsen also sent the draft for revision to Christian Frederik, and kept him updated on the proceedings at Eidsvoll. Falsen's worldviews were strongly influenced by the American Revolution, whose principles and heroes he greatly admired.[73] In this he was strongly influenced by his father, who was also widely read on Greek philosophy and ideas of freedom, something which Falsen also took up. When Falsen studied in Copenhagen, he furthermore became familiar with central enlightenment thinkers including Adam Smith, Immanuel Kant, Montesquieu, and Rousseau. After his studies, Falsen came to read much from authors concerned with ancient Nordic freedom and the *odelsrett*, amongst others the previously mentioned Gerhard Schøning. Falsen also read and befriended Nordahl Brun.[74]

The Adler–Falsen draft, as if to accentuate Falsen's American sympathies, opens with a line that is almost literally a copy of the American Declaration of Independence. The opening paragraph reads:

> All men are born free and equal: they have certain natural, essential and unchangeable rights. These are freedom, security and property.[75]

Paragraph four states that "property is the right which every citizen has, to enjoy and decide over his lands, his income, over the fruits of his labour and diligence."[76] This was all bound to freedom because freedom meant "that a person, as long as he is not intruding on other persons, and let them enjoy the fruits of their labour, may himself enjoy the fruits of his labour and security of his person."[77] We thus see that freedom is inseparably bound with the right to property—that is, to enjoy the fruits of one's labour. This was furthermore connected to popular sovereignty. Paragraph seven states that, "sovereignty is the sum of all those rights which men acquire when entering into society. This sovereignty is vested in the people (or the nation)."[78] In other words, property may be

[73] For the influence of the American Revolution on Falsen and the other men at Eidsvoll, see Skard, Sigmund, *USA i Norsk historie, 1000–1776–1976*, Det Norske Samlaget, Oslo (1976).

[74] My information about Falsen builds first and foremost on Østved, Einar, *Christian Magnus Falsen: linjen I hans politikk*, Aschehoug, Oslo (1945) and on Mykland, Knut, "Christian Magnus Falsen," *Norsk Biografisk Leksikon*. http://nbl.snl.no/Christian_Magnus_Falsen (last edited 13.02.2009, accessed 21.07.2014).

[75] Jæger, Tyco C., *Riksforsmalingens forhandlinger, 3 die del: Grundlovsudkast*, Grøndahl og søns bogtrykkeri, Kristiania (1916), p. 9.

[76] Christian Magnus Falsen and Gunder Adler, April 22, 1814 in Jæger (1916), p. 9.

[77] Christian Magnus Falsen and Gunder Adler, April 22, 1814 in Jæger (1916), p. 3.

[78] Christian Magnus Falsen and Gunder Adler, April 22, 1814 in Jæger (1916), p. 9.

interpreted as one of "all those rights which men acquire when entering into society." In this right all the members of the nation were equal: "All the members of society, regardless of, birth, wealth, or rank are equal in their rights to enjoy the benefits of society."[79] No man was to have privileges, because the people as a whole were sovereign: "Having established that all power flows from the people, all statesmen are their servants, and are accountable to them."[80] Falsen was a living example of this ideology. Belonging to an aristocratic family of the Oldenburg state himself, he officially resigned his title at the Eidsvoll assembly. "I am not amongst the men," he said, "who believe that birth should bestow privileges on a man, which he otherwise would not have had." He did not intend by this to be seen as a man making a "sacrifice" it was rather that he wanted to be "on an equal footing with my fellow citizens."[81] The important point was that all the members of the nation were equal in their rights, of which the most important was the right to property.

As in America the ideas about property and sovereignty were informed by the relative widespread distribution of land in Norway. Falsen saw the creation of the nation state as a return to ancient Nordic freedom; an important point and underlying assumption in Falsen's thinking was that although the right to property was natural, it was also historically conditioned by the Norwegian property structure. In the same way as Jefferson can be seen as a sage of American nationality, Falsen can be seen as one for Norway. In Norway, said Falsen, there had since time immemorial existed free propertied farmers (the *odelsbonde*) who "knew no lord but that of God above and the king bound by law."[82] In the old times of Nordic freedom, wrote Falsen, it was always the men of landed property that constituted the nation, and represented the voice of the people: "sovereignty was vested in the people, which had reserved for themselves legislative power," and the people were constituted by the "men of landed property."[83] Property (or the *odelsrett*) was indeed "the most secure protection of liberty," and liberty the ancient Norwegians had. Falsen wrote, the vision of the past, "the great cliffs

[79] Christian Magnus Falsen and Gunder Adler, April 22, 1814 in Jæger (1916), p. 9.

[80] Christian Magnus Falsen and Gunder Adler, April 22, 1814 in Jæger (1916), p.10.

[81] Christian Magnus Falsen, May 7, 1814 in Olafsen (1914), Vol. 1, p. 201.

[82] Falsen, Christian Magnus, *Norges Odelsret, med hensyn på Rigets constitution*, Bergen (1815), p. 21.

[83] Falsen (1815), p. 22.

of Norway, on whose edges and in whose valleys beneath, the sons of Norway walked free and unbound."[84] Falsen wrote that he could not ever read the Sagas of old without feeling his soul empowered by the vision of "the odelsmend [the propertied farmer] of Norway, in alliance with the king, deciding the laws of the land. The odelsmend of Norway ... free ... masters of their own land."[85] This situation of free propertied men was ancient and natural, Falsen said:

> The natural idea of the division of the lands amongst the citizens has been so common throughout history that one can prove its existence even since the time of Moses, and one can assume that this idea was brought to our north, or even that it is grounded in nature.[86]

It was in any case certain that Norway had never been feudal: "All our ancient history proves that no hereditary aristocracy existed in our north."[87] A landed aristocracy was indeed a disaster for any nation wanting to be free. "Aristocracy," wrote Falsen, had:

> Dismantled all equality between the citizens of Europe. What then do we see in these states? Nothing but aristocracy and slaves, great landowners and unfree peasants, bound to the soil that they were obliged to plow for their masters.[88]

Such a terrible situation of subjugation and slavery did not exist in Norway, and with the framing of the new constitution, one had "by the providence of God almighty, retrieved those rights, that for several centuries made our forefathers a mighty, honorable and famous people."[89] In other words, the new constitution, according to Falsen, ensured, as he had said, a sovereignty based on "the natural idea of the division of the lands amongst the citizens." If the bulk of the people owned land, and represented the will of the people, then one had popular sovereignty. The law, when expressed in this way, was the expression of the

[84] Falsen (1815), p. 9.
[85] Falsen (1815), pp. 9–13.
[86] Falsen (1815), p. 49.
[87] Falsen (1815), p. 24.
[88] Falsen (1815), p. 40.
[89] Falsen (1815), p. 57.

will of the people and protected property. The Adler–Falsen draft's §15 stated that:

> The law, which is a free and sacred expression of the general will, or the will of the whole association, expressed by the majority of its citizens or their representatives, must be the same for all, whether it protects or punishes. It cannot command anything that is not useful for the state … it has to be a secure bulwark against all individuals persons, property and honor. It concerns only action, not opinion.[90]

It was the people themselves who made the laws, and this made them secure in their property:

> The people cannot be bound by any law that they have not themselves given through their representatives. This means that no individual can be bereft of even the smallest amount of property without his own consent or that of the representative assembly.[91]

Division and Unity at the Eidsvoll Assembly and After

This connection between rule of law (popular sovereignty), the security of property, and the ancient landed freedom of the people may also be derived from the records of the Eidsvoll Convention, although it must be emphasized that there was a myriad of opinions voiced at Eidsvoll; many conservative in the direction of absolutism, some only partially congruent with the ideal. The final constitution ended up very similar to Falsen's ideal.[92] That the constitution came to represent Falsen's ideal to a high degree is not surprising if we consider that of the 112 representatives at the convention, 25 were, like Falsen, relatively wealthy lawyers, and furthermore, 15 were theologians who had all studied in Copenhagen under the same intellectual milieu as Falsen. Moreover, fourteen out of the fifteen members of the constitutional committee were state officials like Falsen, five of them lawyers, and all of them

[90] Christian Magnus Falsen and Gunder Adler, April 22, 1814 in Jæger (1916), p. 11.

[91] Christian Magnus Falsen and Gunder Adler, April 22, 1814 in Jæger (1916), p. 11.

[92] In fact, the constitution adopted at the Eidsvoll Convention became more democratic than Falsen had wanted, setting a lower limit to the amount of property needed for enfranchisement.

owned property either landed or real estate. Wedel—Falsen's main opponent—had also studied in Copenhagen. Wedel, however, was a merchant, one of eighteen at the Eidsvoll assembly. It was state officials, the category to which Falsen belonged, who constituted the largest group amounting to 57 in total.[93]

It is common when discussing the negotiations at the Eidsvoll National Assembly to divide the assembly into two major groups: one which advocated for an independent Norwegian state within a loose union with Sweden, and one which advocated full and complete independence. The first group was led by Count Wedel, who had not abandoned his plans of a Norwegian free constitution within a union with Sweden. This group of men, of course, did not conflate Sweden with slavery; for them, it was in everything Danish, and particularly in Prince Christian Frederik himself, that one saw the spectre of absolutism and subjugation. This group was in the minority at the Eidsvoll Convention, and was, for the most part, constituted by merchants and represented commercial and trading interests. This group was labeled by the majority as suspicious at best, as traitors at worst. Christian Frederik, for example, observed the proceedings from outside and was sure, as he wrote in his diary, that they were "plotting evil plans."[94] The second group had Falsen as a main figure, and was working towards a completely independent Norwegian state. Most of the state officials belonged to this group, as well as most of the 37 representatives who were farmers. This group naturally had the support of Prince Christian Frederik, who they envisioned king of the new state. It was therefore perhaps easy for them to conjure up a picture of the Swedish-friendly party as traitors to nationality. The disagreement between these two groups, however, was not as important as what the two groups agreed upon: they were actually both equally nationalist. Much like the infamous dichotomy between the Federalists and the Anti-federalists in early national America, these two camps agreed on the goal, but differed in the means. What should be emphasized is not the difference between the unionist party and the independence party, but their similarities—they were both national.

[93]These numbers are from: Pryser (1999), p. 203; Mestad (2013), p. 11; and Hroch, Miroslav, *Social Preconditions of National Revival in Europe: A Comparative Analysis of the Social Composition of Patriotic Groups in the Smaller European Nations*, Cambridge University Press, Cambridge (1985), pp. 34–35.

[94]Alnæs (1954), p. 84.

Although it is true that many of the constitutions drafted at Eidsvoll by the independence party advocated absolutist or semi-absolutist types of government, I think what matters the most is what was agreed upon in the end: that the new government should be national, that exclusive right to property be absolute and secure through the sovereignty of the people—here was an *amalgamation of the people, sovereignty and property.*

During the course of the negotiations at Eidsvoll the members of the national movement came to believe or at least accept Falsen's idea that within the nation there stood the most robust pillars of liberty (the property of the people)—one could see this now in a new light. It was as if these notions now emerged out of the twilight dusk of absolutism and were presented in the broad day of light under the sun of liberty. The new light made it possible to see distinct people with natural rights, a country and a culture uniquely well suited to safeguard such rights. Flasen wrote that during the age of absolutism, those who had emphasized the propertied freedom of the Norwegian farmer had done so in "a time when one could not speak of the true nature of this right, without attacking the fundamental principles of the state."[95] Once absolutism was anyway gone from Norway this right could be realized and serve as the basis of sovereignty because, as Falsen wrote one year after the Constitutional Convention:

> While the nations of Europe have carried their chains moaning and groaning, and lost all their national worth being, like an animal, treated as a commodity bound to the land which they themselves have fertilized with their sweat, the sons of the North have been practically the only people bestowed with human rights and civic liberties.[96]

It was these rights and liberties that the new constitution drafted at Eidsvoll was to protect. The committee tasked with writing the constitution at Eidsvoll assured the assembly when its preliminary work was done that, "the committee has, during its work, continuously taken into account civic liberty, the security of property and an equal distribution of all rights."[97] This sums up the essence of the national ideology, or, as one member of the convention put it, "no obstacles must now or in

[95] Falsen (1815), p. 10.

[96] Falsen (1815), p. 7.

[97] Falsen et al., May 16, 1814 in Olafsen (1914), Vol. 1, p. 120.

the future be allowed to obstruct the protection of the right to property, unless it is against the general interests of the state."[98] In Norway, as in America, the rights of the individual became based on what was seen as the individual's natural right to the fruits of his labour; "Nature itself," it was said, "proclaims and demands the right of freedom from subjugation for he who by the toil of his hands and the sweat of his brows makes the earth yield fruits." Again we see the centrality of land, "the earth," to have the right to the fruits it yields. This right was "the most natural and fundamental of human rights," and it was therefore, "the most sacred of rights amongst citizens ... and a vital pillar of any just constitution."[99]

The First Form of the Nation: Ancient Liberties and New Freedoms

The Union with Sweden

At the end of the Eidsvoll proceedings, Professor Georg Sverdrup exaltedly exclaimed:

> Restored is the ancient throne of Norway ... May the wisdom and power that was bestowed upon our kings of old, be bestowed also upon he the first, which we, the freemen of Norway, have chosen today out of thankfulness, and as uniformly with the wish of the whole people, to be our king ...[100]

The king that the "freemen of Norway" had chosen was Christian Frederik, but he was soon forced to abdicate the throne. The new Norwegian state was not able to maintain its independence very long. During the summer of 1814, Karl Johan moved his army from the continent to the eastern borders of Norway to claim what had been promised him by the Treaty of Kiel. After a short war in early August, the Norwegian forces surrendered, and Christian Frederik signed a treaty with Karl Johan effectively forcing Christian Frederik to abdicate and leave the country. The Norwegian parliament was thus forced to accept Karl Johan as king and enter in a union with Sweden. The Norwegian Constitution of May 17, 1814 was allowed to be kept largely in the form

[98] A.C. Møller, May 11, 1814 in Olafsen (1914), Vol. 1, p. 262.

[99] A.C. Møller, May 11, 1814 in Olafsen (1914), Vol. 1, p. 263.

[100] Georg Sverdrup, May 17, 1814 in Olafsen (1914), Vol. 1, p. 79.

that it was, but with the necessary amendments to make it compatible with a union with Sweden, in which Norway was not to be an independent kingdom. Because of the union with Sweden the first form of the Norwegian nation was not realized in pure form, as sovereignty was not unitary within the nation; one of the branches of sovereignty—the executive branch—was not connected back inwards to the nation as a whole, but outwards to an external element. Still, as Sverdrup put it, "the freemen of Norway" were vested with legislative power in Norway, and they were seen to represent "the wish of the whole people" of Norway. These freemen were largely the men of property, and it was they who came to secure rule of law and the sovereignty of the people in *the first form of the nation.*

Free Men, Dependent Men and the Happiness of the Whole

Under *the first form of the nation*, it was mostly acknowledged that there were dependent and independent men. Here, dependent men could not be trusted with enfranchisement. Lawyer Henrik Steenbuch (1774–1839) wrote in his commentary to the 1815 constitution that:

> Only a small part of the inhabitants of our state are sufficiently independent and enlightened so as to be suited for enfranchisement. The wellbeing of the whole demands that the people be divided into enfranchised and disenfranchised.[101]

Steenbuch had studied law in Copenhagen, and his interpretation of the constitution was the first academic work on the constitution. Later he taught law at the University of Christiania, where he was an advocate of natural rights theories. He was a defender of the position of the sovereign people in the constitution, and he was an active patriot, publishing works on Norwegian history and law.[102] We can see in Steenbuch's interpretation of the constitution the notion that the "wellbeing of the whole" (or "the will of the whole people" as Sverdrup put it in the quote

[101] Steenbuch, Fredrik, *Bemærkninger over Norges grundlov af 4die November 1814*, Trondheim (1815), p. 90.

[102] Michalsen, Dag, "Henrik Steenbuch," *Norsk Biografisk Leksikon*. https://nbl.snl.no/Henrik_Steenbuch (last edited 13.02.2009, accessed 22.07.2015).

provided in the introduction) is maintained by rule of the few: independent men, the men of landed property. Only such men could rule because they were free. Steenbuch wrote that, "free is he who subsists by himself; independent, he who does not subsist by the will of another." Moreover, wrote Steenbuch, "he who is more or less dependent upon others" could not be granted the right to vote.[103] In 1814 the line between dependent and independent had been relatively clearly drawn in the constitution. Unlike in the American case, the Norwegian national constitution stated specifically who was to be vested with legislative power in the new nation; it was first and foremost men of real property. Paragraph 50 stated that:

> Enfranchisement is to be given only to those Norwegian citizens that are 25 years or older, and have been living in the country for five years, and have either:
>
> a) have an official position in the state bureaucracy
> b) landed property or have leased land for at least five years
> c) is a bourgeois, or have property in a city worth at least 300 rigsbankdallaer.[104]

Although the state officials were given the right to vote regardless of property ownership, property—and especially real landed property—was held as particularly important to the preservation of liberty. Carl Fredrik Erhenvard—a Swedish political refugee to Denmark after his involvement in the murder of Swedish King Gustav 3 in 1792, and friend of Falsen—had sent by request of Falsen a pamphlet that was read at the Eidsvoll Convention. After systematically discussing various constitutions and forms of government the pamphlet concluded that, "it seems to me that ownership of a certain value of real property is a suitable measurement of enfranchisement." This was an axiom Erhenvard held: "we all agree that the enfranchised must own landed property of a certain value."[105] The Adler–Falsen constitutional draft stated that an

[103] Steenbuch (1815), p. 93.

[104] *The Norwegian Constitution of 1814*. https://www.stortinget.no/no/Stortinget-og-demokratiet/Lover-og-instrukser/Grunnloven-fra-1814/ (accessed 03.02.2015).

[105] Carl Fredrik Erhenvard, April 1, 1814 in Olafsen (1914), Vol. 1, p. 178.

individual was independent if he owned property or a certain amount of capital and that, in order to have the right to vote, "one must own property or earn a certain income."[106] The purpose of such restrictions was not exclusion as such; indeed, as was written in the constitutional draft: "The purpose of the foundation of any state is the happiness of the whole."[107] Steenbuch noted the importance of rule of law in his commentary to the constitution: "All agree, that the laws are to govern, and not the men."[108] This was to secure individual property rights through rule by propertied men. Man, wrote Steenbuch, has "a right to support himself, a right he has received not as a gift from his fellow men but from the hand of nature."[109] One could theorize this in the following way, explained Steenbuch: "1) appropriation of property, 2) infringement on this, 3) the creation of an association, and 4) the establishment of a state."[110] This meant that, in actuality, the right to support oneself was maintained by establishing a state which gave the individual certain acquired rights, the first of which was "the right to property."[111] Steenbuch explained:

> To enjoy his natural and acquired rights, the individual enters into a state. By a state or a civic constitution one means a union begun between a certain number of people to secure their natural rights by laws. The main purpose for the establishing of any state must thus be to secure to each individual his external freedom. External freedom the citizen has when his natural and acquired rights know no other restriction than what is necessary for the existence of the state. This freedom of the citizen rests on two foundations: first, that no laws are given that are not strictly necessary for the existence of the state; and, second, that the citizen may do anything that is not against any law of this nature. Different from civic freedom is political freedom. The latter is sustained by the participation of citizens in the legislative power. The citizen is politically free when he obeys no other law than that to which he has given his consent (directly or by a representative); he has civic liberty when he obeys no other law than that which is

[106] Christian Magnus Falsen and Gunder Adler, April 22, 1814 in Jæger (1916), p. 15.

[107] Christian Magnus Falsen and Gunder Adler, April 22, 1814 in Jæger (1916), p. 10.

[108] Steenbuch (1815), p. 83.

[109] Steenbuch (1815), p. VII.

[110] Steenbuch (1815), p. VII.

[111] Steenbuch (1815), p. VII.

> expressed by the general will ... the one may exist without the other, the main purpose of the state is thus only a negative happiness.[112]

Steenbuch here explains a central point about freedom in the first form of the nation. It was men who were politically free (the men of landed property) that were to govern and make laws that expressed "the general will." Moreover, as in America, we see that individuals who have a natural right to property decide to give up some of this natural freedom in order to secure their right to property. Property could be secured only by establishing a civic state where rule by men with property ensured the right to property and the wellbeing of the whole.

Poet, writer and historian Henrik Wergeland (1808–1845), a generation after the constitution was written, expressed very well how the right to property was connected to the happiness of the whole and the rule of law. Wergeland was chronically opposed to the establishment. He was an ardent romantic nationalist and notorious for his drinking habits, lust for women and his stubbornness, which on several occasions led him into fist fights with those who disagreed with him. This was a behaviour somewhat unsuitable to a man of his position: he was the son of a priest and founding father, and he was himself educated to be a priest. Naturally his radicalism and behavior caused him considerable trouble finding a position as a priest. Instead, he spent his time writing poems, prose, and pamphlets/magazines for the public's enlightenment. His literary production was enormous and impressive—for example, in 1830, he published a deep and profound philosophical poem, which was the most voluminous work published in any Nordic language at the time. Wergeland's worldview was built on a personal and romantic/enlightenment Christianity that, for example, rejected the doctrine of hell and that of Jesus as a holy man or God. The central theme of his philosophy was love and enlightenment built on fundamental spiritualism. He saw history as a God-directed story of progress and love, and held love of the nation and individual rights as especially important.[113] Wergeland's national vision was expressed, for example, in his poem *Normandens katechisme* ("The catechism of the Norwegian," 1832). Here, he asked rhetorically, "is the right to property sacred?", and answered:

[112] Steenbuch (1815), p. VIII.

[113] The biographical facts about Wergeland I have taken from Ustvedt, Yngvar, *Henrik Wergeland: En biografi*, Gyldendal Norsk Forlag, Oslo (1994).

> Do not desire what belongs to thy neighbor, but protect his life and property with your own! Only by the security of thy neighbor can your own security be firm. Violate thy neighbor's right, and violate thus your own.[114]

The security of property for the propertied man was also the same for someone who did not have property. For, as Wergeland explained, the nation gave everyone this right: the fatherland was the source of all the power a citizen had, it gave him freedom of religion and of speech, and

> The right to enjoy the fruits which groweth from his sweat, to be secure in his goods and his person, to stand up against whoever subdues right, even if he wears a crown.[115]

The Norwegian had the right to be "secure in his goods and in his person"—the Norwegian was, in other words, free under his constitution; toward the end of the poem, Wergeland asked the Norwegian, "What are you?", and he answered, "Freeborn northman … slavery I hate more than the pest … my father placed my cradle under the sun of liberty."[116] Freedom from slavery meant to live in a state where the right to property was sacred. This being so in Norway, "the working man" was bestowed with "civic honor," and he was "equal to his master in right and rank" to acquire property, a right which was maintained through "reverence to the law – the highest authority, king of the Norwegians."[117]

In Wergeland's romantic vision, there was perhaps no material restrictions to who could be a lawmaker ("I believe that to the parliament, elections should not be by rank, but decided by the degree of enlightenment of a man," he wrote in his *Catechism*),[118] but, as we saw, real property was set as a central qualification to participate in legislation by the 1814 generation. Wergeland also hinted at the importance of landed property for the existence of freedom. In his *History of the Constitution* (*Norges Constitutions historie*, 1841), he referred to the *odelsrett* and

[114] Henrik Wergeland, 1832 in Lassen, Hartvig, *Henrik Wergelands Samlede skrifter tredie bind*, Chr. Tønsbergs forlag, Christiania (1853), p. 9.

[115] Henrik Wergeland, 1832 in Lassen (1853), p. 12.

[116] Henrik Wergeland, 1832 in Lassen (1853), p. 17.

[117] Henrik Wergeland quoted in Sejersted (2001), p. 120.

[118] Henrik Wergeland, 1832 in Lassen (1853), p. 12.

the *odelsbonde* and contrasted the freedom that this right conferred on men against the subjugation of despotic rule. The Norwegians, wrote Wergeland in the first volume of his history, were a "people of odelsmænd, with such a simple and patriotic fear and unwillingness against the corrupting forces of the Danish despotic rule."[119] For such people, the constitution as given at Eidsvoll (with its property rights qualifications for the vote) in 1814 was in perfect correspondence with their nature, because it represented their ancient propertied freedom: "The Norwegian people did not see the constitution as something new and strange; but rather as a restoration, as a *restitio in intergum*, of the old internal state, of its ancient freedom."[120] The emphasis and importance placed on landed property must be understood in relation to the agrarian landed context in which the national movement worked, and indeed for almost half a century there was a consensus in the national movement that the constitution of 1814, with its property qualifications for enfranchisement, was the best way to secure freedom. It was this that constituted popular sovereignty. Indeed, from 1814 till 1869, no attempts were made by the parliament to fundamentally alter the franchise.[121]

The Odelsrett, the Farmer and National Freedom

The debates surrounding the *odelsrett* in 1814 give an indication of the importance of landed property, and how popular sovereignty was understood in relation to this. In his diary from Eidsvoll in 1814, priest and member of the constitutional convention Nicolai Wergeland (father of the previously quoted Henrik Wergeland) noted that the *odelsrett* was contested at Eidsvoll, but he and many others saw it as crucial. Wergeland wrote in his diary:

> I believe that this right [the odelsrett], when our land was ruled by Danish kings and Danish aristocrats, averted the oppression of our farmers ... and that its preservation must be to us a sacred duty, especially considering that our land might very well soon again come under foreign yoke. We who

[119] Wergeland, Henrik, *Norges Constitutions historie, første del*, Kristiania (1841), p. 14.

[120] Wergeland (1841), p. 9.

[121] Langeland (2014), p. 39.

> wanted to secure Norway's freedom, should we destroy the bulwark of this freedom? … should the righteous part of our nation be bereft of this right which makes the small farmer noble and which is just to all families, only because some unjust corrupted men abuse it?[122]

Falsen agreed with Wergeland on the *odelsrett*; moreover, he was one of the strongest advocates of the *odelsrett* and its importance for national freedom in the 1814 generation. One year after the constitutional convention, he published a book whose sole purpose was to show the importance of this right regarding the constitution. He concluded in the book that the *odelsrett* was to the Norwegian "the most sacred of rights which have given him his freedom," and it was a "necessary precondition for its persistence into the future and for future generations."[123] The *odelsrett*, wrote Falsen was not simply a right to property, it was "a right that made him (the farmer) free both from the state and from taxes."[124] Falsen pointed to the ancient Norwegian kingdom to demonstrate the usefulness and common sense of the *odelsrett*:

> It was the men of landed property or the *odelsmend* that exercised legislative power. The right to represent the nation at the Ting, and to take part in the legislation, was, as our history and the old laws demonstrate, not personal; it was attached to the land, and so it had to be, as those that owned land were the only ones that were fit to do military service, and to decide on taxes … that several small landholdings is a safe way and necessary precondition for the securing of the liberty of the people, and a constitutional monarchy's longevity, is a truth on which the politicians and philosophers of recent times all agree.[125]

The right to legislative power (sovereignty) was "attached to the land" and "several small landholdings" were "a safe and necessary precondition for the securing of the liberty of the people." The *odelsrett* secured equality and happiness because it kept the land equally distributed amongst the farmers:

[122] Wergeland, Nicolai, *Fortrolige breve til en ven*, Christiania (1830), p. 108.

[123] Falsen (1815), p. 16.

[124] Falsen (1815), p. 23.

[125] Falsen (1815), p. 32.

> As long as the farms are small, divided between many, we can see that the customs are being respected, that the laws are being respected, in short, that the states remain, perhaps not powerful, but at least they remain happy.[126]

Another supporter of the *odelsrett* asked rhetorically at the Eidsvoll assembly:

> What is the reason that, amongst the nations, only the Norwegian farmer owns his land, and thus enjoys that great right, that nature itself defends, that is, that he who with his labour and the sweat of his brows makes the earth yield fruits, has the right to the fruits of this work, and not be in the position of those that are merely servants of others?

To which he proposed an answer himself:

> has not the odelsrett always been the guardian angel that has preserved the Norwegian farmer from that evil, that in all other lands – to larger or lesser extent – subdues this honorable class?[127]

What was this "evil"? What made men "servants of others"? In the past it had been "hierarchical feudal aristocracy that destroyed all equality between citizens."[128] But in the present, it was moneyed interest. Proponents of the *odelsrett* said that if this right was abandoned, it could easily happen that a few rich men would buy up all the land. Another member of the constitutional convention asserted that the *odelsrett*:

> Stops certain rich citizens from acquiring whole areas of land … and thus domination, which would turn the mass of the citizens, those that work hard and well, into slaves and weaken the power of the state.[129]

The *odelsrett* was "the true pillar of Norway, a bulwark against aristocracy and a security of the wellbeing of the farmer and his noble spirit," and if this pillar were to be removed then:

[126]Falsen (1815), p. 33.

[127]O.E. Holck, April 22, 1814 in Olafsen (1915), Vol. 1, p. 257.

[128]Falsen (1815), p. 40.

[129]O.E. Holck, April 22, 1814 in Olafsen (1914), Vol. 1, p. 259.

> All the land will be in the hands of a few rich men – and behold! Our now noble farmers will sink into the slavery of Europe's past peoples or to that of the Russian slaves of today and inherit their Slavic spirit – I would then look in tears upon my fatherland![130]

Falsen agreed with this. Without the *odelsrett*, he wrote:

> More people would have to subsist by fewer means, and the mass of the people will become miserable … the rich would become hard and unjust; and what could be more natural? They have no right, and this they must surely know for themselves.[131]

The *odelsrett* was to secure the property of the Norwegian from men "who have no right," guaranteeing widespread ownership of land and thus popular sovereignty. In short, the *odelsrett* made the farmer free because it protected his property and capital from aristocrats, merchants and authorities alike. It ultimately secured the Norwegian his freedom to legislate and decide over his property and to tax himself, thus making him sovereign, just as he had done in ancient times. Steenbuch also noted in his commentary on the constitution that, "Odel, in ancient times, meant property free of any taxes," and he noted that in his own day, many saw this as a way in which "the people, by their own right, consented to the taxes they would pay, and thus, by this right, it is almost as if the ancient freedom and *odelsrett* is restored."[132] This point goes straight to the core of the national ideology in the first form of the nation: in order to be free, the legislative power must in the hands of propertied men, so that they themselves can decide over their property and ensure the rule of law. Even some opponents of the *odelsrett*, like Jacob Aall, admitted that the *odelsrett*, had, at least in the past, secured the freedoms of the farmer. In a pamphlet published in 1809, he admitted that the *odelsrett*, although it might not have a place in the future, had nevertheless preserved liberty and sovereignty in old times; it had preserved a nation of farmers "whose property belonged purely and exclusively to themselves." Norwegian farmers were thus "free from the spell of serfdom … that has hindered the cultivation of the soil all over Europe." Indeed, Aall wrote (even though he was in principle against the

[130] W.S. Koren, April 15, 1814 in Olafsen (1914), Vol. 1, p. 160.

[131] Falsen (1815), p. 34.

[132] Steenbuch (1815), p. 89.

right) "if the dissolution of the *odelsrett* were to become the grave of liberty, then it must be protected like a precious artifact."[133] The advocates of the *odelsrett* may be seen as representing how this ideology manifested itself in the first form of the nation: as a propertied democracy.

Division of Powers and Elite Fear of Farmer Rule

It is, however, important to note that, as such, the *odelsrett* was debated before 1814 and continued to be so also in the new nation.[134] In pointing to the above positive views on the *odelsrett*, I do not mean to say that there was a consensus on this. The debates over whether the *odelsrett* was to even continue were fierce, but these debates about property rights demonstrate precisely the importance of landed property in the national ideology. The glorification of the farmer by the elite, however, was neither universal nor persistent, and it even waned in Falsen when he met farmers that did not live up to his expectations. Falsen's friend, the priest Nordahl Brun, who was himself, as we saw, very much a supporter of the *odelsrett* and a farmer during the last decades of the eighteenth century, wrote in a letter to fellow priest Claus Pavels in 1815 that, "I am now worried about the plurality of farmers [in the parliament] ... if this class is to organize our state, then God help us."[135] Pavels himself was also not convinced of the ability of the class of farmers to rule, as they would:

> Bring upon our country a thousand misfortunes ... most people in the higher classes fear a farmers' domination, that would with its majority be able, through legislation, to realize the most unreasonable and damaging projects.[136]

[133] Aall, Jacob, *Fædrelandske ideer*, Christiania (1809), p. 27.

[134] For an overview of such debates before 1814, see Evju, Håkon, "Property, patriotism and self-interest in the debate over Odlesretten, the Norwegian retrait lineager, 1759–1814," *Journal of Intellectual and Political Thought*, Vol. 1, No. 1 (2012), pp. 86–109. And, for a discussion of these debates in a wider context and in the early years of the new Norwegian nation, see Evju, Håkon, "Debating the moral and economic foundations of a democratic polity," *Scandinavian Journal of History*, Vol. 40, No. 5 (2015), pp. 653–676. In this article Evju compares the proponents of the *odelsrett* to those of the same conviction as, for example, the Jeffersonians in America, and its opponents as those who were of ideas that in America might be called Hamiltonian.

[135] Østvedt (1945), p. 290.

[136] Østvedt (1945), pp. 290–291.

It would take time, thought Pavels, before "our citizens, our proprietors and our farmers will be sufficiently cultivated so as to place the well-being of the nation in their hands."[137] Count Wedel was aware of the immaturity of the farmer, too. In the first ordinary parliamentary session of the new nation, he participated in a debate with a farmer who Wedel thought was so rudely spoken that he suggested having the farmer in question expelled from the parliament.[138] The propertied farmer and his possibility to partake in legislation represented the ideal of the new nation's ideas about sovereignty and property, but in practice, thought many, they could not alone uphold the vision that they were supposed to represent.[139] However, in the national ideology, there was in fact a safety mechanism against "farmers' domination"; this safety mechanism was the division of powers which would secure balance. It was this function that the monarch was to have, and this is one reason why monarchism was pervasive at Eidsvoll. As we have seen, this was integrated in Falsen's vision of the propertied farmer when he pointed to the fact that the *odelsbonde*, in ancient times, ruled in cooperation with the king. Just as it had supposedly been in the Medieval Ages, so too was it today. Falsen had written that in the Medieval Ages, "all sovereignty was vested in the people, which thus kept in their hands legislative power, and gave the king accordingly the executive power." The new constitution mirrored this. The final constitution stated that, "the king is vested with the executive power" (§3), while "the people holds the right of legislation" (§49).[140] The king also had a suspensory veto in matters of legislation, and a monarchy was seen as central to the happiness of the nation:

[137]Hommerstad, Marthe, "Et spørsmål om kunnskap? Politisk kompetanse og politisk deltagelse blant bøndene etter 1814," in Langeland (ed.) (2014), p. 92.

[138]Hommerstad (2014), p. 88.

[139]It can be noted here that the distrust was mutual: many farmers had little faith and trust in the new constitution and the parliament. Rather they placed their faith, as they had done for ages past, under the Oldenburg Empire, in the king. That he now resided in Stockholm rather than in Copenhagen did not seem to matter. For a convincing argument about the farmers' opposition to the constitution and the parliament, see Steen, Sverre, *Det frie Norge: på falittens rand*, Cappelen, Oslo (1953), pp. 244–303. A riot of the farmers in 1818 against the parliament is also depicted in detail here.

[140]*Norwegian Constitution of May 1814*. https://www.stortinget.no/no/Stortinget-og-demokratiet/Lover-og-instrukser/Grunnloven-fra-1814/ (accessed 03.02.2015).

> The monarchy should be hereditary under our noble prince Christian Frederik, which is offered the crown of Norway for him and his descendants – Because the history of the world have never provided us with an example where states with an elected executive have remained happy – countries with an elective executive are always prey to discord, the influence of foreign powers, and the most unhappy inner and external disagreements.[141]

Perhaps republics could be happy in their infant years, it was said, but "rarely does this last – it is turned into an aristocracy or an oligarchy."[142] We can also see in the Adler–Falsen constitutional draft the important role that the division of powers and the monarch were given. It did not help simply to respect the universal right to property, as the draft stated:

> Be the foundation of the state ever so strong, it cannot be safe from falling apart if not the various parts of the structure are not in balance. Many states have struggled to find such a balance, and the paths through which it has been attempted have varied a lot. But it seems that this balance has been best secured in those states where the citizens themselves decide on the rules by which they are to be governed, and where they have subjected themselves to an executive power that, although it does not stand above law, is vested with the appropriate means to secure against external or internal usurpation. The separation of the legislative power from the executive power must thus be the main point in any constitution seeking balance...[143]

Balance was a central point. At the Eidsvoll Assembly, delegate Peter Motzfeldt (1777–1854), an army captain, worried that "one single class may be overpowered."[144] He continued:

> The convention has already agreed that the people shall exercise the legislative power through their representatives. But how this is best done without chaos or without danger of the legislative right of the people being violated ... is a big problem.[145]

[141] W.S. Koren, April 15, 1814 in Olafsen (1914), Vol. 1, p. 157.

[142] W.S. Koren, April 15, 1814 in Olafsen (1914), Vol. 1, p. 157.

[143] Christian Magnus Falsen and Gunder Adler, April 22, 1814 in Jæger (1916), p. 3.

[144] Peter Motzfeldt, May 5, 1814 in Olafsen (1914), Vol. 1, p. 224.

[145] Peter Motzfeldt, May 5, 1814 in Olafsen (1914), Vol. 1, p. 223.

His answer was that: "the legislative power of the people is circumscribed – which is a fundamental component – and a security for the freedom of the people."[146] The power of the farmers had to be restricted. This was also pointed to in Erhenvard's pamphlet: even though the pamphlet stated that the farmer was "the only class where the member's personal interest coincides with that of the country," it also had to be admitted that:

> These do not normally have the appropriate knowledge (to rule a state), and taking into consideration that only farmers are members of this class, then one realizes how much ignorance that rules there.[147]

Therefore:

> The executive power should be in the hands of the king through his ministers which are to insure that all that is decided is in correspondence with the laws. Banking, taxation and general legislation, on the other hand, should belong solely to the representatives of the nation.[148]

As Steenbuch similarly noted in his commentary, if the laws were to govern, then one had to "thwart the possibility that the lawgivers act out of passion."[149] For a long time this was done by a strict division of powers in the Norwegian Constitution, separating the elected legislative branch with a royally appointed executive branch. This was to change with the second form of the nation, driven forth by a change in the understanding of property and freedom. We turn to this change in Part II of the book, starting with the American case. Before we do this, however, there will be a discussion on nationalism that stemmed from the agrarian moment.

Summary

This chapter has covered the period between 1770 and 1814. The first section of the chapter dealt primarily with the 1770s and 1780s. The central idea here was that Norway's self-owning farmers were freer than

[146] Peter Motzfeldt, May 5, 1814 in Olafsen (1914), Vol. 1, p. 225.

[147] Carl Fredrik Erhenvard, April 1, 1814 in Olafsen (1914), Vol. 1, p. 175.

[148] Carl Fredrik Erhenvard, April 1, 1814 in Olafsen (1914), Vol. 1, p. 178.

[149] Steenbuch (1815), p. 83.

any other people in Europe, and that this was precisely due to a peculiar Norwegian history which resulted in widespread landownership. The chapter looked at the ideas of scholar Gerhard Schøning (1722–1780), priest Johan Nordahl Brun (1745–1816), and priest Jens Zetlitz (1761–1821). The second section of the chapter dealt with the national movement from January until May 17, 1814 and showed how the idea of widespread landownership became connected to popular sovereignty. This started when Prince Christian Frederik called together a constitutional assembly at Eidsvoll on April 10, 1814, where several constitutional proposals were produced. The chapter focussed especially on the constitutional draft written by Johan Gunder Adler (1784–1852) and Christian Magnus Falsen (1782–1830). The point was to show how, at a time of crisis, loyalty to the Oldenburg state became transformed into a belief that freedom must be built on historical local traditions, and that the most firm pillars of freedom were to be found within Norway. The chapter also discussed *the first form of the nation*, showing how *the amalgamation of property, people and sovereignty* was constituted in such a way that sovereignty of the people, the right to property and the rule of law were seen as secured through a propertied democracy based on landed or real property. The positive position on the special Norwegian allodial right to land—the *odelsrett*—was used to display this.

Nationalism and the Agrarian Moment

This concludes Part I of the book. It encompassed the emergence of nationalism through the independence struggles of the late–eighteenth century colonial American elite, and the early–nineteenth century Oldenburg elite in the Kingdom of Norway. Although these countries are geographically far apart, and belonged to quite different historical contexts—America being a New World, and the Norwegian Kingdom belonging to the Old World—I hope that Part I of this book has displayed fundamental similarities in how and why nationalism emerged in these places.

The first and most important similarity between the two places is the relative widespread ownership of landed property. In both cases, this informed the arguments and the analysis that members of the national movements made. Arguments were made on both sides of the Atlantic that the people were and should be sovereign because they owned landed property. Ownership of landed property, and the securing of this right by laws made by the people themselves, it was argued, was essential for a people and a nation to be sovereign. Based on this there were constructed narratives that used history as its primary logic of justice—Americans and Norwegians had always enjoyed freedom and property in the past, it was thus a perversion that such a freedom should not now be bestowed upon them. It was an historical injustice and they were free by the laws and decrees of history. Adapted to current political contexts and to the current distribution of land in each of the cases, these narratives became the drivers, justifications and inventors of national popular sovereignty in its first form. This was the crux of agrarian nationalism that emerged in these two places, and this agrarian nationalism became an answer to the problem of how to legitimize sovereignty once the imperial bonds were cut off.

Both the American colonies and the Kingdom of Norway were cut off from their respective imperial centres. It happened for different reasons, but the answer was the same—nationalism (i.e., the fusion of landed property and popular sovereignty bound to a specific historical tradition). Nationalism was a new invention of this time—it emerged gradually (albeit much faster in Norway) informed by agrarian societies in response to a crisis in the legitimacy of sovereignty.

In the American colonies the propertied elite started reacting to British policies from the 1760s onwards, and only in 1776 did they become fully nationalist. Before that they tried as far as they could to remain within the Empire, referring to their historical freedoms as Brits. As time went by, the emphasis was increasingly on specific American rights, based, to a large degree, on landholding. When the imperial crisis intensified the colonists simply declared their rights as a distinct people with the right to be free. There were, of course, also so-called loyalists—people who did not want to break with Britain. One might get the impression from this book that nationalism and independence emerged almost effortlessly, frictionlessly, and naturally in colonial America. This was, of course, not the case: there were fierce and violent struggles between loyalists and rebels as part of the revolutionary war between 1775 and 1784—a war that had to be fought and won by the rebels before the US could be established as a nation-state. This aspect was downplayed in the account of colonial America in Chapter 2. This is so because the point of this book is to analyze the victorious, and finally dominant arguments and discourses that promoted independence. These arguments and trains of thought that tell us how the new, American nationalism was.

In Norway too, nationalism emerged in the context of war, although it was not a war between Norwegian nationalists and imperial loyalists. This was the Napoleonic Wars in which the country became entangled by chance. Later, there was a short war of independence (lasting only a few weeks) between Norwegian forces and Swedish troops who came to win the country for Karl Johan—former general for Napoleon, and recently appointed the Swedish king of Sweden, only a few months after independence was declared from Denmark. This aspect of war has not been much emphasized in the chapter on Norway either. It was indeed the outcome of the Napoleonic wars that led to initiation of the Norwegian independence movement, and which made it intensify over a much shorter time than in America. The Norwegian elite was loyal towards the Oldenburg state, just as the colonists were loyal Brits. In fact, it is probably unlikely that a break with the imperial Oldenborg state would have happened at all for Norway in 1814, were it not for the fact that events of the Napoleonic wars separated Norway from Denmark. When this happened the Norwegian elite, led by the Danish prince, started to assert the rights of Norwegians as a free people, based to a large extent upon perceived historical freedoms as a result of landholding, just as in the American colonies. This was not unanimous in Norway either, and there were differences in what exactly were the right actions to take. Some indeed favored a union with Sweden, instead of an independent state led by the former Danish Prince. Indeed, a union with Sweden later became a reality, although not under the circumstances that the supporters of this had favored. This division has not been a focus in this book, and that is because the book has chosen as its subject the more underlying ideological similarities, and to focus on the forces that most strongly shaped the new state during the crucial months of 1814.

The point of this part of the book has been to highlight the similarities between the US and Norway, but there were, of course, local circumstances and peculiarities to each of the cases, one of the most obvious being that Norway became a constitutional monarchy and that the US became a republic. This difference, however, is not as great as it may sound: in both cases a legislative branch was established with powers directly derived from the people in the form of representative democracy. Further, in both cases this representative democracy was restricted, in high degree, to those owning landed or real property. The fact that the executive branch was, in Norway, reserved for the monarch, whereas it was more directly derived from the people in the US, actually represents two sides of the same principle: a balance of power. There were rigorous debates in both nations about how to achieve a balance of power, and practically nobody thought that all power should be in the hands of all the people. The republican and the monarchical principles were different ways of balancing power that were based on the sovereignty of the people through legislation. Furthermore, both were based on popular sovereignty through a property-based democracy in which national sovereignty was understood to be derived from the property of the members of the community. Both the US and Norway became propertied communities and nations.

One important reason the first form of the nation took similar shape in the US and Norway despite their differences was the existence of widespread private landholding. More than anything else, it was this that shaped the national ideology and the new national institutions. For one, wide landownership corresponded to the historical myths invoked about a free, landed people. On the other hand, wide landownership was also what made it realistic to invoke popular sovereignty, because sovereignty was tied to ownership of land. When many people thus owned land, it was natural that sovereignty was popular; sovereignty was not derived from the ownership of a few landholders or kings, but from a wider group of people. It was for the same reason that popular sovereignty took the form of a property-based democracy: only landed property could be the basis of sovereignty. For this reason, it was also important that property became duly protected through the rule of law. This meant that property, in theory, was set down as a universal right for all the members of the nation. It is important to note that this notion was not unanimously seen to be incompatible with the existence of chattel slavery (an institution that specifically denied some people the right to property). This was largely because slaves were not clearly defined as free agents, but were in many regards understood to be a form of property to be protected.

The agrarian moment of nationalism was initiated in America almost forty years before the Norwegian national movement. Between these two events, nationalism also emerged in many other agrarian societies of the time and in many ways. However, American nationalism became the prototype, although the French Revolution probably influenced more places directly. It is outside the scope of this book to explore this, so we shall have to be content with noting the similarity between American and Norwegian nationalisms.

The Norwegians did not copy the colonial Americans, however, although they were certainly aware of, and inspired by, what had happened there, in much the same way that colonial Americans were inspired by British and French before 1776. Neither American nor Norwegian nationalism emerged in a vacuum but they became actualized and formed in the specific way that they did due to the agrarian property relations in each society. It was the very specific American relations of property and power mixed with dominating ideas at the time that for the first time sparked nationalism into being. In Norway, nationalism was a fusion of ideas that had been circulating in the Western world but with a specific focus on Norwegian reality.

By virtue of their peculiar historical developments the American colonies and the Kingdom of Norway, two peripheries of the Western world, situated on each side of the Atlantic, had similar landed property structures, which may account for the very similar developments that happened in the two different places during the agrarian moment of nationalism. This is not to say that these two countries were the only places in which such developments took place. It is likely, for instance, that similar developments and a similar ideology can be found also in revolutionary France—the national revolution *par excellence*. In France too, there had developed a smallholding structure during the century leading up to the revolution, although it was tangled up in its own peculiarities in the power structure of the French absolutist state and its aristocracy.[150] In fact, in most of the Western world between 1776 and 1884, feudal landownership disappeared, giving rise to private property regimes.It is probably not a coincidence that this time period is also generally seen as the heyday of nationalism in this region. Again, going into detail here is outside the scope of this book, but I would like to emphasize that the trends seen in the US and Norway are probably not unique, rather they may serve as very clear examples of a broader moment: agrarian nationalism.

[150]For some discussions on this see Aston, T.H., and C.H.E. Philpin, *The Brenner Debate: Agrarian Class Structure and Economic Development in Pre-industrial Europe*, Cambridge University Press, Cambridge (1985) and Wood, Ellen Meiksins, *Liberty and Property: A Social History of Western Political Thought from the Renaissance to the Present* (2012).

Literature

Aall, Jacob, *Fædrelandske ideer*, Christiania (1809).

Aall, Jacob, *Erindringer som bidrag til Norges historie frå 1800–1815*, Cappelen, Christiania (1844).

Alnæs, Jan Jørgen, *Christian Fredriks dagbok frå 1814*, Gyldendal Norsk Forlag, Oslo (1954).

Bjørnskau, Erik, "Karl 3 Johan," *Norsk Biografisk Leksikon*. https://nbl.snl.no/Karl_3_Johan (last edited 13.02.2009, accessed 26.01.2015).

Bratberg, Terje, "Baroniet Rosendal," *Store Norske Leksikon*. https://snl.no/Baroniet_Rosendal (last edited 2010, accessed 10.02.2016).

Bratberg, Terje, "Jarlsberg," *Store Norske Leksikon*. https://snl.no/Jarlsberg (last edited 2010, accessed 10.02.2016).

Bregnsbo, Michael, "Det politisk intellektuelle offentlige miljø for de kommende grunnlovsfedre. Overgang frå enevælde til forfattining – idemessigemellem-regninger," in Ola Mestad (ed.) (2013).

Brun, Johan Nordahl, *Til Nordmænd: om troskab mod kongen og kiærlighed til fædrelandet* (1773).

Brun, Johan Nordahl, *Tanker om Norges Odels-ret* (1788).

Christensen, Olav, "En nasjonal identitet tar form," in Øystein Sørensen (ed.), *Jakten på det Norske: perspektiver på utviklingen av en Norsk nasjonal identitet på 1800 talet*, Gyldendal Norsk forlag, Oslo (2001).

Dørum, Knut, "Det Norske Skyldssystemet – et særnorsk fenomen?" *Historisk Tidsskrift*, Vol. 101, No. 2 (2001).

Evju, Håkon, "Property, atriotism and self-interest in the debate over Odlesretten, the Norwegian retrait lineager, 1759–1814," *Journal of Intellectual and Political Thought*, Vol. 1, No. 1 (2012), pp. 86–109.

Evju, Håkon, "Debating the moral and economic foundations of a democratic polity," *Scandinavian Journal of History*, Vol. 40, No. 5 (2015), pp. 653–676.

Ersland, Geir Atle, and Hilde Sandvik, *Norsk historie, 1300–1625: eit rike tek form*, Det Norske Samlaget, Oslo (1999).

Falsen, Christian Magnus, *Norges Odelsret, med hensyn på Rigets constitution*, Bergen (1815).

Gjerdåker, Brynjulv, *Til odel og eie: odels og åsetesretten gjennom eit millenium, med vekt på dei 250 siste åra*, Norsk Institutt for Landbruksforskning, Oslo (2001).

Glenthøj, Rasmus, *Skilsmissen: dansk og norsk identitet før og efter 1814*, Syddansk Universitetsforlag, Odense (2012).

Glenthøj, Rasmus, "Enevælde under afvikling. Schlegel og tidens skiftende oppfatelse av kongemakt og konstitution," in Ola Mestad (ed.), *Frihetens forskole: Professor Schlegel og Eidsvollsmennenes læretid i København*, Pax Forlag AS, Oslo (2013).

Grankvist, Rolf, "Gerhard Schøning," *Norsk Biografisk Leksikon*. http://nbl.snl.no/Gerhard_Sch%C3%B8ning (last edited 13.02.2009, accessed 18.07.2014).

Holm, Edvard, *Den offentlige mening og Statsmagten i den dansk-norske stat i Slutningen av det 18de Aarhundrede 1784–1799*, København (1888).

Holmsen, Andreas, *Gård og Gods I Noreg I Eldre tid*, Universitetsforlaget, Oslo (1980).

Hommerstad, Marthe, "Allodial rights and the Norwegian Constitution. Christian Magnus Falsen and the idea of the Norwegian farmer," *Nordic Historical Review*, No. 10 (2010), pp. 83–94.

Hroch, Miroslav, *Social Preconditions of National Revival in Europe: A Comparative Analysis of the Social Composition of Patriotic Groups in the Smaller European Nations*, Cambridge University Press, Cambridge (1985).

Jakobsen, Rolv Nøtvik, "Holberg etter Puffndorf, Guberus etter Darjes, Shlegel før 1814: Om autoritetar og fridom i dansk norsk natur – og folkerett på 1700 talet," in Ola Mestad (ed.) (2013).

Jæger, Tyco C., *Riksforsmalingens forhandlinger, 3 die del: Grundlovsudkast*, Grøndahl og søns bogtrykkeri, Kristiania (1916).

Koth, Halvdan, *Norsk bondereising: fyrebuing til bondepolitikken*, H. Aschehoug & Co., Oslo (1926).

Krag, Claus, *Norges historie fram til 1319*, Universitetsforlaget, Oslo (2000).

Kvestad, Lars, "Frå undersaater til Norske borgere: Utviklinga av eit statsrettsleg frå eineveldet fram mot konstitusjonelt demokrati i 1814," in Langeland (ed.), *Politisk kompetanse: grunnlovas borgar, 1814–2014*, Pax Forlag AS, Oslo (2014).

Langeland, Nils Rune, "Røysteretten som mål på politisk kompetanse," in Langeland (ed.), *Politisk kompetanse: grunnlovas borgar, 1814–2014*, Pax Forlag AS, Oslo (2014).

Langslet, Lars Roar, *Christian Frederik, Konge av Norge (1814), Konge av Danmark (1839–48)*, J.W. Cappelens Forlag, Gjøvik (1998).

Lassen, Hartvig, *Henrik Wergelands Samlede skrifter tredie bind*, Chr. Tønsbergs forlag, Christiania (1853).

Lunden, Kåre, *Norsk Grålysning: Norsk nasjonalisme, 1770–1814 på allmenn grunn*, Det Norske Samlaget, Gjøvik (1992).

Lunden, Kåre, *Nasjon eller union: Refleksjonar og røynsler*, Det Norske Samlaget, Oslo (1993).

Michalsen, Dag, "Henrik Steenbuch," *Norsk Biografisk Leksikon*. https://nbl.snl.no/Henrik_Steenbuch (last edited 13.02.2009, accessed 22.07.2015).

Moseng, Ole Georg, et al., *Norsk Historie II: 1537–1814*, Universitetsforlaget, Oslo (2003).

Mykkland, Knut, *Kampen om Norge*, Cappelen, Oslo (1958).

Mykland, Knut, "Christian August," *Norsk Biografisk Leksikon*. https://nbl.snl.no/Christian_August (last edited 13.03.2009, accessed 26.01.2015).

Nielsen, Yngvar, *Grev Herman Wedel Jarlsberg og hans samtid, 1779–1840*, Alb. Cammermeyer og P.T. Mallings boghandel, Kristiania (1888).

Nygard, Mons Sandnes, *Eigedomsavhending i norsk rettshistorie*, Universitetsforlaget, Oslo (1977).

Olafsen, Arnet, *Riksforsamlingens forhandlinger, 1ste del: Protokoller med bilag og tillæg*, Grøndhal og søns Boktrykkeri, Kristiania (1914).

Olafsen, Arnet, *Riksforsamlingens forhandlinger, 2den del: Adresser og fuldmagter*, Grøndhal og søns Boktrykkeri, Kristiania (1914).

Olsen, Brian Kjær, "Frækhed er frihedens grænse. J.F.W. Schlegel og den republikanske udfordring," in Ola Mestad (ed.) (2013).

Olsen, Gunnar, *Hovedgård og bondegård, studier over stordriftens udvikling I Danmark i tiden 1525–1774*, Kiøbenhavn (1957).

Østerud, Øyvind, *Agrarian Structure and Peasant Politics in Scandinavia: A Comparative Study of Rural Response to Economic Change*, Universitetsforlaget, Oslo (1978).

Østved, Einar, *Christian Magnus Falsen: linjen I hans politikk*, Aschehoug, Oslo (1945).

Pryser, Tore, *Norsk Historie 1814–1860: Frå Standssamfunn mot klassesamfunn*, Det Norske Samlaget, Oslo (1999).

Rasmussen, Carsten Porskrog, *Det Danske godssystem. Udvikling og afvikling 1519–1919*, Århus (1987).

Sars, Ernst, *Historisk indledning til Grundloven*, Folkeskriftsselskabet, Kristiania (1887).

Schøning, Gerhard, *Om Norges Riiges historie: første del, rigets ældste historie frå det begyndelse til Harald Haarfagres tider*, Kiøbenhavn (1771), p. 289.

Seip, Jens Arup, *Teorien om det opinionsstyrte eneveldet*, Universitetsforlaget, Oslo (1958).

Seip, Jens Arup, *Utsikt over Norges historie*, Gyldendal Norsk Forlag (1974).

Sejersted, Francis, *Demokratisk Kapitalisme*, Pax Forlag AS, Oslo (2000).

Sejersted, Francis, *Demokrati og rettstat*, Pax Forlag AS, Oslo (2001).

Siggurdson, Jon Vidar, *Det Norrønne samfunnet: Vikingen, Kongen, Erkebiskopen og Bonden*, Pax Forlag AS, Oslo (2008).

Skard, Sigmund, *USA i Norsk historie, 1000–1776–1976*, Det Norske Samlaget, Oslo (1976).

Skeie, John, *Odels og Aasetesretten*, Gyldendal Norsk Forlag, Oslo (1950).

Skrubbletrang, Fridlev, *Det Danskelandbosamfund 1500–1800*, Odense (1978).

Steen, Sverre, *Det frie Norge: på falittens rand*, Cappelen, Oslo (1953).

Steen, Sverre, *1814*, J.W. Cappelen Forlag AS, Oslo (1989).

Steenbuch, Fredrik, *Bemærkninger over Norges grundlov af 4die November 1814*, Trondheim (1815).

Storsveen, Odd Arild, *Norsk patriotisme før 1814*, KULT's skriftserie nr 88, Oslo (1997).

Sørensen, Øystein, *Kampen om norges sjel: norsk idehistorie bind II*, Aschehoug, Oslo (2001).

The Norwegian Constitution of 1814. https://www.stortinget.no/no/Stortinget-og-demokratiet/Lover-og-instrukser/Grunnloven-fra-1814/ (accessed 03.02.2015).

Ustvedt, Yngvar, *Henrik Wergeland: En biografi*, Gyldendal Norsk Forlag, Oslo (1994).

Wergeland, Nicolai, *Fortrolige breve til en ven*, Christiania (1830).

Wergeland, Henrik, *Norges Constitutions historie, første del*, Kristiania (1841).

Zetlitz, Jens, *Sange til den norske bondestand* (1795).

PART II

Industrial Moment: Land to Labour

This part explores the industrial moment in which American and Norwegian nationalism became transformed. The industrial moment is defined here as the second half of the nineteenth century, and this is the time period on which this part will focus. Certain important developments must be traced back a bit earlier though, so this part also deals with the first half of the nineteenth century to some extent.

The main events dealt with in this part are the abolition of slavery in the US and the coming of parliamentary democracy in Norway . These two processes or events are not immediately as comparable and similar as the two independence struggles during the agrarian moment. However, the aim of this part is to show that these two processes exemplify the industrial transformation of nationalism, which I have called the *transvaluation of property*. What this means is that the central aspect of the right to property went from primarily being understood as a right to land to being understood as the right to own the fruits of one's labour. The exploration and explication of this transformation is the central topic of this part of the book.

Chattel slavery, its *raison d'être* and, ultimately, its abolition and dissolution in the US is the first topic of this part. The focus will be on key public figures and their position on slavery in the lead-up to the Civil War (1861–1865), The most important point is to show how republicans and abolitionists, through their discussions of chattel slavery, point to the *transvaluation of property*—or the shift from land to labour.

When moving to Norway, there will first be a brief discussion of the early labour movement during the 1850s to show how the *transvaluation of property* was an emergent discourse even as early as this. Then the discussion will focus on suffrage debates and follow these debates as they became part of the movement for parliamentary democracy during the 1870s and 1880s. The main point is to show how these debates demonstrate, much like the debates over slavery in the US, the shift from land to labour in the understanding of property.

It will be pointed out here how both cases display the same conceptual developments in national ideology, as well as in how the state became organised. Developments in the industrial moment compliment those in the agrarian moment. Together, it will be suggested, these two developments can form the basis of a more general theory of the emergence and transformation of nationalism in these countries, and perhaps also for other Western countries.

CHAPTER 4

The Industrial Moment in America—"Irrepressible Conflict"

The industrial transformation of nationalism in America had its roots in the country's "peculiar institution"—chattel slavery—stemming from a time way before industrialisation. There were inherent antagonisms between that institution and the American national ideology, and when the American nation gradually industrialized these antagonisms surfaced and became resolved in the Civil War. We must therefore start looking at the industrial transformation of nationalism in America by going back to the problem of slavery in the age of revolution.

The Problem of Slavery in the Age of Revolution

"In summary … slavery has always embodied a fundamental contradiction arising from the ultimately impossible attempt to define and treat men as objects."[1] David Brion Davis summed up in this way the core of the problem of slavery in the age of revolution. Americans were always aware of this. Samuel Johnson asked in 1775: "How is it that we hear the loudest yelps for liberty amongst the drivers of negros?"[2] Many agreed with Johnson, seeing an obvious contradiction between slavery

[1] Davis, David Brion, *The Problem of Slavery in the Age of Revolution: 1770–1823*, Cornell University Press, Ithaca and London (1975), p. 82.

[2] Samuel Johnson, 1775, quoted in Cogliano, Francis D., *Revolutionary America 1763–1815: A Political History*, Routledge, London (1999), p. 183.

E. M. Fuglestad, *Private Property and the Origins of Nationalism in the United States and Norway*,
https://doi.org/10.1007/978-3-319-89950-3_4

and the universal rights of liberty proclaimed in the *Declaration of Independence* a year later. One American proclaimed in 1794:

> If anything can sound as a solecism in the ears of all mankind, it will be this story – That in the United States of America, societies are formed for the promotion of freedom. Will not the inquiry instantly be made "are the United States of America not free? Possessed of the best country, the wisest government, and the most vitreous inhabitants, on the best face of the earth; are they still enslaved?" No – America is not enslaved; she is free ... but this replay must be mixed with one base ingredient. The slavery of Negros is still suffered to exist."[3]

However, as Benjamin Franklin wrote, "slavery is such an atrocious debasement of human nature, that its very expiration, if not performed with solicitous care, may sometimes open a source of serious evils."[4] Slavery did indeed pose a problem for the founders and subsequent generations, a problem about how to treat "men as objects."

The status of the slave remained ambiguous all the way up until the Civil War. But the very national revolutionary ideology of liberty helped sustain and reinforce the idea of the slave as fundamentally an object—as property. I quote at some length from Winthrop D. Jordan's classic study of American attitudes towards slavery. He writes about the revolutionary ideology:

> the revolutionary ideology was of limited benefit to the American Negro. For one thing, ideas about freedom and equal rights were intimately linked with the concept of private material property. As Locke had said, men possessed a "property" in both themselves and their possessions ... American revolutionaries saw no reason to readjust this view of private property as a basic natural right; more important, they rarely thought of the right of private property as distinct from, much less antagonistic to, other natural liberties. Arbitrarily deprive a man of his possessions, and you have a slave.... one of the most common antislavery arguments was that enslaved Negros were being wrongly deprived of the fruits of their labor. The absence of any clear distinction between what are now called "human" and

[3]Theodore Dwight, 1794 quoted in Jordan, Winthrop D., *White Over Black: American Attitudes Towards the Negro, 1550–1812*, University of North Carolina Press, Chapel Hill (1968), p. 333.

[4]Davis (1975), p. 84.

> "property" rights formed a massive roadblock across the route to abolition of slavery. It was obvious that compulsory manumission would violate the right of masters to their own property. Insofar as slaves were property, their masters possessed an inherent right to dispose of them as they wished. A revolution carried forward in the name of this right was a in this sense a serious and enduring impediment to compulsory abolition.[5]

In this way, slavery and slave labour came to be seen by many as fundamental to the preservation of freedom. Indeed, in the first form of the nation, slave labour was compatible with the fundamental ideas of property and freedom.

The Continuum of Slavery and Freedom: The Slave as Property Under the Constitution

Slavery as freedom may appear as a contradiction: not necessarily so. François Furstenberg has suggested seeing the positions of slavery and freedom conceptually on a continuum as being interconnected: "freedom and slavery stood, not in dialectical contradiction to, but in tension with, each other."[6] As we saw in the previous chapter, when the colonists declared themselves free from what they saw as the tyranny of the British in 1776, it was as subjects or slaves of tyranny claiming to be free. It was a political act of asserting rights and acquiring the means to be free. As we saw, property was essential to this; not to have the right to property was to be a slave. Property must thus be essential to understanding the continuum of slavery and freedom, because it was the medium making men free. What matters here is that, although the colonists saw themselves as slaves of despotism under British rule, they never saw themselves as property as such; they were potentially free men. Slaves, however, were understood by many on the continuum of slavery and freedom as real property—as the medium making a man free.

Slaves had, since before the revolution, been seen primarily as property, not as persons or free individuals. During the Continental Congress debates about taxation, Thomas Lynch (born 1749) from South

[5] Jordan (1968), pp. 350–351.

[6] Furstenberg, François, "Beyond freedom and slavery: Autonomy, virtue, and resistance in early American political discourse," *Journal of American History*, Vol. 89, No. 4 (March, 2003), p. 1296.

Carolina said (in a statement that might be seen to foreshadow the Civil War) that if slaves were not to be seen as a man's real property, then there could very well be "an end to the confederation … our slaves being our property why should they be taxed more than the land, sheep, cattle, horses, etc.?"[7] It was clear that slaves were fundamentally seen as property, at least by the proponents of slavery. Slaves, said William Paterson (born 1745) of New Jersey, were actually understood by the slave holders "in no light but as property. They are not free agents, have no personal liberty, no faculty of acquiring property, and like other property, entirely at the will of the Master."[8] It was also recognised by many that the federal constitution represented a protection of slave property. As George Tucker, attorney and politician, put it in 1806, the constitution was framed with "a cautious eye" to the subject of slavery "and was meant to embrace the case of free citizens, or aliens only, and not by a side wind to overturn the right of property."[9] Scholars in modern times have made the same observation. Pascal Larkin wrote in 1930:

> The constitution not only assumed that property in human beings is lawful, but it helped to convert the presumption that property is the reward of industry into a prejudice against state inference with property, however acquired.[10]

Or in the words of a more recent scholar:

> Surely, the author of the fifth amendment, James Madison, of Virginia, who himself owned many slaves, did not intend to deprive southerners of their slaves through this clause … if slaves were 'property' then masters could not 'be deprived of their property' without due process … From the perspective of 1789, the only possible interpretation of the three-fifth clause of the amendment was to assume that slaves were property.[11]

[7]Finkelman, Paul, "Slavery in the United States: Persons or property," in Allain Jean (ed.), *The Legal Understanding of Slavery: From the Historical to the Contemporary*, Oxford University Press, Oxford (2012), p. 116.

[8]Finkelman (2012), p. 117.

[9]Thomas Jefferson, quoted in Kantz, Stanley, "Jefferson and the right to property," *Journal of Law and Economics*, Vol. 19, No. 3 (1976).

[10]Larkin, Pascal, *Property in the Eighteenth Century: With Special Reference to England and Locke*, Cork University Press, Dublin and Cork (1930), p. 164.

[11]Finkelman (2012), p. 120

The three-fifth clause referred to in the quote stated slaves were to count for three-fifths of a person when it came to representation in the House of Representatives, in which the states were represented by population size. This clause thus gave proportionally more power to the slave-owning class.[12] Hence, indirectly, the constitution helped maintain the position of the slave on the continuum of slavery and freedom as the medium making men free. However, there were contradictions in these very same property assumptions that eventually (but not inevitably) led to division of the American nation and to the abolition of slavery. Alexander Hamilton can provide us with an example of this, as we shall see below.

A Glimpse of the Future: Hamilton's Vision

One can find in Alexander Hamilton's writings in the early national period an embryo of the future national form, a form in which property in one's labour came to be the central defining factor for freedom, and thus demanded liberation of the slaves, as we shall see later. Hamilton was born in the British West Indies in 1757. He was well read and, as a teenager in the early 1770s, he published an essay in a local paper which was so well received that money was gathered from the community to send him to school in New Jersey. When the Revolutionary War started he became involved in action, and promoted to lieutenant. Just before the end of the war, he married to wealth and land in New York, and when the Constitutional Convention gathered, Hamilton served as a delegate from New York County. After the convention he became one of the strongest advocates for the new constitution. In this regard, he participated in writing *The Federalist Papers* (1788). Under Washington's presidency, Hamilton became Secretary of the Treasury, and at this time he wrote "Report on manufactures" (1791), another document which displays his contribution to the national ideology.[13] In the report, Hamilton asserts the equal worth of wealth or capital to landed property. "It seems to be overlooked," Hamilton wrote, that:

[12] For a discussion on this see Wills, Gary, *"Negro President": Jefferson and Slave Power*, Houghton Mifflin, Boston and New York (2003), especially pp. 1–15 and 50–62.

[13] Carnes, C. Mark, and John A. Garraty (eds.), *American National Biography*, Vol. 9, Oxford University Press, New York and Oxford (1999), pp. 905–912.

> Land is itself a stock or capital, advanced or lent by its owner to the occupier or tenant, and that the rent he receives is only the ordinary profit of a certain stock in land, not managed by the proprietor himself, but by another to whom he lends or lets it, and who, on his part, advances a second capital to stock and improve the land, upon which he also receives the usual profit. The rent of the landlord and the profit of the farmer are, therefore, nothing more than the ordinary profits of two capitals belonging to two different persons, and united in the cultivation of a farm.[14]

The important thing about landed property was not that it was landed or real as such, but that it was essentially "a stock of capital":

> Both together make the ordinary profits of two capitals employed in a manufactory: as in the other case the rent of the landlord and the revenue of the farmer compose the ordinary profits of two capitals employed in the cultivation of a farm.[15]

To Hamilton, the "preference founded upon a discrimination between the different kinds of industry and property" was not meaningful. It was through different applications of an individual's skills or labour in the accumulation of capital that individual freedom was realised:

> It is a just observation that minds of the strongest and most active powers for their proper objects fall below mediocrity, and labor without effect if confined to uncongenial pursuits. And it is thence to be inferred that the results of human exertion may be immensely increased by diversifying its objects. When all the different kinds of industry obtained in a community, each individual can find his proper element, and can call into activity the *whole vigor of his nature*.[16]

For Hamilton, this was integrated into a general vision of government and sovereignty. If labour and commerce were to prosper, according to Hamilton, a strong federal government was needed:

[14] Alexander Hamilton, December 5, 1791 in Syrett, Harold and Jacob E. Cooke (eds.), *The Papers of Alexander Hamilton*, Vol. 10, Columbia University Press, New York and London (1966), p. 243.

[15] Alexander Hamilton, December 5, 1791 in Syrett and Cooke (1966), Vol. 10, p. 244.

[16] Alexander Hamilton, December 5, 1791 in Syrett and Cooke (1966), Vol. 10, p. 255.

> If we are in earnest about giving the union energy and duration, we must abandon the vain project of legislating upon the states in their collective capacities; we must extend the laws of the federal government to the individual citizens of America.[17]

It was important to Hamilton's vision of national freedom that the federal government had complete power over certain things:

> The government of the union must be empowered to pass all laws, and to make all regulations which have relation to them … to commerce, and to every other matter to which its jurisdiction is permitted to extend.[18]

The Hamiltonian vision was very much contested in the early national period. A quick visit to Jefferson can serve as a reminder of this. It can also indicate the general conflict line about the nature of federal sovereignty and of private property which was present from the beginning, and which became central for the formation of *the second form of the nation* and the abolition of slavery.

Jefferson's Dinner Party

Although the Americans had adopted a national constitution the nature of its sovereignty was very much federative, and the federal government was not, in many important matters, “extended to the individual citizens of America” as Hamilton wished. Many shunned every attempt to make the national government stronger. This divide was, in many ways, a continuity from the Federalist/Anti-federalist debates around the constitution.[19] However, this time the sides were divided in the Democratic-Republican Party, on the one side, and the Federalist Party, on the other. We could also call the former group Jeffersonian, as they were advocates of relatively more power to the states, less interested in commerce and industry, and in general propagated an agrarian model of society. The Federalists in many ways can be associated with Hamiltonianism, a vision that propagated a strong federal government, and which encouraged

[17] Alexander Hamilton, December 18, 1787 in Cooke (1961), p. 148.

[18] Alexander Hamilton, December 18, 1787 in Cooke (1961), p. 149.

[19] Discussed in the previous chapter.

commerce and industry.[20] The central difference between these two groups, when it came to national sovereignty, might be summed up by an anecdote that Jefferson refers to in the so-called *Anas* (an autobiographical work by Jefferson covering the time period from 1791 to 1806). Here, Jefferson explains the difference between himself (Republican-Democrat) and Alexander Hamilton (Federalist). The "real ground of the opposition," wrote Jefferson, was whether to "restrain the administration to republican principles" or to allow "the constitution to be constructed into a monarchy, and to be warped into all the principles and pollutions of ... the English model." Hamilton, as Jefferson saw it, was undoubtedly an advocate for the latter position, while he himself was a protector of true republican principles. To give weight to this, Jefferson referred to a dinner party that he hosted, where Hamilton was one of the guests. At this party, Hamilton revealed, according to Jefferson, that he was:

> Not only a monarchist, but for a monarchy bottomed on corruption. In proof of this I will relate an anecdote, for the truth of which I attest the God who made me. Before the President set out on his Southern tour in April 1791. he addressed a letter of the 4th. of that month, from Mt. Vernon to the Secretaries of State, Treasury & War, desiring that, if any serious and important cases should arise during his absence, they would consult & act on them, and he requested that the Vice-president should also be consulted. This was the only occasion on which that officer was ever requested to take part in a cabinet question. Some occasion for consultation arising, I invited those gentlemen (and the Attorney genl. as well as I remember) to dine with me in order to confer on the subject. After the cloth was removed, and our question agreed & dismissed, conversation began on other matters and, by some circumstance, was led to the British constitution, on which Mr. Adams observed "purge that constitution of it's corruption, and give to it's popular branch equality of representation, and it would be the most perfect constitution ever devised by the wit of man." Hamilton paused and said, "purge it of it's corruption, and give to it's popular branch equality of representation, & it would become an *impracticable* government: as it stands at present, with all it's supposed defects, it is the most perfect government which ever existed." And this was assuredly the exact line which separated the political creeds of these

[20] There are many accounts on these two parties. Cogliano (1999), pp. 137–159 provides a good overview.

> two gentlemen. The one was for two hereditary branches and an honest elective one: the other for a hereditary king with a house of lords & commons, corrupted to his will, and standing between him and the people. Hamilton was indeed a singular character. Of acute understanding, disinterested, honest, and honorable in all private transactions, amiable in society, and duly valuing virtue in private life, yet so bewitched & perverted by the British example, as to be under thoro' conviction that corruption was essential to the government of a nation.[21]

Hamilton's political views were complex, and it would be wrong to classify him as a monarchist.[22] To Jefferson, Hamilton's ideas of federal government represented monarchism and corruption from which the colonies had won independence less than a decade earlier; it represented arbitrary government that could and would interfere with the property of Americans, and which endangered the sovereignty of the people by encouraging commerce instead of securing landed property. In a sense, this is exactly what happened during the Civil War, when the federal government assumed stronger powers and encroached on the slave property of the slaveholding Americans of the south. This was the resolution of what one commentator called an "irrepressible conflict."

American Transvaluation: The Second Form of the Nation

"Irrepressible Conflict"

By 1861, changes in the American economic structure led to what William Henry Seward (an anti-slavery Republican) in 1858 called "an irrepressible conflict between opposing and enduring forces"[23]—the Civil War. The cause of the conflict, said Seward, was the existence of

[21] Thomas Jefferson, February 4, 1818 inLooney, Jefferson J. (ed.), *The Papers of Thomas Jefferson: Retirement Series*, Vol. 12, Princeton University Press, Princeton and Oxford (2015), pp. 425–462.

[22] For a quite recent overview of Hamilton's thoughts see Federici, Michael P., *The Political Philosophy of Alexander Hamilton*, Johns Hopkins University Press, Baltimore (2012).

[23] Seward, William, "The irrepressible conflict" (1858), p. 1. https://archive.org/stream/irrepressiblecon00insewa#page/n0/mode/2up/search/%22the+laborers%22 (accessed 30.01.2015).

two different "systems" in America. They were "two radically different political systems—the one resting on the basis of servile or slave labor, the other on the basis of voluntary labor of freemen."[24] The essence of the conflict was about the nature of national property rights, about different ways of understanding labour: free labour and slave labour. It could be seen as a class conflict between a slave-owning class (a slavocracy), on the one side, and an alliance of bourgeoisie/petty bourgeoisie interests and small farmers, on the other, as, for example, Charles Beard and Barrington Moore have suggested.[25] Seward also sensed this. Seward was born in 1801 to a prosperous farmer in Florida, New York. He became involved in politics as a Whig during the 1830s, and during the 1840s and 1850s came to mark himself as a strong anti-slavery agitator. Seward was close to becoming the Republican candidate for president, but was considered too radical. However, when Lincoln was elected president, he became Secretary of State.[26] To Seward, slavery was a perversion of the national ideas of property and freedom, it was "intolerable, unjust, and inhuman toward the laborer" and the whole principle of this kind of labour was wrong:

> The laborers who are enslaved are all negroes, or persons more or less purely of African derivation. But this is only accidental. The principle of the system is that labor in every society, by whomsoever performed, is necessarily unintellectual, groveling, and base; and that the laborer, equally for his own good and for the welfare of the State, ought to be enslaved. The white laboring man, whether native or foreigner, is not enslaved only because he can not as yet be reduced to bondage.[27]

[24]Seward (1858), p. 1.

[25]Beard, Charles, *The Rise of American Civilization, Vol. 2: The Industrial Era*, Macmillan, New York (1931), pp. 3–122. See also Moore, Barrington, *Social Origins of Dictatorship and Democracy: Lord and Peasant in the Making of the Modern World*, Beacon Press, Boston (1966). Lincoln's election as president did represent the coming of a new class into power. In the 60 years between Washington's election as the first US president and 1850, slaveholders controlled the presidency for 50 years. All the presidents to be re-elected in this period were slave holders. As the slaves were counting for representation, the slave states always had one third more seats in Congress than their free population would have warranted. These details are from Wills (2003), p. 6.

[26]Carnes, C. Mark, and John A. Garraty (eds.), *American National Biography*, Vol. 19, Oxford University Press, New York and Oxford (1999), pp. 676–680.

[27]Seward (1858), p. 1.

The system of slave labour did not honour labour as a good thing in itself. The free labour system, on the other hand, wrote Seward, "conforms to the divine law of equality which is written in the hearts and consciences of men, and therefore is always and everywhere beneficent."[28] This last assertion became the ruling idea, as it were, of American nationalism in its second form. The free labour system represents the *transvaluation of property* and was incompatible with chattel slavery. This happened because the mode of production changed from being an agrarian economy to becoming increasingly industrialised and market oriented.

The New Sociological Frame and Expression of Nationalism: Republicanism, Slavery and Abolitionism

While America remained largely rural until the mid-nineteenth century the country also experienced the fastest growing urbanisation in its history over this period, and simultaneously more and more spheres of life became interwoven in a market economy. In 1800, 70% of people in the north had been agricultural labourers, many of them on farms that were only partly immersed in market relations; by 1860 the number of agricultural labourers had fallen to 40%. Urban dwellers had risen from 6% in 1810 to 21% in 1860, while the percentage of people engaged in non-agricultural labour rose from 21 to 45% in the same period. In the south the number of agricultural labourers remained at 80%, and only one out of 10 people lived in urban areas. The new nation also grew enormously in the period from 1800 to 1860, when the population doubled and doubled again, the geographical size swelled and the economy boomed. In 1860, over 30 million people lived in the US. Growing wealth was not, however, equally distributed amongst this growing population. Four million people were slaves and had no, or at best very little, wealth, and the top 5% of free adult males owned over 50% of the wealth, while the bottom half of the population owned only 1%. Slave-driven southern agrarian exports constituted three fifths of American exports, and cotton from this region made up three quarters of the world supply of that commodity, and the bulk of this was produced by

[28] Seward (1858), p. 1.

slaves.[29] However, it was the new form of mechanised production that sprawled across northern cities that came to be the dominant economic form by 1860.

Already by the 1830s, industry and manufacturing had changed the social structure considerably: wage labour was more common, and thus, an increasing number of people found themselves without the property needed for enfranchisement. Accordingly, by 1830 a nationwide movement for universal male suffrage had arisen and by the end of the 1830s, universal male suffrage had been introduced in many states. Democratic reforms happened in four waves:

1. 1801 to the War of 1812. Reductions in property qualifications in Maryland, South Carolina and New Jersey. Defeat of similar efforts in Massachusetts, Rhode Island, Connecticut and New York.
2. 1815–1828. Reforms in Connecticut, Massachusetts and New York. Only Rhode Island, Louisiana, Virginia maintained powerful property barriers.
3. 1830–1840. Beginning with the Virginia Convention in 1829, Mississippi, North Carolina, and Georgia expanded the suffrage.
4. The Dorr War in Rhode Island (1841–1842). This attempt at suffrage expansion failed initially, but in its aftermath property qualifications for enfranchisement were abandoned.[30]

Despite these events, suffrage was not high on the agenda in national politics, but it can be seen as a symptom of the ***transvaluation of property***, or the shift from land to labour. Chattel slavery created the conflict that most drastically changed the nation on the basis of the new (transvalued) understanding of property. It could be said that both expanded franchise and the conflict over slavery were the results of what Charles

[29]This account of socioeconomic development rests mainly on Macpherson, James M., *Battle Cry of Freedom: The Civil War Era*, Oxford University Press, Oxford (1988), pp. 6–47 and another of his books, *Ordeal by Fire: The Civil War and Reconstruction*, Princeton University Press, New York (1982), pp. 5–31.

[30]Wilentz, Sean, "Property and power: Suffrage reform in the United States, 1787–1860," in Donald W. Rogers (ed.), *Voting and the Spirit of American Democracy: Essays on the History of Voting and Voting Rights in America*, University of Illinois Press, Urbana and Chicago (1992).

Sellers called "The Market Revolution"—the expansion of capitalist market relations,[31] but it was abolitionism that consolidated the new transvalued understanding of property.[32] In one form, abolitionism was very much religiously based, and emerged partly out of what has been called the Second Great Awakening that took place in the 1830s.[33] It was held that every man was equal under God, and that not even the constitution could justify slavery. Despite these religious foundations, I argue that the most important underlying idea was the *transvaluation of property*,[34] and, as pointed to above, that the conflict was essentially a class conflict brought about by changing economic relations.[35] The Republican Party

[31] Sellers, Charles, *The Market Revolution: Jacksonian America 1815–1846*, Oxford University Press, Oxford (1991).

[32] This is not to say that slave economy was not compatible with market society or capitalist property. It was only not compatible with capitalist property as understood in *the second form of the nation*. For some accounts on slave economy and capitalism see Baucom, Ian, *Specters of the Atlantic: Finance Capital, Slavery and the Philosophy of History*, Duke University Press, Durham (2005); Fogel, Robert, and Stanley Engerman, *The Economics of American Negro Slavery*, Little Brown, Boston (1974); Genovese, Eugene, *The Political Economy of Slavery: Studies in the Economy and Society of the Slave South*, MacGibbon & Kee, London (1966) (this book proposes that slavery was not capitalist); Moore (1966); and Shore, Laurence, *Southern Capitalists: The Ideological Leadership of an Elite, 1832–1885*, University of North Carolina Press, Chapel Hill (1986).

[33] For a recent account of this see Delbanco, Andrew, *The Abolitionist Imagination*, Harvard University Press, Cambridge, MA (2012). For an account on how religious ideas were also in fact used to justify slavery see Daly, John Patrick, *When Slavery Was Called Freedom: Evangelicalism, Proslavery and the Causes of the Civil War*, University Press of Kentucky, Kentucky (2002).

[34] For further support of this position see Haskell, Thomas L., "Capitalism and the origins of the humanitarian sensibility, Part 1," *American Historical Review*, Vol. 90, No. 2 (April, 1985); and Haskell, Thomas L., "Capitalism and the origins of the humanitarian sensibility, Part 2," *American Historical Review*, Vol. 90, No. 3 (June, 1985).

[35] The emergence of radical Jacksonians and "free soilers" might also point to this, and it might be said that elements from these traditions merged to form the Republican ideology of the 1850s and 1860s. An explicit explication of this can be found in TenBroek, Jacobus, *The Antislavery Origins of the Fourteenth Amendment*, University of California Press, Berkeley and Los Angeles (1951). See also Wilson, Major L., *Space, Time and Freedom: The Quest for Nationality and the Irrepressible Conflict, 1815–1861*, Greenwood Press, Westport and London (1974). For a discussion of the Jacksonians and anti-slavery see Earle, Jonathan, *Jacksonian Antislavery and the Politics of Free Soil: 1824–1854*, University of North Carolina Press, Chapel Hill and London (2004).

became the clearest expression of the new class interests and the *trans-valuation of property*, the shift from land to labour.

It was Republicanism, as it emerged in the late 1850s, that represented the national ideology in its newborn second form. And the social base of the Republicans was precisely the new middle class of wage earners. One contemporary asked rhetorically who supported the Republicans, and answered himself:

> Precisely those who would most naturally be expected to – the great middling class – The highest class, aristocratically associated and affiliated, timid, afraid of change, and holding in their hands the sensitive cords of commerce, and the lowest class, ignorant, derived with name, fed by the rich man's money, and led by the rich man's finger, – these are the forces arrayed against Republicanism, as a whole … those who work with their own hands, who live and act independently, who hold the stakes of home and family, of farm and workshop, of education and freedom, as a mass, are enrolled in the republican ranks.[36]

The Republican Party stood for a vision in which slavery became unacceptable, although abolition was not directly or officially propagated by Republicans in office until after the Civil War had commenced. However, at the time of the Civil War the abolition of slavery became seen, at least by Republican President Abraham Lincoln, as a direct continuation and fulfilment of what had been initiated at the revolution. Lincoln believed, he said, that the *Declaration of Independence* was "thought to include all"—something which was not, at the present, the case. On the contrary, held by Lincoln, it was used to "aid in making bondage of the negro universal and eternal."[37] The assertion in the *Declaration of Independence*, held Lincoln, was placed there "for future use," to be a "stumbling block to all those who in after times might seem to turn a free people back into the hateful paths of despotism."[38]

[36]Geinapp, Williamson, "Who voted for Lincoln," in John L. Thomas (ed.), *Abraham Lincoln and the American Political Tradition*, University of Massachusetts Press, Amherst (1986).

[37]Abraham Lincoln, June 26, 1857 in Basler, Roy P., *The Collected Works of Abraham Lincoln*, Vol. 2, Rutgers University Press, New Brunswick, NJ (1953), p. 404.

[38]Abraham Lincoln, June 26, 1857 in Basler (1957), Vol. 2, p. 406.

The Issue of Federal Sovereignty and Slavery

Lincoln's vision could not easily be realised, and it met its own stumbling block in the constitution. The constitution, as we have seen, had since the beginning protected the system of slave property in the states where it already existed. Here lay one source of the "irrepressible conflict" of which Seward spoke: it was the nature of American sovereignty. It was this that had allowed the development of two "radically different political systems." Seward wrote:

> The two systems have existed in different States, but side by side within the American Union. This has happened because the Union is a confederation of States. But in another aspect the United States constitute only one nation. Increase of population, which is filling the States out to their very borders, together with a new and extended network of railroads and other avenues, and an internal commerce which daily becomes more intimate, is rapidly bringing the States into a higher and more perfect social unity or consolidation. Thus these antagonistic systems are continually coming into closer contact and collision results.[39]

In this passage the conflict over slavery is connected to the federative nature of the American state; to the fact that the US was, de facto, a confederacy—a union consisting of sovereign states—and yet in another "aspect," considered "only one nation." One central issue in the matter of slavery became whether the national government had the right to impose its will on the states and new territories on the issue of slave property. Several compromises and decisions were made on this issue during the first half of the nineteenth century—for example, the Missouri debates, 1819–1820; the nullification crisis of 1832; the Compromise of 1850; and the Kansas–Nebraska Act, 1854.[40] However, with the Supreme Court's Dread Scott decision of 1857 (decided by Chief Judge Roger B. Taney, 1777–1864, from Maryland), the issue flared up again in a "fire" that could not be stopped. The Dread Scott decision decided three important questions:

[39] Seward (1858), p. 2.

[40] Macpherson (1982), pp. 51–70.

1. Could prolonged residence in a free state or territory make runaway slave Dread Scott free?
2. Did Scott, as a black slave, have the right as a citizen to sue in a federal court?
3. Was the Missouri Compromise (an 1820 decision that had prohibited slavery in certain new territories, including where Scott had resided) valid?

All the answers given to these questions in the Court's decision reinforced slavery: the Dread Scott decision stated that Scott was still a slave, that he was not, as a black and a slave, an American citizen, and that the Missouri Compromise was unconstitutional, meaning that Congress had no authority to exclude slavery in new territories.[41] Southerners celebrated this decision as once and for all making slavery a principle of American nationality. One southern newspaper exclaimed: "Southern opinion upon the subject of southern slavery … is now the supreme law of the land … Opposition to southern opinion upon this subject is now opposition to the constitution, and morally treason against the Government."[42] This was brought forth by southern men and by a peculiar slavery ideology that had developed in the south of the American nation, which adhered to the property assumptions of the *first form of the nation*.

The Southern Antebellum Vision: Chattel Slavery as National Freedom

The southern antebellum opinion on the subject of slavery was derived from an ideology of labour and sovereignty that can, in one sense, be traced back to certain Jeffersonian notions of sovereignty and property. This is in no way to say that Jefferson was a proto-antebellum slave apologist. Indeed, central antebellum pro-slavery men outright rejected the fundamental ideas on which Jefferson built his vision. But Jefferson, as we have seen, asserted that real independence was created through tilling the earth. Following from this, Jefferson believed, as we have seen, that those who labored at "the work bench" or in "manufacture" suffered from a "depravity of morals, a dependence and corruption, which renders them an undesirable accession to a country whose morals are

[41] Macpherson (1982), pp. 99–100.

[42] Macpherson (1982), p. 100.

sound." Such men were unfree because they were at the will of the masters who paid them. This is not so different from how the slaves were seen in the antebellum southern slave ideology, as we shall see below. While Jefferson thought that the factory workers could "quit their trades and go to laboring the earth," the slaves in the antebellum pro-slavery ideology had no such option.

In the slave ideology there was a central assertion that both the slave and the wage labourer were unfree, and that only by slavery could free society exist. Slavery was thus reasserted and firmly placed on the continuum of slavery and freedom. Jefferson also pointed to this connection; he knew that the labour of the slave was part of the reason why he himself could be independent.[43] He said that, "[I will not] willingly sell my slaves as long as there remains any prospect of paying my debt with their labour."[44] It was this notion that the pro-slavery ideology carried to its extreme. In the south, as George S. Alexander put it, chattel slavery became "the exclusionary response to the task of realizing the political task of property."[45] Many pro-slavery men of the antebellum era – for example, the plantation owner and attorney James H. Hammond of South Carolina—claimed that every society, in order to subsist in freedom, was dependent on a class of labourers, and held that the best way to maintain a state of independence was through chattel slavery; only thus could private property and liberty exist.[46] He wrote:

> The idea that slavery is so necessary to the performance of the drudgery so essential for the sustenance of man, and the advance of civilization is undoubtedly the fundamental ground on which the reason of the institution rests.[47]

[43]For more on this point see Morgan, Edmund S., "Slavery and freedom: the American paradox," *Journal of American History*, Vol. 59, No. 1 (June, 1972).

[44]Quoted in Cohen, William, "Thomas Jefferson and the problem of slavery," *Journal of American History*, Vol. 56, No. 3 (December, 1969), p. 516.

[45]Alexander, George S., *Commodity and Property: Competing Visions of Property in American Legal Thought*, University of Chicago Press, Chicago and London (1997), p. 214.

[46]Genovese, Eugene, and Elizabeth Fox, *Slavery in Black and White: Class and Race in the Southern Slaveholders New World Order*, Cambridge University Press, Cambridge (2005), p. 2.

[47]Quoted in Shore (1986), p. 19.

Hammond (born 1807) was a slave owner planter and lawyer who, during his career, was governor of South Carolina and a United States senator. By the outbreak of the Civil War, he was one of the wealthiest men in the south, owning more than 300 slaves. Hammond was a Democrat and outspoken pro-slavery ideologist, and delivered a variety of speeches on the matter.[48] Many other men of the south agreed with Hammond. Slave labour was by many seen to be the best way to secure liberty from the corruption and dependence that free wage labour created. Some pro-slavery men held that labour in factories and manufacturing was in fact binding men in a form of slavery worse than that of chattel slavery, and if chattel slavery was to be abandoned, then all of society would fall into a position of dependence.

George Fitzhugh—a lawyer from Virginia, self-appointed sociologist and devoted slave apologist—wrote about forms of enslavement and proclaimed that, "capital commands labour as master does slave."[49] Was it not better, then, to have slavery institutionalised? At least, it was asserted, the slave had a master who was obliged to feed him and house him, which was more than one could say of the masters of the industrial factory slaves of the north. "Capital is a cruel master," wrote Fitzhugh, and the free capitalist economy was nothing less than a "free slave trade, the commonest, yet the cruelest form of trades."[50] Fitzhugh was born in 1806 and became a distinct advocate of slavery. He was often seen as representing the essential slavery ideology. Fitzhugh operated his own law business from his mansion in Port Royal, Virginia, during the antebellum and Civil War eras (he was also treasurer for the Confederacy during the Civil War). He was not politically active, but he wrote extensively on the issue of slavery, notably his books *Sociology for the South, or, the Failure of Free Society* (1854), and *Cannibals All!, or Slaves without Masters* (1857).[51] This ideology, propagated by Fitzhugh and the members of the slave aristocracy, as Eugene Genovise put it, "located the primary social manifestations of evil precisely in the system of wage labour

[48] Carnes, C. Mark, and John A. Garraty (eds.), *American National Biography*, Vol. 9, Oxford University Press, New York and Oxford (1999), pp. 955–956.

[49] Greenfeld, Liah, *Nationalism: Five Roads to Modernity*, Harvard University Press, Cambridge (1993), p. 478.

[50] Quoted in Greenfeld (1993), p. 478.

[51] Loewenberg, Robert J., "John Locke and the antebellum defense of slavery," *Political Theory*, Vol. 13, No. 2 (May, 1985).

and celebrated slavery as an alternative to it."[52] Just as the revolutionaries of the 1770s saw nationality as the realization of human nature, so too did the pro-slavery ideology see slavery as natural and as crucial in fulfilling nationality. Fitzhugh wrote:

> Nature has made them slaves; all that law and government can do is modify, and mitigate their slavery. The wise and vitreous, the brave, the strong, in mind and body are by nature born to command and protect, and law but follows nature in making them rulers, legislators, judges, captains, husbands, guardians, committees, and masters.[53]

But this vision built, in many ways, on a completely different social vision from that of the north and one of the founding fathers. Slave owner Alexander Stephens (1812–1883) from Georgia, who became Vice-President of the Confederacy, was another typical advocate of slavery. He became a member of the Georgia legislature, and in the 1850s a prominent member of the Democratic Party. He played a pivotal role in the passing of the Kansas–Nebraska Act (1854), but retired from politics (only temporarily it proved) in 1858, believing that the issue of slavery was settled and safe. However, the formation of the Confederacy in 1861 saw the return of Stephens to politics.[54] In his infamous "Cornerstone speech" given that year, he elaborated on southern values and said that southern society was:

> Founded upon exactly the opposite idea [from the founders]; its foundations are laid, its corner stone rests upon that great truth, that the negro is not equal to the white man; that slavery – subordination to the superior race – is his natural and normal condition.[55]

In the end, the antebellum vision became a downright rejection of many founding values, and this was openly admitted: as Stephens explained about the Confederate constitution:

[52] Quoted in Alexander (1997), p. 228.

[53] Quoted in Greenfeld (1991), p. 478.

[54] Carnes, C. Mark, and John A. Garraty (eds.), *American National Biography*, Vol. 20, Oxford University Press, New York and Oxford (1999), pp. 658–661.

[55] Cleveland, Henry, *Alexander H. Stephens, Public and Private, with Letters and Speeches Before, During and Since the War*, National Publishing, Philadelphia (1866), p. 721.

> The new constitution has put at rest, forever, all the agitating questions relating to our peculiar institution. African slavery as it exists amongst us – the proper status of the negro in our form of civilization. This was the immediate cause of the late rupture and present revolution. Jefferson in his forecast, had anticipated this, as the "rock upon which the old Union would split." He was right. What was conjecture with him, is now a realized fact. But whether he fully comprehended the great truth upon which that rock stood and stands, may be doubted. The prevailing ideas entertained by him and most of the leading statesmen at the time of the formation of the old constitution, were that the enslavement of the African was in violation of the laws of nature; that it was wrong in principle, socially, morally, and politically. It was an evil they knew not well how to deal with, but the general opinion of the men of that day was that, somehow or other in the order of Providence, the institution would be evanescent and pass away. This idea, though not incorporated in the constitution, was the prevailing idea at that time. The constitution, it is true, secured every essential guarantee to the institution while it should last, and hence no argument can be justly urged against the constitutional guarantees thus secured, because of the common sentiment of the day. Those ideas, however, were fundamentally wrong. They rested upon the assumption of the equality of races. This was an error.[56]

However, as Stephens also explained, the rejection of some values of the founders did not mean that the Confederate constitution did not protect the true and original liberty:

> It amply secures all our ancient rights, franchises, and liberties. All the great principles of Magna Carta are retained in it. No citizen is deprived of life, liberty, or property, but by the judgment of his peers under the laws of the land.[57]

It was not the southern system that was against the law of nature, as northerners and the founders had held. On the contrary, it was the southern system that was in concordance with the laws of nature:

> Many governments have been founded upon the principle of the subordination and serfdom of certain classes of the same race; such were and are in violation of the laws of nature. Our system commits no such violation of nature's laws. With us, all of the white race, however high or low, rich or poor, are equal in the eye of the law. Not so with the negro. Subordination

[56] Cleveland (1866), p. 721.

[57] Cleveland (1866), p. 718.

> is his place. He, by nature, or by the curse against Canaan, is fitted for that condition which he occupies in our system.[58]

The pro-slavery ideology stuck to the idea that it was crucial to organize property relations in a way so that some did not have to alienate their labour, while others (namely African Americans) were bound, as it were, to do so, in order to create freedom for society as a whole. In the words of Virginia lawyer, and from 1843 until his death in 1844, Secretary of State Abel P. Upshur[59]: for a free society to exist, it was necessary that "one portion of mankind shall live upon the labours of another person."[60] We might also invoke Hammond again, in the introduction to his "Cotton is King" speech (1858):

> In all social systems there must be a class to do the menial duties, to perform the drudgery of life. That is, a class requiring but a low order of intellect and but little skill. Its requisites are vigor, docility, fidelity. Such a class you must have, or you would not have that other class which leads progress, civilization, and refinement. It constitutes the very mud-sill of society and of political government; and you might as well attempt to build a house in the air, as to build either the one or the other, except on this mud-sill. Fortunately for the South, she found a race adapted to that purpose to her hand. A race inferior to her own, but eminently qualified in temper, in vigor, in docility, in capacity to stand the climate, to answer all her purposes. We use them for our purpose, and call them slaves. We found them slaves by the common "consent of mankind"…[61]

It was this vision that the south hoped was safe after the Dread Scott decision, not only within the American nation as it was, but also in lands yet to be American.[62]

[58] Cleveland (1866), p. 722.

[59] Carnes, C. Mark, and John A. Garraty (eds.), *American National Biography*, Vol. 22, Oxford University Press, New York and Oxford (1999), pp, 116–117.

[60] Quoted in Shore (1986), p. 29.

[61] Hammond, James, *Speech of Hon. James H. Hammond of South Carolina on the Admission of Kansas Under the Lecompton Constitution*, Lemuel Towers, Washington (1858), pp. 13–14. http://babel.hathitrust.org/cgi/pt?id=loc.ark:/13960/t7jq19w-4m;view=1up;seq=3 (accessed 13.01.2016).

[62] For an interesting perspective on history and time and the issue of slavery see Wilson (1974).

The Republican Ideology: Free Labour, or to Own Oneself

"We are men with rights of men … but we are poor men; obliged to labour for our daily bread, dependent on those who choose to employ us"[63] complained the working men of Charlestown in the early 1840s. We might contrast this complaint against the sentiment of the northern version of *The Battle Cry of Freedom* written about two decades later, which asserted that "although he may be poor, no man shall be a slave."[64] The working men of Charlestown saw themselves as unfree wage slaves, poor and thus dependent. But in the Republican ideology, wage was freedom. It did not matter if one was poor; every man was free if he owned the fruits of his labour. One Republican said, "the great idea and basis of the republican party as I understand it, is free labour." The Republicans were, as another Republican put it: "not only … the anti slavery party but emphatically … the party of free labour."[65]

Abraham Lincoln became the towering leader of the Republican Party in the lead-up to the Civil War and remained so throughout the war years. Like Jefferson for revolutionary America, Lincoln looms over the Civil War era as an enormous giant. Born in 1809 in rural Kentucky on a small farm, and later rising to become a successful lawyer and President of the United States, he, in many ways, embodied the ideology of the self-made man and the American dream. Lincoln is remembered, of course, first and foremost as the president who abolished slavery and saved the union. His ideas about nationality and property are very much connected to this, and are displayed throughout his letters and speeches. Particularly useful are his debates over slavery and popular sovereignty with Stephen Douglas (1858).[66] In a debate with Douglas, Lincoln said that the right to property for which the south fought (slave or real property) was for him only secondary. Republicans, he said, did not "hold the liberty of one man to be absolutely nothing, when in conflict with

[63]Quoted in Tomlins, Christopher L., *Law Labor and Ideology in the Early American Republic*, Cambridge University Press, Cambridge (1993), p. 10.

[64]This is from verse 3 of the Union version of the song, reprinted on the first page of the Preface in Macpherson (1988).

[65]Quoted in Foner, Eric, *Free Soil, Free Labor, Free Men: The Ideology of the Republican Party Before the Civil War*, Oxford University Press, New York (1970), p. 11.

[66]Carnes, C. Mark, and John A. Garraty (eds.), *American National Biography*, Vol. 13, Oxford University Press, New York and Oxford (1999), pp. 662–673.

another man's right of property." Rather, he said, the Republicans were for "both the dollar and the man, but in case of conflict, the man before the dollar."[67] Gradually a *transvaluation of property* happened, which saw all men as free if they had the right to the fruits of their labour in the form of wages. This was based on a fundamental universalism of equality. Lincoln wrote in 1854:

> Equality in society alike beats inequality, whether the latter be of the British aristocratic sort or the domestic slavery sort. We know southern men declare that their slaves are better off than hired labourers amongst us. How little they know whereof they speak ... Twenty five years ago I was a hired labourer. The hired labourer of yesterday labours on his own account today, and will hire others to labour for him tomorrow. Advancement – improvement in condition – is the order of things in a society of equals. As labour is the common burden of our race, so the effort of some to shift the burden on to the shoulders of others is the great durable curse of the race. Originally a curse for transgression upon the whole race, when as by slavery, it is concentrated on a part only, it becomes the double-refined curse of God upon his creatures. Free labour has the inspiration of hope; pure slavery no hope.[68]

Labour might have been a curse on mankind, but if shared equally in a system of free labour it could lead to "Advancement –improvement in condition" and have the "inspiration of hope." What happened was that freedom through property came to mean, first and foremost, the right to the fruits of one's labour. Lincoln explained in an argument about slavery:

> That each man should do precisely as he pleases with all that which is exclusively his own, lies at the foundation of the sense of justice there is in me. I extend the principle to communities of men as well as to individuals ... the doctrine of self government is right, – absolutely and internally right. Or perhaps I should rather say that whether it has any application here depends upon whether a negro is not or is a man. If he is not a man, in that case he who is a man may, as a matter of self government, do just

[67] Quoted in Wilentz, Sean, *The Rise of American Democracy: Jefferson to Lincoln*, W. W. Norton, New York and London (2005), p. 793.

[68] Abraham Lincoln, September 17, 1859 in Basler, Roy P. (ed.), *The Collected Works of Abraham Lincoln*, Vol. 3, Rutgers University Press, New Brunswick, NJ (1953), p. 462.

> what he please with him. But if the negro is as a man, is it not to that extent a total destruction of self-government to say that he, too, shall not govern himself. When the white man governs himself, that is self government; but when he governs himself and also governs another man, that is more than self government – that is despotism.[69]

What distinguished *the second form of the nation* in notions of freedom was that the crucial thing was to be the proprietor of oneself, of one's labour. It was this idea that became tied up with self-government, not ownership of land. Leading abolitionist Wendell Phillips asked rhetorically about the slave: "Does he not own himself?"[70] Moreover, Frederick Douglass, the freed slave, wrote after becoming a freed man, an earner of wages through his labour: "I was now my own master."[71] To Lincoln, this universalism of self-ownership included also the slave: he was "a man" and had the same right to self-government as other men. Other men could not do "just what he please with him." When Lincoln said that he put the "man before the dollar," this is what he meant. In Republican ideology, this came to be seen as the fulfilment of national freedom. There is a clear dichotomy between chattel slavery and freedom here: "I believe each individual is naturally entitled to do as he pleases with the fruit of his labour, so far as it in no way interferes with any other man's rights and only by giving every man the right to the fruits of his labour," Lincoln said against slavery.[72] Slavery was wrong because it denied men this right; it denied slaves their humanity. The pro-slavery man "says that, upon the principle of equality, slaves should be allowed to get into a new territory like other property." But this was to deny the slave his national right as a man, it was to define him as real property, which was wrong. Lincoln said:

> This is strictly logical if there is no difference between it and other property … but if you insist that one is wrong and the other is right, there is no use to institute a comparison between right and wrong … The democratic policy everywhere carefully excludes the idea that there is any wrong in it. That is the issue … it is the same principle in whatever shape it develops

[69]Abraham Lincoln, October 16, 1854 in Basler (ed.) (1953), p. 265.

[70]Quoted in Foner (2000), pp. 164–166.

[71]Quoted in Foner (2000), p. 66.

[72]Abraham Lincoln, June 10, 1858 in Basler (1953), Vol. 2, p. 493.

> itself, it is the same spirit that says "you toil and work and earn bread, and I'll eat it." No matter in what shape it comes, whether from the mouth of a king, who seeks to bestride the people of his own nation and live by the fruit of their labour, or from one race of men as an apology for enslaving another race, – it is the same tyrannical principle.[73]

In this way, Lincoln, and much of the north, identified slavery with tyranny, restricting the rights of the nation to the slaves. However, there was "no reason in the world" said Lincoln why:

> The negro is not entitled to all the natural rights enumerated in The Declaration of independence, the right to life liberty and the pursuit of happiness. I hold that he is as much entitled to this as the white man … in the right to eat the bread, without the leave of anybody else, which his own hands earns, he is my equal…[74]

Popular Sovereignty

Lincoln connected the right to the fruits of one's labour to the idea of popular sovereignty. When Democrat Stephen Douglas claimed slavery consistent with popular sovereignty, Lincoln protested.[75] This became what is now known as the Lincoln–Douglas debates. Douglas was born in Vermont in 1813, and went on to be a lawyer and congressman. He married the daughter of a plantation owner in Mississippi, and later started his own plantation in Greenville. From his entry into politics, Douglas was a staunch Democrat; however, on the issue of slavery, he stood for a middle position, believing that it should always be up to the people of a state to decide if a state should be a slave state or not. Douglas is famous for the Kansas–Nebraska Act (1854), which contained issues of popular sovereignty and the spread of slavery to new states.[76] Douglas's main point was that the people of each state should decide whether or not it was to be a slave state. For Douglas, popular sovereignty was "the sacred right of self government." Lincoln saw

[73] Abraham Lincoln, October 15, 1858 in Basler (1953), Vol. 3, p. 315.

[74] Abraham Lincoln, August 21, 1858 in Basler (1953), Vol. 3, p. 16.

[75] Macpherson (1982), pp. 86–87.

[76] Carnes, C. Mark, and John A. Garraty (eds.), *American National Biography*, Vol. 6, Oxford University Press, New York and Oxford (1999), pp. 805–808.

through this and claimed that, as it was, popular sovereignty was nothing but "a mere deceitful pretence for the benefit of slavery."[77] In order to see what real popular sovereignty was, Lincoln posited one had to look to the *Declaration of Independence*: "I suppose that Judge Douglas will claim that he is the inventor of the idea that the people should govern themselves," but one should not forget "that in that old Declaration of independence … there is the origin of popular sovereignty."[78] The Declaration, according to Lincoln, made everyone in the US—whether slave or immigrant—connected to the founding fathers and part of the freedom that they had won, "as though they were blood of the blood, and flesh of the flesh, of the men who wrote that Declaration."[79] Moreover, he asked: if one were "making exceptions" to the Declaration of Independence, "where will it stop?"[80] Universality was the only right way to interpret the Declaration; it applied to the whole American nation. This universalism and the notion of property that was underlying its freedom were incompatible with southern ideology. Thus, when Lincoln was elected president in 1860, the southern slave states soon began seceding from the union, seeing their freedom and right to property threatened.

"We All Declare Freedom": The Question of Nationality in the Civil War Era

Both the northern and the southern visions claimed supremacy within the American nation, both claimed to represent freedom and the security of property. This was not lost on contemporaries. Eric Foner writes, and quotes from Lincoln:

> "We all declare freedom," Lincoln observed in 1864. "But in using the same word we do not all mean the same thing." To the North, freedom meant for "each man" to enjoy "the product of his labour": to the

[77] Abraham Lincoln, quoted in Burton, Orville Vernon, *The Age of Lincoln*, Hill & Wang, New York (2007), p. 70.

[78] Abraham Lincoln, July 10, 1858 in Basler (1953), Vol. 3, pp. 488–489.

[79] Abraham Lincoln, July 10, 1858 in Basler (1953), Vol. 3, p. 500.

[80] Abraham Lincoln, July 10, 1858 in Basler (1953), Vol. 3, p. 500.

> southern whites, it conveyed mastership – the power to do as they please with other men, and the product of other men's labour.[81]

Both parties referred to what they saw as a specific American national freedom. The South Carolina "Declaration of immediate causes which induce and justify the secession of South Carolina from the Federal Union," for example, begins by telling the story of the creation of the American nation by revolt from Britain, and states that "two great principles" were then asserted by the colonies: "namely; the right of a state to govern itself; and the right of a people to abolish a government when it becomes destructive of the ends of which it was instituted."[82] It was accordingly asserted that:

> The Government thus established is subject to the two great principles asserted in the Declaration of Independence; and we hold further, that the mode of its formation subjects it to a third fundamental principle, namely: the law of compact. We maintain that in every compact between two or more parties, the obligation is mutual; that the failure of one of the contracting parties to perform a material part of the agreement, entirely releases the obligation of the other; and that where no arbiter is provided, each party is remitted to his own judgment to determine the fact of failure, with all its consequences.[83]

The writers of the South Carolina declaration felt, in 1860, that the federal government no longer respected these principles: "We affirm that these ends for which this Government was instituted have been defeated, and the Government itself has been made destructive of them by the action of the non slaveholding States." Because of this, South Carolina joined other southern states to form a confederacy to preserve liberty. The confederacy was created to preserve the original liberties asserted in the *Declaration of Independence*, according to its author. Jefferson David, President of the Confederacy, plantation owner and military man

[81] Foner, Eric, *The Story of American Freedom*, W. W. Norton, New York (2000) [1998], p. 97.

[82] "Declaration of immediate causes which induce and justify the secession of South Carolina from the Federal Union." http://avalon.law.yale.edu/19th_century/csa_scarsec.asp (accessed 30.01.2015).

[83] http://avalon.law.yale.edu/19th_century/csa_scarsec.asp (accessed 30.10.2015).

(colonel in the war with Mexico in 1848)[84] wrote years after the Civil War that:

> The southern states had rightfully the power to withdraw from a Union into which they had, as sovereign communities, voluntarily entered; that the denial of that right was a violation of the letter and spirit of the compact between the states; and that the war waged by the Federal Government against the seceding states was in disregard of the limitations of the Constitution, and destructive of the principles of the Declaration of Independence.[85]

Indeed, he wrote that those who deemed supporters of the confederacy rebels or traitors were: "ignorant of the nature of the union, and the powers of the states." Like the anti-slavery proponent Seward, Davis also pointed to sectionalism and different systems as the cause of the conflict. However, the difference was that Davis did not see this as an "irrepressible" conflict:

> Sectional issues appear conspicuously in the debates of the Convention which framed the Federal Constitution, and its many compromises were designed to secure an equilibrium between the sections, and to preserve the interests as well as the liberties of the several states. African servitude at that time was not confined to a section, but was numerically greater in the South than in the North, with a tendency to its continuance in the former and cessation in the latter. It therefore thus early presents itself as a disturbing element, and the provision of the Constitution, which were necessary for its adoption, bound all the States to recognize and protect that species of property.[86]

For a long time, Davis wrote, those who wanted to abolish slavery—the peculiar "species of property"—were "Pseudo-philanthropists, and fanatics." However, in the lead-up to the Civil War, this notion was "seized upon" by "political demagogues … to acquire power."[87]

[84] Carnes, C. Mark, and John A. Garraty (eds.), *American National Biography*, Vol. 6, Oxford University Press, New York and Oxford (1999), pp. 201–205.

[85] Davis, Jefferson, *The Rise and Fall of the Confederate States of America*, Appleton & Co., New York (1912) [1881], p. V.

[86] Davis (1912), p. VI.

[87] Davis (1912), p. VI.

This destroyed the equilibrium within the union. His Vice President agreed with him: "Those at the North … we justly denominate fanatics."[88] However, it would be a misunderstanding, wrote Davis, to think that the Confederacy was fighting for the extension of slavery or for enslavement of more people. No, it was simply the right of any free man, "to go, with his slaves, into territory (the common property of all) into which the non-slave holder could go with *his* property of any sort."[89] Many southerners believed that the north—and specifically the Lincoln administration—wanted to thwart the right to enjoy slave property, and saw this as an imposition of tyranny. John C. Calhoun wrote that "what was once a constitutional federal republic" was "converted in reality, into one as absolute as that of the Autocrat of Russia."[90] Interestingly, Lincoln too used the same image, but against the south:

> As a nation, we began by declaring that all *men are created equal.* We now practically read it, *all men are created equal except negros* … When it comes to this, I shall prefer emigrating to some country where they make no pretense of loving liberty – to Russia, for instance, where despotism can be taken pure, and without the base alloy of hypocrisy.[91]

This was the same freedom understood differently. The two different principles of property underlying the concept of freedom and sovereignty held in the north and the south were not reconcilable. Both claimed the other as its antithesis or a perversion, both claimed to represent the original American freedom. However, whereas the south saw no contradiction in preserving American freedom without the existing federal union, the north saw the union as essential to the preservation of American freedom. As Frederick Douglass observed in 1862, after the Civil War had commenced, "Liberty and Union have become identical."[92] To Lincoln, the issue was first and foremost about the preservation of the union:

[88] Cleveland (1866), p. 271.

[89] Davis (1912), p. 7.

[90] Quoted in Greenfeld (1993), p. 475.

[91] Abraham Lincoln to Joshua Speed, August 21, 1855 in Basler (1953), Vol. 2, p. 323.

[92] Foner (2000), p. 99.

> I would save it in the shortest way under the constitution … My paramount objective is to save the union, and is not either to save or destroy slavery. If I could save the union without freeing any slave, I would do it, and if I could save it by freeing all the slaves, I would do it … what I do about slavery and the colored race I do because I believe it helps to save the union.[93]

However, that Lincoln said his goal was not "either to save or destroy slavery" should not be interpreted to say that he was indifferent to slavery—he was not.[94] As we have seen, his rhetoric was one of equality in the right to free labour, but he would not sacrifice the union for it, for the Americans freedom was too ingrained with it. Union was freedom, freedom was union, the freedom of the Americans could not be detached from the historical reality of its existence through the union because "We are historically connected with it."[95] In the same way that many revolutionary Americans saw their freedoms inseparably connected with Britain, so too did Republicans now see their freedoms inseparable from the union. In this sense, it was in fact the confederates who most firmly stuck to the principles of 1776, both in that they initiated a break from the existing political body (as with the revolution of 1776) and in that they more strongly empathised with landed freedom (again as in 1776).

Lincoln foresaw the inevitability of a crisis due to the two different visions of freedom in 1858, "a house divided against itself cannot stand. I believe this government cannot endure permanently half slave half free."[96] The issue would not be dissolved, he thought, before "a crisis has been reached and passed."[97] In the northern vision the new

[93]Abraham Lincoln to Horace Greeley, August 22, 1862 in Basler, Roy P. (ed.), *The Collected Works of Abraham Lincoln*, Vol. 5, Rutgers University Press, New Brunswick, NJ (1953), p. 388.

[94]Foner writes that "there is no reason to doubt Lincoln's empathic declaration." However, one has to be aware that his attitudes towards slavery formed slowly and gradually. See Foner, Eric, *The Fiery Trail: Abraham Lincoln and American Slavery*, W. W. Norton, New York (2010), p. 3.

[95]Abraham Lincoln, June 10, 1858 in Basler (1953), Vol. 3, p. 499.

[96]Abraham Lincoln to George Robertson, August 15, 1855 in Basler (1953), Vol. 2, p. 318.

[97]Abraham Lincoln, July 10, 1858 in Basler (1953), Vol. 2, p. 491.

property assumptions could only be fully realised within the union and in the whole union. A break was not an option. Seward too referred to this in his "irrepressible conflict" speech. There could be no liberty without union, and the union had to be completely based on the system of free labour—no half-way was possible. It was a matter of total liberty or total slavery:

> The United States must and will, sooner or later, become either entirely a slave-holding nation or entirely a free-labor nation. Either the cotton and rice-fields of South Carolina and the sugar plantations of Louisiana will ultimately be tilled by free labor, and Charleston and New Orleans become marts for legitimate merchandise alone, or else the rye-fields and wheat-fields of Massachusetts and New York must again be surrendered by their farmers to slave culture and to the production of slaves, and Boston and New York become once more markets for trade in the bodies and souls of men. It is the failure to apprehend this great truth that induces so many unsuccessful attempts at final compromise between the slave and free States, and it is the existence of this great fact that renders all such pretended compromises, when made, vain and ephemeral.[98]

The Civil War became the "crisis" that Lincoln foresaw, and it consolidated national unity and free labour ideology (i.e., the notion of a right to one's labour as the essential property right necessary to liberty and sovereignty). Through the Civil War the economic system of the north was victorious over the agrarian slave system of the south; as a consequence of this the Republicans understood America finally to be a unified and thus a fully free nation. Republican Charles Sumner asked the question, "Are we a nation?" after the northern victory in the Civil War in his pamphlet by the same title. Sumner was born in 1811 as the son of a lawyer in Boston, who went on to study law himself and practised for a short time. He was, however, more interested in learning and philosophy, and early on became a convinced anti-slavery man. His anti-slavery rhetoric sparked fury on the pro-slavery side, and in 1856 he was assaulted by pro-slavery Congressman Preston Brooks. The attack made him unable to participate in politics for three years, but by the start of the Civil War, he was back into politics, and strongly urged Lincoln to

[98] Seward (1858), p. 2.

make the Civil War a cause of abolition from the outset.[99] Thus, Sumner saw preservation of liberty and preservation of the union as identical. He asked in his "Are we a nation?" pamphlet whether the US after the war (in 1867) had "that essential indestructible unity which belongs to a nation ... just government, to protect the citizens of all the rights of citizens."[100] His answer was positively affirmative. Sumner chronicled the political story of the early national period, emphasizing especially the *Declaration of Independence* and the constitution. From this, he declared that "we are one nation ... Side by side with the growth of national unity was a consistent dedication to human rights."[101] Being a nation meant having certain "responsibilities", amongst the first of which was "equality the first of rights."[102] This was everything that the Confederacy had fought against, he wrote: their cause was a "rebellion instigated by hostility to the sacred principles of the Declaration of independence." Such rebellions could not be allowed to occur in the future if liberty was to be preserved. Thus, to secure the safety of liberty, "the national unity must be preserved."[103] Sumner's wish was realised and enforced with the reconstruction amendments (the 13th, 14th and 15th amendments), which granted the federal government unprecedented powers over the states, freed the slaves and ensured their rights.[104]

It was the Civil War that cemented the new transvalued notion of property in America, and at the same time strengthened a unified state power for an industrial wage-based economy. In Norway, these processes happened in less dramatic circumstances, although it was certainly not without *any* drama, as we shall see. We now turn to the industrial moment in the development of nationalism in Norway.

[99] Carnes, C. Mark, and John A. Garraty (eds.), *American National Biography*, Vol. 21, Oxford University Press, New York and Oxford (1999), pp. 137–139.

[100] Sumner, Charles, "Are we a nation?" Young Men's Republican Union, New York (1867), p. 1. https://archive.org/stream/arewenationaddre00sumn#page/n1/mode/2up (accessed 30.01.2015).

[101] Sumner (1867), p. 30.

[102] Sumner (1867), p. 31.

[103] Sumner (1867), p. 1.

[104] This, of course, is not to say that equality and rights were actually secured for African Americans. I am fully aware of the troubles of reconstruction and the century of continued oppression that burst into new battles during the 1950s and 1960s.

Summary

This chapter has demonstrated how the *amalgamation of property, people and sovereignty* became constituted in such a way that the right to property became more abstract and separated from real property. This was connected to the strengthening of national sovereignty and the idea of property as a right to the fruits of one's labour, and explored primarily through the abolition of slavery. The chapter introduced William Seward's "irrepressible conflict" speech in order to set the scene for the conflict about slavery. The chapter then proceeded to look at the pro-slavery ideology in the antebellum and Civil War eras, and the Republican ideology as it existed by the early 1860s, with focus on the notion of property. The Republican ideology became the most popular and forceful expression of the nation in its second form, and it was Republicanism that came to reiterate and create a successful continuum of the original national idea into the 1860s. The south, of course, also claimed to do this, as did abolitionists but, as it happened it was the Republicans who succeeded. The main proponents of the Republican ideology were Abraham Lincoln and William Seward. For the slavery ideology, the chapter invoked the President of the Confederacy, Jefferson Davis, and slavery ideologues such as Georg Fitzhugh, John C. Calhoun and James H. Hammond.

Literature

Alexander, George S., *Commodity and Property: Competing Visions of Property in American Legal Thought*, University of Chicago Press, Chicago and London (1997).

Basler, Roy P., *The Collected Works of Abraham Lincoln*, Vol. 2, Rutgers University Press, New Brunswick, NJ (1953).

Basler, Roy P., *The Collected Works of Abraham Lincoln*, Vol. 3, Rutgers University Press, New Brunswick, NJ (1953).

Basler, Roy P. (ed.), *The Collected Works of Abraham Lincoln*, Vol. 5, Rutgers University Press, New Brunswick, NJ (1953).

Baucom, Ian, *Specters of the Atlantic: Finance Capital, Slavery and the Philosophy of History*, Duke University Press, Durham (2005).

Beard, Charles, *The Rise of American Civilization, Vol. 2: The Industrial Era*, Macmillan, New York (1931).

Abraham Lincoln quoted in Burton, Orville Vernon, *The Age of Lincoln*, Hill & Wang, New York (2007).

Carnes, C. Mark, and John A. Garraty (eds.), *American National Biography*, Vol. 6, Oxford University Press, New York and Oxford (1999).
Carnes, C. Mark, and John A. Garraty (eds.), *American National Biography*, Vol. 9, Oxford University Press, New York and Oxford (1999).
Carnes, C. Mark, and John A. Garraty (eds.), *American National Biography*, Vol. 19, Oxford University Press, New York and Oxford (1999).
Carnes, C. Mark, and John A. Garraty (eds.), *American National Biography*, Vol. 20, Oxford University Press, New York and Oxford (1999).
Carnes, C. Mark, and John A. Garraty (eds.), *American National Biography*, Vol. 22, Oxford University Press, New York and Oxford (1999).
Cleveland, Henry, *Alexander H. Stephens, Public and Private, with Letters and Speeches Before, During and Since the War*, National Publishing, Philadelphia (1866).
Cogliano, Francis D., *Revolutionary America 1763–1815: A Political History*, Routledge, London (1999).
Cohen, William, "Thomas Jefferson and the problem of slavery," *Journal of American History*, Vol. 56, No. 3 (December, 1969).
Daly, John Patrick, *When Slavery Was Called Freedom: Evangelicalism, Proslavery and the Causes of the Civil War*, University Press of Kentucky, Kentucky (2002).
Davis, David Brion, *The Problem of Slavery in the Age of Revolution: 1770–1823*, Cornell University Press, Ithaca and London (1975).
Davis, Jefferson, *The Rise and Fall of the Confederate States of America*, Appleton & Co., New York (1912) [1881].
Delbanco, Andrew, *The Abolitionist Imagination*, Harvard University Press, Cambridge, MA (2012).
Earle, Jonathan, *Jacksonian Antislavery and the Politics of Free Soil: 1824–1854*, University of North Carolina Press, Chapel Hill and London (2004).
Federici, Michael P., *The Political Philosophy of Alexander Hamilton*, Johns Hopkins University Press, Baltimore (2012).
Finkelman, Paul, "Slavery in the United States: Persons or property," in Jean Allain (ed.), *The Legal Understanding of Slavery: From the Historical to the Contemporary*, Oxford University Press, Oxford (2012).
Fogel, Robert, and Stanley Engerman, *The Economics of American Negro Slavery*, Little Brown, Boston (1974).
Foner, Eric, *Free Soil, Free Labor, Free Men: The Ideology of the Republican Party Before the Civil War*, Oxford University Press, New York (1970).
Foner, Eric, *The Story of American Freedom*, W. W. Norton, New York (2000) [1998].
Foner, Eric, *The Fiery Trail: Abraham Lincoln and American Slavery*, W. W. Norton, New York (2010).

Furstenberg, François, "Beyond freedom and slavery: Autonomy, virtue, and resistance in early American political discourse," *Journal of American History*, Vol. 89, No. 4 (March, 2003).

Geinapp, Williamson, "Who voted for Lincoln," in John L. Thomas (ed.), *Abraham Lincoln and the American Political Tradition*, University of Massachusetts Press, Amherst (1986).

Genovese, Eugene, *The Political Economy of Slavery: Studies in the Economy and Society of the Slave South*, MacGibbon & Kee, London (1966).

Genovese, Eugene, and Elizabeth Fox, *Slavery in Black and White: Class and Race in the Southern Slaveholders New World Order*, Cambridge University Press, Cambridge (2005).

Greenfeld, Liah, *Nationalism: Five Roads to Modernity*, Harvard University Press, Cambridge (1993).

Hammond, James, *Speech of Hon. James H. Hammond of South Carolina on the Admission of Kansas Under the Lecompton Constitution*, Lemuel Towers, Washington (1858), pp. 13–14. http://babel.hathitrust.org/cgi/pt?id=loc.ark:/13960/t7jq19w4m;view=1up;seq=3 (accessed 13.01.2016).

Haskell, Thomas L., "Capitalism and the origins of humanitarian sensibility, Part 1," *American Historical Review*, Vol. 90, No. 2 (April, 1985).

Haskell, Thomas L., "Capitalism and the origins of humanitarian sensibility, Part 2," *American Historical Review*, Vol. 90, No. 3 (June, 1985).

Jordan, Winthrop D., *White Over Black: American Attitudes Towards the Negro, 1550–1812*, University of North Carolina Press, Chapel Hill (1968).

Kantz, Stanley, "Jefferson and the right to property," *Journal of Law and Economics*, Vol. 19, No. 3 (1976).

Larkin, Pascal, *Property in the Eighteenth Century: With Special Reference to England and Locke*, Cork University Press, Dublin and Cork (1930).

Looney, Jefferson J. (ed.), *The Papers of Thomas Jefferson: Retirement Series*, Vol. 12, Princeton University Press, Princeton and Oxford (2015).

Macpherson, James M., *Ordeal by Fire: The Civil War and Reconstruction*, Princeton University Press, New York (1982).

Macpherson, James M., *Battle Cry of Freedom: The Civil War Era*, Oxford University Press, Oxford (1988).

Moore, Barrington, *Social Origins of Dictatorship and Democracy: Lord and Peasant in the Making of the Modern World*, Beacon Press, Boston (1966).

Morgan, Edmund S., "Slavery and freedom: The American paradox," *Journal of American History*, Vol. 59, No. 1 (June, 1972).

Robert, J., "John Locke and the antebellum defense of slavery," *Political Theory*, Vol. 13, No. 2 (May, 1985).

Sellers, Charles, *The Market Revolution: Jacksonian America 1815–1846*, Oxford University Press, Oxford (1991).

Seward, William, "The irrepressible conflict" (1858), p. 1. https://archive.org/stream/irrepressiblecon00insewa#page/n0/mode/2up/search/%22the+laborers%22 (accessed 30.01.2015).

Shore, Laurence, *Southern Capitalists: The Ideological Leadership of an Elite, 1832–1885*, University of North Carolina Press, Chapel Hill (1986).

Sumner, Charles, "Are we a nation?" Young Men's Republican Union, New York (1867), p. 1. https://archive.org/stream/arewenationaddre00sumn#page/n1/mode/2up (accessed 30.01.2015).

Syrett, Harold, and Jacob E. Cooke (eds.), *The Papers of Alexander Hamilton*, Vol. 10, Columbia University Press, New York and London (1966).

TenBroek, Jacobus, *The Antislavery Origins of the Fourteenth Amendment*, University of California Press, Berkeley and Los Angeles (1951).

Tomlins, Christopher L., *Law, Labor and Ideology in the Early American Republic*, Cambridge University Press, Cambridge (1993).

Wilentz, Sean, "Property and power: Suffrage reform in the United States, 1787–1860," in Donald W. Rogers (ed.), *Voting and the Spirit of American Democracy: Essays on the History of Voting and Voting Rights in America*, University of Illinois Press, Urbana and Chicago (1992).

Wilentz, Sean, *The Rise of American Democracy: Jefferson to Lincoln*, W. W. Norton, New York and London (2005).

Wills, Gary, *"Negro President": Jefferson and Slave Power*, Houghton Mifflin, Boston and New York (2003).

Wilson, Major L., *Space, Time and Freedom: The Quest for Nationality and the Irrepressible Conflict, 1815–1861*, Greenwood Press, Westport and London (1974).

CHAPTER 5

The Industrial Transformation in Norway—The Will of the People

The industrial moment that transformed Norwegian nationalism was framed around debates on how the separation of powers in the constitution should be interpreted. These debates led to the formation of a broad social movement that vindicated what in practice became parliamentary democracy. We start the discussion on the industrial transformation in Norway by looking at the forces that changed the social structure of Norway during the decades between 1850 and 1880.

Socio-economic Foundations

The second form of the nation in Norway must be seen against the background of the general social and economic development during the nineteenth century. Up until 1884 it was still a small elite of state officials (practically the same in number as in 1814) and the bourgeoisie, along with the self-owning farmers, who ruled the country.[1] Indeed, while the

[1]Seip characterises this period in Norwegian history as *Embetsmansstaten* ("the official state"). He writes, "One can say that before 1814 the state officials ruled the country in the name of the king, after 1814, they ruled it in the name of the people." See Seip, Jens Arup, *Et regime foran underangen: kampen mellom men og idealer i årene førparlamentarismens seier I Norge*, Gyldendal Norsk Forlag, Oslo (1965) [1945], p. 13. Sejersted uses the term *Rettsstaten* ("the rechtsstaat" or rule of law), implying rule by the bourgeoisie or, more specifically, the rule of property: "The self interest of the bourgeoisie is one of the

E. M. Fuglestad, *Private Property and the Origins of Nationalism in the United States and Norway*,
https://doi.org/10.1007/978-3-319-89950-3_5

propertied precondition for the suffrage in 1814 made Norway one of the most democratic countries in Europe at the time (7% of the population had the vote), these same qualifications had actually slightly decreased the percentage of enfranchised by 1891, making Norway one of the least democratic countries in Europe.[2] Amongst the disenfranchised were landless tenants and a new group of different kinds of wage labourers who had emerged in the latter half of the nineteenth century. Norway had seen rapid population growth, urbanisation and industrialisation in the century that unfolded after 1814. There was a great emigration from Norway during this century—primarily to the US—and the number of people who emigrated from Norway in the course of the century was almost equal to the number of people living in Norway in 1801; however, despite this, the population in Norway had increased from 884,000 to almost two million by the end of the nineteenth century. Most of these people still lived in rural areas, and farming remained a dominant livelihood; the number of farms actually expanded, and self-owning farmers remained dominant, but an increasing group of landless tenants, functionaries and industrial and skilled workers set a firm mark on the relations between property and appropriation by the end of the century. During the 1840s, large factories began to appear, especially around Oslo, but also in the other big cities such as Bergen and Trondheim. In 1850 there were still no more than 12,000 industrial workers in Norway, but by 1875 the number had risen to 44,000 while the number of skilled artisans and functionaries had reached 35,000. In 1870 there were also 53,000 *husmen* or "crofters"[3]—independent tenants who can be classified along with wage workers in opposition to

most fundamental preconditions for the emergence of the rechtsstaat and the decline of arbitrary monarchical power." See Sejersted, Francis, *Demokrati og rettsstat*, Pax Forlag AS, Oslo (2001), p. 137. However, as Nerbøvik writes, it was probably a mix of both, and they do not exclude each other. See Nerbøvik, Jostein, *Norsk Historie 1860–1914: Eit bondesamfunn i oppbrot*, Det Norske Samlaget, Oslo (1999), p. 211. My view is perhaps more in tune with Sejersted as I focus on the centrality of private property.

[2]Langeland, Nils Rune, "Røysteretten som mål på politisk komeptanse," in Nils Rune Langeland (ed.), *Politisk Kompetanse: grunnlovas borgar*, Pax Forlag AS, Oslo (2014), p. 48.

[3]Østerud has used the English term crofter for this group of people. See Østerud, Øyvind, *Agrarian Structure and Peasant Politics in Scandinavia: A Comparative Study of Rural Response to Economic Change*, Universitetsforlaget, Oslo (1978), p. 96.

the self-owning farmers.[4] The number of people living in cities was also growing; by 1875, 25% of the population lived in cities and there was an especially intense period of industrialisation from 1860 to 1875 in which the number of industrial workers quadrupled.[5] One way of understanding this is relating it to what has been called *det store hamskiftet* ("the great transformation") in the agricultural sector.[6] This refers to a change in economics from a predominantly self-sufficient economy to a more capitalist market economy. It has been contested whether the Norwegian agrarian sector was not also integrated into a market economy way before the 1860s, but this is not the place to engage in debates about this. There was, in any case, an expansion or intensification of capitalist market relations in the nation as a whole in the years after the 1860s, and the term *det store hamskiftet* explains the change from a pre-industrial to an industrial society. Jørn Sandnes writes:

> *Det store hamskiftet* is an umbrella term covering social, economic and cultural changes in rural Norway at a time when changes were no longer slow and occasional, but fast and pervasive, tending strongly towards a market economy.[7]

It might also be useful to invoke Edvard Bull's term *kapitalismens frigjørende fase* ("the liberating phase of capitalism"), by which he meant that the time between 1860 and 1920 was one where wage labour relations opened up possibilities for the class of people who were below the self-owning farmers in the pecking order, and who became manufacturers producing tools and providers of raw materials for food production.[8] Changes in a burgeoning industrial society brought about an economic and social crisis; after general growth from the 1840s to the 1860s, the 1870s and 1880s were marked by economic depression, stagnation and

[4]The numbers are from Pryser, Tore, *Norsk Historie, 1814–1860: frå standssamfunn til klassesamfunn*, Det Norske Samlaget, Oslo (1999), pp. 166–170.

[5]Nerbøvik, Jostein, *Norsk Historie 1860–1914: Eit bondesamfunn i oppbrot*, Det Norske Samlaget, Oslo (1999), pp. 79–85.

[6]The term was first used in Krokan, Inge, *Det store hamskifet i bondesamfunnet*, Det Norske Samlaget, Oslo (1976) [1942].

[7]Quoted in Pryser (1999), p. 181.

[8]Bull, Edvard, "Fra bøndenes og husmennenes samfunn til den organiserte kapitalisme," in Ottar Dahl (ed.), *Makt og motiv: Festskrift til Jens Arup Seip*, Gyldendal Norsk Forlag, Oslo (1975).

massive emigration.[9] It is also significant, as Østerud writes, that these changes "made the rural population as a whole more similar to the urban bourgeoisie, the middle class."[10] The changes in socio-economic relations brought to the fore different ideas about property and freedom and thus of political rule—it brought about a *transvaluation of property*.

Transvaluation in Norway: The Second Form of the Nation

There had been changes in the way people thought about property and freedom as early as the first form of the nation. For example, in 1850 members of the newly-emerged radical labour movement wrote in their newspaper that the right to labour was the central right. This was "the new right that knocks on the door of the constitution," and "the claim is that work shall be organised in such a way so that every human being can make a living."[11] Marcus Thrane, the leader of the radical labour movement, said that the right to make a living was opposed to the prevalent claim that "property is sacred"—the right that was really sacred, according to Thrane, was that of labour. These notions became the foundation on which the second form of the nation was built, and universal male suffrage was a logical conclusion of these notions. The labour movement demanded this as the means by which the people could secure their property rights to labour, but their demands were met with firm conformism to the existing property regime and the rules of enfranchisement. The labour movement soon lost its unity and dissolved. However, similar notions, when adopted by the mass of the national movement in the decades after 1850, became a powerful force that changed the form of the nation.

[9] It is interesting to note that at this time it was America that most immigrants went to, and many of those who went were people who did not themselves own their own land, or who were deeply in debt. It was precisely the promise of land, of a property of one's own in America that to a large extent drove them. This may indicate the pervasiveness of the notions of the first form of the nation, both in Norway and the US. For a short overview of Norwegian emigration to the US see, Østrem, Nils Olav, *Norsk utvandringshistorie*, Det Norske Samlaget, Oslo (2006).

[10] Østerud (1978), p. 244.

[11] Quoted in Bull, Edvard, *Arbeiderklassens historie I: arbeiderklassen blir til*, Tiden Norsk Forlag, Oslo (1985), p. 55.

As in America, the inner meaning of property and the freedom associated with it changed. It was still the same words applied and still the same fundamental meaning, but the content of the concept became subject to transvaluation. Freedom increasingly became understood as having the right to the fruits of one's labour, not just to own real property. We might remember that Falsen, for example, had included in his concept of property from 1814 the right, which "every citizen has, to enjoy and decide over his lands, his income, over the fruits of his labour and diligence." Moreover, Wergeland had written similarly that freedom for the individual meant "the right to enjoy the fruits that grow from his sweat, to be secure in his goods and his person." Indeed, Falsen had also included income from labour as property qualifying for enfranchisement in his constitutional draft: "one must own property or earn a certain income." Because of the change in the mode of production to a more industrialised or wage-based society a shift gradually happened from land to labour as the focal point of freedom. This can be seen in the debates about suffrage reform.

Suffrage Reform: Johan Sverdrup Versus A.M. Schweigaard

It was what came to be known as the Venstre coalition that drove the change from land to labour in Norway. This was a broad and diverse coalition that was constituted of small farmers, rural religious conservatives, city radicals and intellectuals, teachers, and a large group of functionaries.[12] Until the early 1880s the Venstre coalition was not a party in the modern sense of the word, but it is possible to detect a continuum from the 1850s until the 1880s. A good example of a member of this coalition is Johan Sverdrup (not to be confused with Professor Georg Sverdrup from the early stages of the national movement).

Sverdrup was born in 1816, the son of a farmer. In 1841 he graduated in law, and worked as a solicitor from 1851, until he bought a farm in the late 1860s. His career in national politics started in the early 1850s when he became a member of parliament, distinguishing himself as an idealistic radical akin to the French revolutionary tradition, or, as some have said, to Abraham Lincoln.[13] One of Sverdrup's

[12] Mjeldheim, Leiv, *Folkerørsla som vart parti: Venstre frå 1880 åra til 1905*, Universitetsforlaget, Bergen (1984), pp. 101–105.

[13] Halvdan Koht makes this comparison in his three-volume biography of Sverdrup.

first suggestions was universal suffrage in local government; it was not adopted, but the debate came up again at the national level in the 1860s and 1870s.[14] In 1869, 21 suggestions were present in parliament as how to modify the franchise, all of which proposals broadening suffrage based on income or taxes in various ways.[15] The idea of transvaluation was implicit in this—none of the parliamentary drafts suggested universal male suffrage, but because they were based on income or tax payments, they set, in theory, no limits to enfranchisement and thus the idea that only real property could confer independence on an individual was abandoned. Contemporary critics saw this as well, commenting that if "the floodgates of democracy were opened" it would be impossible to stop it again, and it would go further than anyone would want, ending "at its opposite, at its counter point, after absolute democracy, follows absolute domination, Caesarism."[16] Johan Sverdrup, however, had no fear of this and said that "the greatest capital a country can have, is its people, with this no amount of landed property can compete."[17] Even the wording is interesting here such as the fact that he compares the people to capital, and directly confronts the rule of landed property. Despite this, Sverdrup saw no conflict between wage labourers and the old propertied voters. It was not the case, he said, as some thought, that "the high and the low are at war with each other"; on the contrary, "they are bound to each other by tradition, work, property and family."[18] When it came to enfranchisement, said Sverdrup, the issue was:

> A question of common sense in our time. About new industries, new wealth, new interests, new developments and new social formations. It regards the new economical, moral and intellectual forces in our society. It is a matter about newly sprung antagonisms that demand equality. It is

[14]For information on Sverdrup I have relied on Halvdan Koht's three-volume biography.

[15]Danielsen, Rolf, *Det Norske storting gjennom 150 år, Bind 2: tidsrommet 1870–1908*, Gyldendal Norsk Forlag, Oslo (1964), pp. 25–26.

[16]Quoted in Danielsen (1964), pp. 29–30.

[17]Johan Sverdrup, April 29, 1873 in Lars Havstad, *Johan Sverdrup: taler i stortinget, 1851–1880*, Græbes bogtrykkeri, København (1882), p. 354.

[18]Danielsen (1964), p. 31.

> new and old that demand amalgamation or, if one wants to call it so, the idea of unification ... a state system more fitted to the future with demands for people's representation ...[19]

Sverdrup here quite directly says that the expansion of suffrage is an adaptation to a new proto-industrial reality, with its new forms of wealth and capital. This implied different conceptions of property and freedom that did not see the wage worker as dependent and dangerous to the nation's freedom. It was now possible to combine wage earners and propertied farmers in the same understanding of freedom. As in Lincoln's America, wage labour was seen as a freedom in itself, a way to raise one's position. Another debater, farmer and member of parliament Ole Gabriel Ueland (1799–1870), agreed with Sverdrup that to include a new class of voters would not be dangerous, and he pointed to the possibility of the wage labourer improving his position: "the new classes will feel a natural affinity to the older voters and groups and will share their interests ... the wage worker has as his goal to one day become a farmer."[20] Indeed, expanded suffrage was, said Ueland, a "fulfilment of the principles of the constitution"—this is exactly the same rhetoric that Lincoln used in America, when he claimed his principles as a fulfilment of the *Declaration of Independence.* Others in Norway invoked the "liberal tradition upon which our constitution is built."[21] There was no contradiction now between including wage labourers in politics and preserving the freedom of the constitution. On the contrary, including wage labourers would be a realisation of the principles of the freedom set down in the constitution. However, not everyone thought so, and Sverdrup's movement met powerful ideological resistance from people who claimed to also represent the principles of the constitution and the unity of the nation. A considerable proponent of Sverdrup's during the first decades of his career as a member of parliament was A.M. Schweigaard—a conservative professor of law and economy and one of the most distinguished politicians and intellectuals in Norway during the nineteenth century.

[19] Johan Sverdrup, April 29, 1873 in Havstad (1882), p. 342.

[20] Quoted in Danielsen (1964), p. 30.

[21] Quoted in Kaartvedt, Alf, *Det Norske Storting gjennom 150 år*, Bind 1, Gyldendal Norsk Forlag, Oslo (1964), p. 65.

In recent years, Schweigaard has been recognised as one of the most important nation builders in the nineteenth century, having a consistent and pervasive nationalist worldview. He exemplifies well the principles of the first form of the nation. He excelled in primary school and was the best student of his class, and in 1828 he graduated with the best results ever produced in Norway up until that time. At the age of 25 he was proclaimed by his friend as "the greatest son that Norway had produced." When he was 27, he travelled to Germany and France where he wrote a polemical critique in German of Hegelian idealist philosophy and of German law, published in French and Danish academic journals. In 1840 he became professor of law, political economy and statistics at the University of Christiania (as Oslo was called during the whole nineteenth century), where he became an advocate of an empiricist and utilitarian approach to science, greatly influencing the study of these subjects. From the mid-1830s until 1870, he applied his academic principles in a long career as a member of parliament, where he marked himself as a very distinguished conservative.[22] This is clear in his ideas about suffrage. Schweigaard pointed to the absurdity of universal democracy as opposed to a propertied democracy; he wondered what would happen if the people decided that landed property was to be equally distributed amongst the propertyless? It was clear to him that this would not work because: "the foundations of the state would burst asunder."[23] Such a majority could not make rights and could not alone make law. There had to be a rule in which men who were truly independent could make law. Schweigaard believed that the main issue in expansion of suffrage "was to draw a line which could prevent the person who paid one shilling in taxes from getting an influence equal to the person paying 19/20."[24] It was clear to Schweigaard that a constitution needed to have a clear and fixed measurement for who would be entitled to vote. "In England, one has, since the year 1216, held real property as a precondition for enfranchisement", said Schweigaard. This pointed to the stability and common

[22]These facts are based on Lund, Carl, *A.M. Schweigaard som stortingspolitiker*, Universitetsforlaget, Oslo (1958). See Slagstad, Rune, *De nasjonale strateger*, Pax Forlag AS, Oslo (1998).

[23]A.M. Schweigaard, quoted in Seip, Jens Arup, *Utsikt over Norges historie*, Gyldendal Norsk Forlag, Oslo (1974), p. 109.

[24]A.M. Schweigaard, quoted in Lund (1958), p. 299.

sense of having property qualifications to be able to vote, "one could invoke the whole world experience all the way back to Severius Tullius"[25] to prove this. The question of enfranchisement was, to Schweigaard, a question about taxation: "at its core this is a question about taxation." It was clear to him that those with real property and wealth should be in charge of taxation. Otherwise, said Schweigaard (talking about expansion of enfranchisement to local government), one could end up with the absurd situation where, for example, those receiving poor relief, "themselves will have a say in how much money they shall receive."[26] Schweigaard here continues the line of argument from 1814: the distinction between dependent and independent individuals based on ownership of wealth. It was important to Schweigaard to keep political power in the hands of those to which it had been bestowed by the constitution in 1814.

Schweigaard based his argument on what we might call a realist position. He defended the existing propertied conditions for the vote because it was based on actual and tangible things; he had little sympathy for his opponents' "general arguments, which could be applied to anything and nothing." If something was to be done for the masses, he said, it should be to give them corn or potatoes. It was not the franchisee itself that did good, but material security—this had to come first. "Did not the propertyless hold a grant to land as the fundamental thing, more so than merely to be granted the right to vote?"[27] Schweigaard asked rhetorically. However, apparently they did not think so, at least not according to Johan Sverdrup. Discussing the nature of the propertied qualifications for voting, Sverdrup asked the parliament:

> Imagine that each of us are asked to propose what we deem to be land of such value that it may confer enfranchisement. How many different opinions would we get? I think it would be about as many different answers as there are representatives in this hall.[28]

[25] A.M. Schweigaard, quoted in Sørensen, Øystein, *Anton Martin Schweigaards politiske tenkning*, Universitetsforlaget, Oslo (1988), p. 174.

[26] A.M. Schweigaard, quoted in Sørensen (1988), p. 181.

[27] A.M. Schweigaard, quoted in Lund (1958), p. 298.

[28] Johan Sverdrup, June 19, 1878 in Havstad (1882), p. 376.

One had to realise the consequences of dividing men into enfranchised and disenfranchised on account of the size of the property, said Sverdrup: "Is half a shilling to distinguish a dependent man from an independent man, a self-sustained man, sufficiently enlightened to be an empowered man in our society?"[29] Sverdrup further pointed to what he saw as the absurdity and the inconsequence of confining the franchise to men of landed property. He asked: "is it reasonable that a house worth 150 spd is compared to the capital which is found in the skill and labour of a man? Show me he who can honestly say; no, a laboring man is not worth 150 spd …"[30] Instead, Sverdrup suggested basing enfranchisement on taxes, and by doing so, "securing the intellectual and economic independence which had been the purpose of the constitution." This proposition was "an expression of an acknowledgement and respect for the worker." We can see clearly from this that Sverdrup invokes the language of labour in order to expand the national political community, just as Republicans and abolitionists did in America a few decades before the abolition of slavery. The right to property became interwoven with popular sovereignty and linked to property through the right to the fruits of one's labour. Property and sovereignty understood in this way implied full democracy said Sverdrup. The constitution, he held:

> Rests on the acknowledgement, that the rights of the people, specifically the right to legislation through their sovereignty. Though this system is still in its first stages; what has happened so far is only the temporary step of our culture and experience towards the realisation of the natural state form, democracy, cleansed through its fight for existence.[31]

Another liberal in the parliament, the priest Nils Nilsen Dahl, argued in much the same way as Sverdrup that an expansion of suffrage was a natural consequence of the changing socio-economic structure of society. Classes of people existed now in the 1850s who did not exist in 1814. It was therefore natural to expand suffrage:

[29] Johan Sverdrup, June 19, 1878 in Havstad (1882), p. 376.

[30] Johan Sverdrup, April 29, 1873 in Havstad (1882), p. 349.

[31] Johan Sverdrup, quoted in Koht, Halvdan, *Johan Sverdrup I, 1816–1869*, Aschehoug, Kristiania (1918), p. 117.

> Solicitors and doctors were in those days enfranchised on account of being state officials, teachers' seminars did not exist, constables and church cantors did not have the same amount of influence then, and free candidates to the university or high schools were not common.[32]

However, the idea that suffrage qualifications should change in accordance with social reality, or that democracy (understood as universal male suffrage) was "the natural state form" could not be realised without first dealing with the overarching issues of government ministers' accountability. The historian Rolf Danielsen writes:

> The majority required [for expansion of the franchise] in the parliament could only be achieved when the issue of expanded franchise became intimately interwoven with the issue of the government members responsibility to the parliament, when expansion of the franchise had become an integrated part of the complex conflict that in the end was to split the representatives in two clearly divided groups.[33]

It was when this conflict over government ministers' accountability to the parliament intensified in the 1880s that the Venstre movement gathered strength behind Johan Sverdrup against the conservatives in a potent social movement. This conflict was the outer expression of the *transvaluation of property* in Norway, in the same way that the abolition of chattel slavery became so in the US. In what follows, I will spend some time on the debates relating to the ministers' accountability to the parliament—which has become known as the issue of parliamentary democracy. The debates relating to this issue were not directly concerned with the shift from land to labour, they were more about good government and the role of the sovereignty of the people versus the king. It is nevertheless important to give an overview of this because this issue and suffrage reform became interconnected in the 1880s, and both were carried through in the name of the sovereignty of the people. It was only suffrage reform that invoked the shift from land to labour, but parliamentary democracy was instrumental in making suffrage reform come about. The debates over parliamentary democracy were made within the

[32]Nils Nilsen Dahl, quoted in Sørensen (1988), p. 174.

[33]Danielsen (1964), p. 31.

already existing system of suffrage, by men who already had the vote and who understood themselves to represent the people because of this the shift from land to labour was not invoked in this instance, but instead the sovereignty of the people versus the government or the king. Suffrage reform and parliamentary democracy were expansions of the sovereignty of the people in different directions: suffrage reform downwards, including more people (hence the language of land to labour); and parliamentary democracy upwards, inferring the power of the government by the representatives of the people.

The Issue of Access and Responsibility of Government Ministers to the Parliament

Parliamentary Democracy

The proponents of parliamentary democracy presented the issue in the form of a bill that gave government ministers access and accountability to the parliament. From 1872 to 1880, propositions that the ministers of the king (the government) should meet in the parliament and be held responsible for their policy were put forward and passed several times by the parliament. This required a change in the constitution and, in theory, such a change would mean that parliament would be vested with complete sovereignty within the nation (i.e., parliamentary democracy). This proposal was, however, always denied sanction by the king, who assumed the right to veto in constitutional matters. When the proposal was denied sanction for the third time in 1880 the parliament put forward an impeachment act against the (king's) government.[34] It had come to be seen by a majority as unacceptable that the king should be able to veto the decisions of the parliament. As one debater put it in 1880, to grant the king absolute and unchecked executive power meant in practice to "turn over the *odelsrett* that the nation had to the kingdom of Norway, to give it away, and replace it with a bond of serfdom."[35]

[34] Kaartvedt, Alf, *Kampen mot parlamentarisme, 1880–1884: den konservative politikken under vetostriden*, Universitetsforlaget, Bergen (1967), pp. 63–95 and 122–160.

[35] Quoted in Kaartvedt (1967), p. 84.

Early Debates

This issue of closer integration between the legislative and the executive branch had been present since the new Norwegian state was founded in 1814. During the first years after 1814, Christian Magnus Falsen had put forward suggestions that would give the ministers access to the parliament. Falsen wanted to create an efficient and balanced state by unifying sovereignty—that is, by creating closer bonds between the legislative and the executive branch. At first quite firm on the importance of a strict division of powers, he later held that this was not as important as "unity and order,"[36] which was to be created by giving more sovereignty to the executive branch. There was a dangerous "great abyss,"[37] Falsen had said, between the legislative branch and the executive branch, and it was imperative that a bridge be built over it. Falsen's suggestion was never realised due to protest from the parliament, but others took up the idea. Lawyer and statesman Frederik Stang (1808–1884)[38] also emphasised the unity of the nation and its will, and favoured a reform that gave government members admission to the parliament. His interpretation of the constitution from 1833 stressed this, and his underlying idea can be summed up by his famous statement:

> The primary principle of a constitutional monarchy is undoubtedly that the general will, cleansed and moderated by the forms through which it must work towards its goal, must be the animating force of all state organisms.[39]

Interestingly, this idea is very similar in wording to Sverdrup's statement displayed above, but with the opposite intention. The point for Stang was to effectively coordinate state powers and a stronger executive branch, yet keep the division of powers intact. From the 1830s to the 1870s, Stang and Schweigaard became the leading statesmen and nation builders in Norway, both stressing the centrality, activity and unity of the state and its important purpose for nation building.[40] In their student

[36] Quoted in Seip (1974), p. 96.

[37] Quoted in Kaartvedt (1964), p. 439.

[38] For biographical information about Stang see Svare, Bjarne, *Frederik Stang* (2 Vols.) Aschehoug, Oslo (1939–1950).

[39] Quoted in Kaartvedt (1964), p. 441.

[40] Seip (1974) and Slagstad (1998).

days, Stang and Schweigaard had been members of *Intelegentz*—a group of gifted students with Count Wedel as their patron. The centralised, interventionist liberalism that this group stood for became the ruling ideology during the 1830s and 1840s, but the idea of a strong, unified state apparatus was promoted by the conservatives only as long as they felt that they would be controlling the state and could keep the farmers at a safe distance.

Early Opposition from the Farmers

The ideology of Stang, Schweigaard and *Intelegentz* was antagonistic to many interests of the farmers in the parliament during the 1830s and 1840s who wanted the state to spend as little money as possible and keep government members separated from the parliament. 1833, during the first so-called farmers' parliament, Farmer Ole Gabriel Ueland became a main opponent, especially to Schweigaard in the parliament. The farmers in the parliament in the 1830s and 1840s feared a closer relationship between the legislative and the executive branch because they believed it would make the government stronger and more able to impose additional taxes and measures on them.[41] Farmer Hans Barlien (1772–1842) wrote, in his interpretation of who according to the constitution (as it stood in 1836) had the ultimate power in the nation, "here, in our country, the people have the absolute veto," which meant that the parliament was absolutely "unrestricted" in its power.[42] He felt its powers should not be interfered with by the government, and it was clear that this was according to the spirit of the constitution. According to Barlien:

> If the parliament stays true to the spirit of the constitution and the will of the people, then the laws will be just ... thus, the Norwegian people have secured for themselves a larger part of the powers of the state than any other country in Europe.[43]

[41] For an overview of the farmers' opposition and its leader see Bergsgård, Arne, *Ole Gabriel Ueland og bondepolitikken*, Aschehoug, Oslo (1932). Primary sources that I have used here are Barlien, Hans, *Bemerkninger til Norges grunnlov* (1836); and Nergaard, John, *En odelsmands tanker om Norges nærværende forfatning*, Christiania (1830). The latter was particularly important in getting farmers elected to the parliamentary session of 1833.

[42] Barlien (1836), p. 88.

[43] Barlien (1836), p. 94.

Barlien here proposes the need for antagonism between the power that the people "have reserved for themselves" and the government. The government was dangerous and sovereignty was vested solely in the people: "all of the power of the state befalls the people, the people are masters in their house, in the people lies sovereignty."[44] To maintain this, it was important that power was divided. The point about keeping the powers of the state separate was to avoid infringements from state officials, to avoid, as Farmer John Nergaad (1795–1885) wrote, "taxes and expenses ... in the 15 or 16 years that now have passed [since independence], the expenses of the state have continued to grow, and has now reached double the original."[45] It was for this reason that the farmers should elect their own men to the parliament, and not state officials or other elites, wrote Nergaard. Moreover, it was exactly this that happened: the parliamentary session of 1833 had more farmer members of parliament than ever before (hence the "farmers' parliament"). *Intelegentz* regarded this with suspicion; it was a result of the unfortunate "demagogical element" of the constitution, wrote one of its members.[46] The farmers, with their anti-centralisation and anti-tax policies, did not understand the essentials of running a nation-state: "If one looks at the actual skill and knowledge that the farmer representatives bring to the parliament," he continued:

> Then one sees without doubt that not a single one of them fulfil the requirements that one would generally expect of a representative to the national assembly. Only superficial knowledge of the laws of the country, a little historical reading, a bit more of religious reading. And their practical knowledge of economy is restricted to the workings of the fields where they live, and the ways of livelihood there ... some idea of what in matters of economics and politics concerns our country; that is what is missing in the farmers representatives, and will be missing for some time.[47]

However, the farmers remained relatively strong in the parliament in the coming decades. Moreover, they were joined by increasing numbers of a new middle class of wage earners who prospered from the 1850s.

44 Barlien (1836), p. 55.

45 Nergaard (1830), pp. 4–5.

46 Fougstad, Carl, *Det Norske storting 1833*, Christiania (1834), p. 11.

47 Fougstad (1834), p. 18.

Together they acquired considerable strength in the parliament and proposed a closer unification between the parliament and the government in order to strengthen their own position.

The Final Debates

The new initiatives for unification of sovereignty did not originate with the classical farmers' opposition, but from Johan Sverdrup, who primarily represented the new classes of officials, functionaries and clerks.[48] In 1869 (this wasalso the year in which suffrage reforms started to be seriously debated), Sverdrup and his followers managed to get a bill proposing annual parliamentary meetings be sanctioned (beforehand, parliament had met only every three years). Annual parliamentary sessions not only strengthened the position of the parliament, but also brought about closer cooperation between the legislative and the executive branch. The conservatives now feared that integration between the two state powers would give parliament too much power.

During the 1860s and 1870s, Sverdrup gained support from Ueland and the farmers' opposition. He further gained support from the new farmers' opposition of the late 1860s led by farmer Søren Jaabæk. Seeing this broad coalition gathered in parliament every year, the conservatives saw the imperative of keeping the government (the executive branch) separate from the legislative branch. They viewed with unease the populist and demagogical developments in Europe (the revolutions of 1848, and the rule of Napoleon the III in France) and believed the monarchical aspect of the Norwegian constitution was the only bulwark against this.[49] Frederik Stang, Prime Minister from 1873 to 1880, now actively opposed bills suggesting ministers be responsible to parliament. Indeed, Stang's ministry became the most powerful bulwark against such attempts.[50] Schweigaard perhaps summed up the fear of the conservatives when he said that parliamentary reform would be as if "in a way we have two governments."[51] This was not, however, what Sverdrup wanted. Instead, he wanted, as he famously said in the Parliamentary Hall, "all power and force

[48] Mjeldheim (1984), pp. 101–105.

[49] Langeland (2014), p. 42.

[50] Kaartvedt (1967), pp. 20–33 and 50–63.

[51] Kaartvedt (1964), p. 510.

united here in this hall."[52] It was precisely this (i.e., parliament assuming powers of government) that the conservatives feared. In the conservatives' minds, there could be only one executive and it should be the King's government. Division was crucial to the conservatives in the 1870s and 1880s. Professor of law T.H. Aschehoug, who wrote a three-volume interpretation of the constitution between 1875 and 1885, said that "there is nothing I fear more than absolute and overwhelming power in one hand. The power must be divided if the state is to be free."[53] The main conservative newspaper, supporting strict division of powers, wrote in 1871 that the central issue at stake was whether the people:

> Wanted to keep our constitution as passed on to us, the constitutional monarchy, liberty safeguarded through division of powers, and security against abuse and inference, and on the other hand, whether they adhered to the principle that 'division of powers is nonsense', that power should be located only in one place, namely in those men, that it is declared represents the will of the people ... which have been the end of republics of old and new alike, tyranny.[54]

The conservative position here is basically a continuation of the prevalent policy in 1814: power must be divided, the people cannot be granted unlimited power. However, this conservative assertion Sverdrup believed was founded on a misconception. Discussing the matter during annual parliamentary sessions, Sverdrup said that it may have been true that the purpose of the constitution in 1814 had been "to secure against arbitrary inference, rather than the possibility for the people to self-government."[55] However:

> When the constitution had been working for some time, and the circumstances had changed and developed ... it became clear, after much discord and work, that the decisions of the constitution did not correspond to its purpose. The government had power enough, but the power of the people did not have its rightful influence on matters.[56]

[52] Koht (1922), p. 68.

[53] Koht, Halvdan, *Johan Sverdrup II, 1870–1880*, Aschehoug, Kristiania (1922), pp. 66–67.

[54] Koht (1922), p. 168.

[55] Johan Sverdrup (1868) in Havstad (1882), p. 287.

[56] Johan Sverdrup (1868) in Havstad (1882), pp. 287–288.

The Will of the People

Sverdrup thought it natural that the sovereignty of the people should have absolute expression through expanded democracy. He asked, when discussing the bill advocating annual parliamentary sessions:

> If, in a society, there are forces that know what they want, and have the will to carry it through based on our current constitutional frame, if here is agreement amongst the electorate, then I cannot for the life of me understand, why anyone should have the right to stop them?[57]

What was needed, said Sverdrup, was parliamentary democracy to make the ministers of the government accountable to the parliament, to the people:

> That the cause of prolongation [of the parliamentary meetings], this one cause, have been so strongly discussed, points to another important matter that is even less satisfactory, that of the access and accountability of the ministers to the parliament.[58]

However, since the king always vetoed such a suggestion, the king's veto in matters of constitutional change became a great obstruction to this cause. Sverdrup said, "if one wants to grant the king an absolute veto in matters of constitutional change, then one has violated the will of the people. One has wounded the tree of liberty at its roots."[59] The cause of parliamentary democracy to Sverdrup was part of a broader critique of the whole system of the state:

> The relationship between a government and the people's representatives cannot be reduced to one single cause which happens to surface from everyday politics … it is about the whole system.[60]

Here, Sverdrup himself suggests exactly what the quote from Danielsen above suggested, and what I have suggested with him: that suffrage reform and parliamentary democracy were interconnected in a broader

[57] Johan Sverdrup (1868) in Havstad (1882), p. 280.

[58] Johan Sverdrup, February 13, 1873 in Havstad (1882), p. 91.

[59] Johan Sverdrup, May 19, 1851 in Havstad (1882), p. 20.

[60] Johan Sverdrup, February 13, 1873 in Havstad (1882), p. 97

critique of *the first form of the nation*—a critique of "the whole system" by the new middle class. It was the issue of access and accountability of ministers to parliament that became the tipping point of the system, because it was connected to the veto power of the king. When the bill was passed for the third time by parliament but denied sanction by the king, Sverdrup said again:

> Is the king to have an absolute veto in matters of the constitution? Should the people then not have legislative power on this important matter, in the very matter of popular sovereignty, its power over their own faith and that of coming generations?[61]

It was clear to Sverdrup that the king's veto and the government's unwillingness to cooperate meant, "the government have not shown respect for the general will, nothing is more certain."[62] In an effort to overcome this, Sverdrup and his followers put forward an impeachment act against the government (although it was the king who wielded the veto, it was his government that was formally responsible for such a policy according to the constitution). Since 1882 was an election year for parliament, Sverdrup waited until after the election to propose the Impeachment Act. This allowed him in the lead-up to the campaign to raise the support needed for the Impeachment Act. In the end, Sverdrup got more than 60% of the vote, This led to the Venstre coalition emerging as a political party.[63] Sverdrup now felt ready for an impeachment trial. However, although Venstre had a parliamentary majority, it was uncertain how the impeachment would end: it was not a given that the judges would find in favour; the Conservatives were discussing plans of a *coup d'état* and local Venstre parties all over the country were training for war. In the end, however, the trial ended peacefully and in favour of Sverdrup and Venstre: the government resigned, and on July 26, 1884 Sverdrup was appointed Prime Minister on a parliamentary basis. After this, parliamentary praxis became the norm in political life and suffrage reforms were carried through gradually during the next decades—universal male suffrage was achieved in 1898 and female suffrage in 1913. Indeed, even as early as 1881 Sverdrup and his followers managed to

[61] Johan Sverdrup, June 2, 1880 in Havstad (1882), p. 158.

[62] Johan Sverdrup, February 13, 1873 in Havstad (1882), p. 103.

[63] Nerbøvik (1999), pp. 150–162.

carry through suffrage reform based on income, and the very first issue that Sverdrup dealt when he became Prime Minister was further expansion of suffrage. I do not mean to say, however, that the expansion of universal enfranchisement was an inevitable outcome of Sverdrup and Venstre's rule and the coming of parliamentary democracy. There were tensions and conflicts about this, and Venstre split up into many factions soon after it acquired power. Pressure from the newly formed Labour Party was arguably important for universal suffrage. An important factor in why the franchise was expanded relatively easily in the 1880s was that there was a new economic crisis that made fewer people wealthy enough to benefit from suffrage expansion based on income.[64] Nevertheless, in any event it was the Venstre movement that opened "the floodgates of democracy", which even their critics pointed out. Without the victory of Venstre, suffrage expansion would most probably have been delayed.

Summary

Initially, the timeframe covered in this chapter was 1830–1884, and the chapter explained how *the amalgamation of property, people and sovereignty* became constituted in such a way that the right to property became more abstract and separated from real property. Instead, it became more connected to the individual as the owner of one's own labour power. This was explored primarily through the unification of national sovereignty resulting from the implementation of parliamentary democracy. The chapter traced this development to the first years of the nation's existence, when it was normally the elite—Falsen, for example—who wanted to unify the two branches of government in order to create more efficient rule, while the mass of the people, particularly the farmers, were against it.

The chapter then moved on to the 1860s, when the social basis of the conflict changed. The people wanted to unify sovereignty by bringing about parliamentary democracy, making the parliament in effect the only medium of sovereignty. Then, during the 1870s farmer and solicitor Johan Sverdrup became the unequivocal leader of the coalition (known as the Venstre movement) that advocated parliamentary democracy. It is mostly through his speeches that this section built its argument. As with the Republicans in America, Sverdrup's fight for parliamentary

[64] Langeland (2014), pp. 41–51.

democracy was connected to a changed conception of property that can be traced back at least to the 1850s as meaning primarily the right to the fruits of one's labour, and which went hand in hand with the vindication of expanded suffrage. The chapter first looked at the suffrage debate and then moved on to the debate about unification of sovereignty. The chapter also looked at counter-arguments in regard to both suffrage expansion and parliamentary democracy, primarily through the writings of lawyer, professor and Member of Parliament Anton Martin Schweigaard (1808–1870) and his friend, lawyer and Prime Minister Frederik Stang (1808–1884).

Nationalism at Its Industrial Moment

In this part of the book (Part II) we have followed two different, yet conceptually interlinked social movements in the US and Norway. Unlike the agrarian moment of Part I, where we followed the two similar independence struggles of the US and Norway, Part II first followed the peculiar and distinct American movement for the abolition of chattel slavery, and then looked at the Norwegian movement towards parliamentary democracy and universal male suffrage. The intention of Part II was to show that, despite these two movements being different, they display the same ideological and intellectual transformations: something I have called *the transvaluation of property*, or a shift from land to labour. What is more, the American abolition of slavery and the Norwegian movement for parliamentary democracy were both movements that strengthened and unified central state power and reinterpreted the constitution. In America, this happened through the new powers that the federal government assumed when it decided to abolish slavery, with implementation of the 14th and 15th amendments. In Norway the implementation of parliamentary democracy and later universal male suffrage were the consequence of the Impeachment Act of 1884 and the unification of legislative and executive powers in parliament. Finally, it can be argued that these two movements were the most important and fundamental political changes that occurred in these two nations during the first century of their existence.

The movement for the abolition of chattel slavery and the movement for parliamentary democracy explicitly challenged the assumptions made about property and sovereignty in the *first form of the nation*. Most important was abandoning the idea that it was only real, landed property that could be the basis of sovereignty and individual freedom. The right to property was still held as a crucial, fundamental right, but the right to property was increasingly understood as dual, encompassing also the right to the fruits of one's labour. In this way the freedom of the individual and the sovereignty of the nation could be derived from, and belong to, everyone who worked. In such a vision, it did not make sense to confine sovereignty only to the men of landed property. The right to property, understood in this way, also demanded the abolition of chattel slavery, so that slaves too could have the right to the fruits of their labour.

The transformation of nationalism at the industrial moment represents a continuation of the national ideology that formed during the agrarian phase. It points to how the original property rights elemen,t coupled with the idea of popular sovereignty, were central to the national ideology all the way from its agrarian origins through its industrial transformation. What changed was the interpretation of these concepts and the way in which they were put together.

In America, by the late 1850s large forces within the American nation had been mobilised on both fronts of the cause of slavery. The south, led by a Democratic Party backed by large landholders and slave owners, defended the property assumptions of the *first form of the nation*. The north, driven by the Republican Party and a broad alliance of intellectuals, wage earners and farmers, propagated the new vision of *transvaluation*, or the shift from land to labour. An important factor that contributed to the shift from land to labour in the north was decline in the importance of smallholding farming, although smallholding remained a relatively prominent feature of life also in the north. Smallholding farming nevertheless gradually fell in the shadow of emerging industry and artisan work in the mushrooming cities and towns of the north. This meant that the total proportion of people who lived off the land decreased, and that an increasing amount of people earned their livelihoods from waged work. This was different from the south, which remained largely agricultural—and slave driven. In the end, it was the northern vision that was victorious. In much the same way that the first emergence of nationalism was strongly connected with the emergent smallholding property structure during the seventeenth and eighteenth century, so too was the *transvaluation of property* or the shift from land to labour strongly connected with the demise of this kind of property structure and the emergence of industrial forms of property capital.

In Norway the cause of parliamentary democracy had built up momentum by 1884. An important reason why parliamentary democracy became the main issue through which *transvaluation* was carried out in Norway was the monarchical structure of the Norwegian state. This meant, amongst other things, that the government was appointed by the king and was clearly separate from the parliament. It also meant that the king could veto parliamentary bills. Radical reforms thus became efficiently blocked by conservative forces, constituted by relatively wealthy intellectuals and state officials within the government and the monarchy. It was for this reason that radical forces within the parliament needed to thwart the power of the government and the king in order to carry through any reform. As in America, the impediment to reform in Norway was also strongly related to the gradual decline in importance of smallholding farming. It is true that Norway, even more so than the US, remained very much an agricultural economy during the latter decades of the nineteenth century. But Norway saw growth in cities and industries as well, and experienced huge population growth during the course of the nineteenth century. Most of these people were not smallholding farmers due to the scarcity of suitable land; thus, the proportion of tenants increased, as did employment in artisan professions and in occupations such as clerks and teachers. As in America an increasing number of people became dependent on wages for their living. The social movement that finally carried through parliamentary reform (and which carried with it the transvalued notion of property) in 1884 was a complex and diverse movement with various interests, ranging from large farmers to smallholders and tenants, from city intellectuals to clerks and teachers.

Like the development of American and Norwegian nationalism at the agrarian moment the transformations during the industrial moment were probably not unique. Additionally, there is reason to believe that what happened in these two societies is representative of a trend in the development of European and American societies at the time. Indeed, by the turn of the nineteenth century, but universal male and female suffrage had become common in most of Western Europe and North America, and traditional forms of bondage and servitude had been dismantled. Within the first two decades of the twentieth century universal suffrage and free labour relations marked even greater parts of Europe and the Americas. We do not know, of course, whether internal developments were driven by the same logic, but given that Europe and America saw roughly the same kind of material transformations as the US and Norway, and similar political ones, it does at least seem like a plausible hypothesis.

Literature

Barlien, Hans, *Bemerkninger til Norges grunnlov* (1836).

Bergsgård, Arne, *Ole Gabriel Ueland og bondepolitikken*, Aschehoug, Oslo (1932).

Bull, Edvard, "Fra bøndenes og husmennenes samfunn til den organiserte kapitalisme," in Ottar Dahl (ed.), *Makt og motiv: Festskrift til Jens Arup Seip*, Gyldendal Norsk Forlag, Oslo (1975).

Bull, Edvard, *Arbeiderklassens historie I: arbeiderklassen blir til*, Tiden Norsk Forlag, Oslo (1985).

Danielsen, Rolf, *Det Norske storting gjennom 150 år, Bind 2: tidsrommet 1870–1908*, Gyldendal Norsk Forlag, Oslo (1964).

Fougstad, Carl, *Det Norske storting 1833*, Christiania (1834).

Havstad, Lars, *Johan Sverdrup: taler i stortinget, 1851–1880*, Græbes bogtrykkeri, København.

Kaartvedt, Alf, *Det Norske Storting gjennom 150 år*, Bind 1, Gyldendal Norsk Forlag, Oslo (1964).

Kaartvedt, Alf, *Kampen mot parlamentarisme, 1880–1884: den konservative politikken under vetostriden*, Universitetsforlaget, Bergen (1967).

Koht, Halvdan, *Johan Sverdrup I, 1816–1869*, Aschehoug, Kristiania (1918).

Koht, Halvdan, *Johan Sverdrup II, 1870–1880*, Aschehoug, Kristiania (1922).

Krokan, Inge, *Det store hamskifet i bondesamfunnet*, Det Norske Samlaget, Oslo (1976) [1942].

Langeland, Nils Rune, "Røysteretten som mål på politisk komeptanse," in Nils Rune Langeland (ed.), *Politisk Kompetanse: grunnlovas borgar*, Pax Forlag AS, Oslo (2014).

Lund, Carl, *A.M. Schweigaard som stortingspolitiker*, Universitetsforlaget, Oslo (1958).

Mjeldheim, Leiv, *Folkerørsla som vart parti: Venstre frå 1880 åra til 1905*, Universitetsforlaget, Bergen (1984).

Nerbøvik, Jostein, *Norsk Historie 1860–1914: Eit bondesamfunn i oppbrot*, Det Norske Samlaget, Oslo (1999).

Nergaard, John, *En odelsmands tanker om Norges nærværende forfatning*, Christiania (1830).

Østerud, Øyvind, *Agrarian Structure and Peasant Politics in Scandinavia: A Comparative Study of Rural Response to Economic Change*, Universitetsforlaget, Oslo (1978).

Østrem, Nils Olav, *Norsk utvandringshistorie*, Det Norske Samlaget, Oslo (2006).

Pryser, Tore, *Norsk Historie, 1814–1860: frå standssamfunn til klassesamfunn*, Det Norske Samlaget, Oslo (1999).

Seip, Jens Arup, *Et regime foran underangen: kampen mellom men og idealer i årene førparlamentarismens seier I Norge*, Gyldendal Norsk Forlag, Oslo (1965) [1945].

Seip, Jens Arup, *Utsikt over Norges historie*, Gyldendal Norsk Forlag, Oslo (1974).

Sejersted, Francis, *Demokrati og rettsstat*, Pax Forlag AS, Oslo (2001).

Slagstad, Rune, *De nasjonale strateger*, Pax Forlag AS, Oslo (1998).

Sørensen, Øystein, *Anton Martin Schweigaards politiske tenkning*, Universitetsforlaget, Oslo (1988).

Svare, Bjarne, *Frederik Stang* (2 Vols.), Aschehoug, Oslo (1939–1950).

PART III

Conclusions

CHAPTER 6

The Nation as a Propertied Community

This book has tried to display the nation as a propertied community, and nationalism as a property rights ideology. That is to say that the nation may be understood as a community of property holders, a society where all full members of society are seen to have an unalienable right to private property. As we have seen, in the historical time period to which this book has been confined, the two cases investigated went from being agrarian societies to becoming burgeoning industrial societies. This transition, and the idea of the nation as a propertied community, can be used as the basis for a more general theory of nationalism. It suggests that to understand nationalism in the later form (industrial—that is, modern), it is important to grasp it in its first form: nationalism emerged and formed in agrarian societies—that is, in societies where the main source of wealth was land, and where a large majority of people lived off the land. This landed, agrarian form of nationalism is in effect a "missing link" between pre- or proto-national forms of society (feudal, absolutist, mercantilist, etc.), and the fully modern industrial form identified famously by Ernest Gellner. Nationalism was both a *product of* and a *reaction to* an agrarian political model and the material relations that supported it:

1. Nationalism was a product of agrarian relations in the ways in which sovereignty, freedom and property were understood. These

E. M. Fuglestad, *Private Property and the Origins of Nationalism in the United States and Norway*,
https://doi.org/10.1007/978-3-319-89950-3_6

concepts were derived from, and understood in, an agrarian absolutist context.[1]

2. Nationalism was a reaction to the existing agrarian frame because the meanings of sovereignty, property and freedom became modified and adapted to the material relations of each of my cases. In this reaction, these agrarian concepts became the foundations for further capitalist, democratic and industrial development.

In essence, nationalism emerged out of the changes in agrarian landed property structures that made land rights a purely economic right, detached from feudal privileges and structures, and which also made land rights more widespread. It was out of such a situation that popular sovereignty based on propertied freedom emerged, and became in effect nationalism in its first form—a propertied community where land had special significance.[2] One important point to note about this agrarian aspect of nationalism is that the core concepts of nationalism (popular sovereignty, property and freedom) were all formed and adjusted to an agrarian social structure, contrary to the dominating Gellnerian modernist point that nationalism is a product of industrial society.[3] However, despite (or indeed, perhaps precisely because of) the agrarian origins of nationalism and its property assumptions, they were also compatible, and particularly favourable to, industrial society as this new base or mode of production led to an inner alteration—*transvaluation*—of the basic property ideas of nationalism. This led to the nation in its second form—a propertied community where the idea of an individual's right to the fruits of his labour was seen as the essence of the property right. So, nationalism, although agrarian and landed in its origins, is also ideologically functional to industrial society. This is one of the key insights into the development of nationalism that this book has sought to offer.

[1]In the case of the US, these ideas and notions were the "rights of Englishmen" inherited from Britain (see American chapters). In Norway the notions and ideas not only came from the imperial state of which it was part, but also from ideological currents stressing the peculiarity of Norwegian property relations (see chapters on Norway). In both cases the ideas were formed by the agrarian capitalist character of their societies.

[2]For other perspectives on how the class relations of my cases affected the idea of popular sovereignty see Koth, Halvdan, "Trongen til demokrati I 1814," *Historisk tidsskrift*, No. 38 (1947) (Norwegian case); and Morgan, Edmund S., *Inventing the People: The Rise of Popular Sovereignty in England and America*, W.W. Norton & Co., New York (1988). It is argued here that the elite constructed popular sovereignty and included the farmers purely for instrumental reasons.

[3]Gellner, Ernest, *Nations and Nationalism*, Blackwell, Oxford (2006) [1983].

The Theory

I have stressed again and again throughout this book the importance of relative widespread ownership of land, and the lack or dissolution of feudal or semi-feudal structures for the emergence of nationalism in the US and Norway. This was, as I see it, an important precondition for the first stage of national development. Widespread ownership of individual, exclusive property in land was a decisive factor for how the idea of national sovereignty developed during the agrarian moment. What was equally important was the creation of a historical narrative based on perceived long traditions of distribution of land and self-government in the US and Norway. These narratives were not fully constructed; they were grounded in the historical reality of these two countries, both of which actually did have traditions of self-government going back several centuries. This of course took different forms. In the US, it was through the establishing of the colonies and their forms of local government (although some debaters drew the line back to the Norman conquest of the Anglo-Saxon kingdom). In Norway, it was through the establishment of the Viking and medieval kingdoms and the forms of local government that had existed there. These traditions were of course highly idealised, especially when it came to the extent of freeholding and distribution of power, and through this the influence of common people in the governing of the states. Still, these narratives became the nerve centre of the national ideology in the US and Norway during the agrarian moment. They were fundamental to the national imagination that formed during the agrarian moment, and these narratives became central in the argument for national independence at that time. To fully understand the emergence of nationalism as it is presented in this book it is important to understand and remember that the historical narratives about property, freedom and self-government were very important, and that the reality of widespread ownership that existed at the time of the national revolutions during the agrarian moment was one of the most crucial parts of this narrative. The justifications and arguments used were historical in their logic. The history of the American colonies and the Kingdom of Norway were used to exemplify and pinpoint the truthfulness and the just cause of the nationalists. The current distribution of property in the two places became a support for these claims, it both informed the thinking about the past, and became the tangible form to which the national imagination could cling in the present. The historical narrative also continued to play an important part in the industrial moment, but landed property became less important. Instead, there was a focus on more abstract rights to freedom, still historically grounded, but now primarily based in the history of new nation-states established during the agrarian moment.

If we were to make a conceptual historical sketch of the emergence and development of nationalism in the US and Norway, it would look like this:

1. First, the gradual dissolution of what we could call either the society of orders, the *ancien régime* or feudalism—concepts I use here as stereotypes—to allude to a very general idea of a social form where property rights and sovereignty were still tangled up in various ways in webs of privileges and dues, aristocracy, religion, in hierarchical and rigid social structures.
2. Then the emergence of capitalist conceptions of exclusive, economic property in land, which led to land sales and distribution of land amongst farmers, creating relatively widespread smallholding based on much more exclusive property rights. Simultaneously, with this there emerged historical narratives that accentuated the historical freedoms and property rights of the people living in the American colonies and the ancient Norwegian kingdom. These narratives became the basis of the national ideology when the different imperial crises developed in the British and the Oldenburg Empires. The reality of relatively widespread landholding at the time provided an inspiration for assertions of freedom and theories of popular, national sovereignty. This was the first stage—the birth—of nationalism and nation-states in the US and Norway.
3. Later, landed property came to lose its importance for the understanding of popular sovereignty and freedom because wage work gradually became more dominant. When this happened, there emerged new historical narratives that focussed on the freedoms that were perceived to be created at the national revolutionary moments, but it was no longer reasonable to talk about nations of smallholders. Instead, the ideas about freedom and sovereignty adapted to the new reality of emerging wage work. The original and primarily propertied freedom became understood more widely to include all labouring men of the nation. In the next section we discuss some central topics that have been brought to the surface during this study and which will clarify.

Slavery and Freedom: Agrarian and Industrial Visions

A central theme of the development of nationalism, from the agrarian moment to the industrial moment, has been the continuum of slavery and freedom. Today, slavery is hardly ever used in political discourse, but the notion of freedom on which nationalism in the US and Norway was based gained, as we have seen, its meaning from debates about slavery in various forms. The language of slavery in the national ideology belongs to a long tradition of political thought going back at least to Aristotle, and which became especially prominent in English and Western political thought from the seventeenth century onwards. The Bible was an important inspiration for this, but other historical examples, such as Roman slavery, were also invoked. It is of course also significant that chattel slavery existed (and was rebelled against) in large parts of the world in the time period that the national movements of this book emerged.[4] The idea of slavery was integrated into the broader language of property and freedom as an idea of "the other," so to speak—something that Norwegians and Americans were not. In the cases explored in this book, we must also view the language of slavery in relation to its actual property relations, which with its peculiarities framed the notions of freedom and slavery so that in the US it was compatible with chattel slavery, and both cases it came to hold landed property as essential to freedom in the *first form of the nation.*

Slavery and Freedom in the First form of the Nation (The Agrarian Moment)

The form of rule in *the first form of the nation* was that of a sovereign people who made laws, but that political power was actuality confined primarily to men of real property. Freedom came to be defined primarily against feudalism and ancient slavery. These negations of freedom were understood both in economic and political terms: both political and economic freedom were held to be necessary components of freedom:

[4]Buck-Morss, Susan, "Hegel and Haiti," *Critical Inquiry*, Vol. 26, No. 4 (Summer, 2000). See also Furstenberg, François, "Beyond freedom and slavery: Autonomy, virtue, and resistance in early American political discourse," *Journal of American History*, Vol. 89, No. 4 (March, 2003).

one could not exist without the other. In both cases, feudalism, slavery and subjugation were seen as something that belonged to the distant past and/or to other places, so that the members of the national movement saw themselves as unique and free. Freedom was historical: the freedom that the members of the national movement claimed was done so on account of belonging to a tradition of freedom. The national identity implied here was first and foremost a historical construction, based on the ideals and characteristics of the distant past. In this vision not to be free was defined as any person subject to arbitrary rule—that is, a situation in which the individual had no say in political decisions which affected him and thus his right to property. In other words, it was believed that, in order for individuals to enjoy the economic freedom to property, it was vital that the individual also had political freedom—that is, that they made the laws to which they were themselves subject, that they were sovereign.

Because it was landed property that was seen to make individuals free in the first form of the nation,[5] landless wage labourers, for example, were considered more or less unfree, in a similar situation to that of the chattel slave: neither had real property, and neither were therefore free. The difference was of course that the slave was himself seen as a form of property. There is a conceptual similarity here: neither the slave nor the wage labourer had the right to the fruits of their labour exclusive to themselves. The slave was forced to yield all the fruits of his labour to his master, and was thus dependent on him completely. The wage labourer was dependent on his employer for his wage, and was therefore not completely free.

[5]We have seen in the chapters on America that there was no necessary contradiction between asserting landed freedom and having slaves. In Norway, this issue has not been explored because there was no chattel slavery in Norway. Yet I have indicated that the idea was the same in Norway, and a comment from Christian Magnus Falsen, central member of the national movement, may reinforce this. A point had been made against Falsen's argument about the special propertied freedom of the Norwegian farmer, saying that in ancient times the *odelsrett* (see Chapter 3 and 5) coexisted with the institution of slavery. To this Falsen replied that slavery had existed in both Rome and Greece, even among the ancient Jews. Were these societies thus not worthy of being called free societies? Obviously they were. See Falsen, Christian Magnus, *Som man raaber I skoven faar man svar*, Dhal, Enke og Søn, Bergen (1815), pp. 10–11. While this is not to say that Falsen supported chattel slavery, it points to the general understanding of property, freedom and slavery, where freedom was primarily landed freedom and with which chattel slavery could coexist.

Slavery Dismantled: The Second form of the Nation (The Industrial Moment)

In the second form of the nation the language of slavery started disappearing from the main political discourse in the US and Norway, as industrial capitalism and mass politics started to consolidate. Despite this shift, there were people who still maintained the original meaning of slavery and thus posed a critique of capitalist labour relations. That is worth taking note of because the core of the critique was in many ways Marxian (even predating Marx). Most important in this conservative critique was that only real property could confer freedom on men and nations. It was held that freedom was based on rights to real material wealth, that it was not enough to have a right to vote or to one's labour. The men who held this view were mostly Conservatives and have been deemed backward-looking and anti-progressive, mostly because they wanted to deny the masses the right to vote and denied the slaves their freedom. However, as William Scott observed:

> If nothing else the defenders of property qualifications [for the vote] had understood the implications of contemporary changes [the coming of industrial society]. The reformers, however, denied the importance of widespread property holding and concerned themselves with abstract liberty and equality for all men.[6]

Scott was writing about the franchise debates in the US, but his general argument applies to Norway as well. The meaning of freedom became more abstract. Property now meant the abstract right to the fruits of one's labour: this made men free. On this logic, it was possible to assert that all men were independent and thus give all men the right to vote. Membership of the political community was now based on putting labour into the system, not on the ownership of physical property. Yet the Conservatives saw something lost here. The question from Norwegian Conservative A.M. Schweigaard in relation to the suffrage expansion as quoted earlier is telling. He had asked: "Did not the propertyless hold a grant to land as the fundamental thing, more so than merely to be granted the right to vote." It was real wealth that mattered,

[6] Scott, William, *In Pursuit of Happiness: American Conceptions of Property from the Seventeenth to the Twentieth Century*, Indiana University Press, Bloomington and London (1977), p. 77. The text in brackets are my insertions.

not some abstract right to labour, or as Shweigaard put it, it was not enough to appeal to "general arguments which could be applied to anything and nothing."

There is something to be said here for the Conservative (and in the US pro-slavery) position on property (which is in no way to say that I agree with or support the slavery ideology): they did see, or admit more clearly than others, that freedom in capitalist society is based on real economical wealth, on ownership of the means of production and of capital. Norwegian historian Nils Rune reflected on this. Writing about the Norwegian founding fathers of 1814, he states:

> [Real] Property is freedom. It is the only true form of freedom in a capitalist society... The founding fathers of 1814 knew this well, only he who owned or administered real property could be a free sovereign citizen.[7]

This is also what was implicit in Morris Cohen's assertion that property is sovereignty, as referred to in the introduction: to have a property right to something gives an individual freedom and power to dispose over the wealth and resources that the property right covers, and thus the right to limit and control those who do not have such rights. The right to property is exclusive; a right to property is thus sovereignty, but if this right is alienated, as it is in a wage labour relation, there is no real sovereignty, no freedom in the positive sense. The pro-slavery men, for example, critiqued capitalist labour relations because they created an unfree society, cold and merciless, ruled by capital—a society that gave individuals no rights at all, that guaranteed them not even a minimum of subsistence and, least of all, freedom. In short, the wage labourers were in fact *wage slaves* in the Conservative view. George Fitzhugh's assertion quoted earlier, that "Capital commands labour as master does slave," may serve as a summary statement here. This point was completely dismissed by the majority of the national movement during this phase—it was in fact seen to be a complete and utter perversion of what freedom really meant. Freedom came to mean to own one's labour, and it came to be seen as rigorously egalitarian—it was no longer accepted that a society could be free if only those owning landed property were seen to be truly independent.

[7] Langeland, Nils Rune, *Kveldsseta: historiske essay*, N.W. Damm & Søn AS (2003), p. 21.

The people who ushered in the second form of the nation with the transvalued notion of property and freedom may be considered capitalist revolutionaries or reformers in the sense that the political changes they advocated fully accepted all the implications of an industrial capitalist ideology: private ownership and all individuals as free alienators of their labour. The *transvaluation of property* thus became a way of legitimising industrial capitalist labour and property relations: fewer and fewer people owned real property and the economic system was in increasing degree founded on ownership of the means of production by the few. This is not to say that the members of the national movement of *the second form of the nation* were consistent and conscious capitalist apologists. The main concern of these people was to realise national propertied freedom in what was seen as a logical and necessary conclusion of the national ideal. Thus, both these reformers and the Conservatives were advocating the same fundamental freedom, but with different understandings of what distribution of property was the most essential to freedom. However, only the Conservatives retained the original ideas of slavery and freedom.

With the transvalued notion of property, there was no space for the language of slavery, apart from those critiquing capitalism, because such language completely undermined the foundations of freedom in the second form of the nation—if the wage labourers were seen as unfree slaves, then the nations would be nations of slaves. There was, in short, no one left to be slaves. Nationalism created a society of free men (as claimed by its proponents) under conditions which Marxists (and the national Conservatives) would see as an unfree society.

Property, Wealth and Democracy in Industrial Society

Nationalism and Perpetual Growth

The debates about slavery and freedom were connected to issues of poverty and wealth, and nationalism may have become at its industrial moment a force that legitimised continued and expanding growth based on the exploitation of labour power. For Ernest Gellner, one of the fundamental characteristics of modern industrial society is that it is founded on perpetual growth: "Industrial society is the only society ever to live by and rely on sustained and perpetual growth."[8] It is the imperative of perpetual growth and the constant remobilisation of labour that nationalism, as described by Gellner, sustains. This book also supports this conclusion, but for different reasons: nationalism sustains a society of perpetual growth because it legitimises industrial labour and property relations. That is, nationalism, in its industrial form, propagates a vision of freedom that sees all individuals as free proprietors of their own alienable labour power, because the right to private property is held as a fundamental right connected to popular sovereignty. Nationalism is thus not only practically but also ideologically functional to industrial society. Because the right to property was based on the idea of the right to the fruits of one's labour, property could mean both having real property and, more simply, not to be denied the right to the fruits of one's labour. Because property was understood dually in this way the national vision could, without violating the universal right to property, result in the creation of industrial societies where ownership of the means of production and capital could be confined to a minority, while the majority were confined to alienate their labourpower. Thus, by seeing all men as free and unlimited proprietors of their labour power when connected to a sovereign people, nationalism lays the foundation of free and unlimited growth and accumulation. In this light, we might juxtapose nationalism with Protestantism as Max Weber saw it: in a similar fashion as Weber saw the Protestant notion of the calling as a precondition for capitalist growth, we might say that the nationalist conception of property and sovereignty was also a precondition for industrial growth.[9]

The Relationship Between Democracy and Property

It is implicit in what has been said above that the way in which the sovereignty of the people was understood was different in the first and the second form of the nation: the sovereignty of the people in *the first form of the nation* was understood as a restricted representative democracy, and this was because the understanding of freedom was tied to real landed property. In *the second form of the nation* the sovereignty of the

[8] Gellner (2006), p. 22.

[9] Weber, Max, *The Protestant Ethic and the Spirit of Capitalism*, Routledge, London and New York (1992) [1905].

people became understood as a universal democracy, and again this was related to how property freedom was understood. Universal democracy became a potent idea when propertied freedom became understood primarily as the right to the fruits of one's labour. Hence, property and forms of representative rule (democracy) were always interconnected in the national ideologies of the US and Norway. This suggests an answer to Therborn's paradox referred to in Chapter 1[10]: in the early nineteenth century (*the first form of the nation*), property and democracy were incompatible due to the underlying definition of freedom as landed property. The propertyless were thus unfree and a danger to the preservation of property. Later (*the second form of the nation*), freedom became understood as self-ownership of one's labour, thus all who laboured were free and would have an interest in the preservation of property rights and the political system.

The National Property Ideals and the Distribution of Wealth

One of the central claims in Thomas Piketty's recent and acclaimed study *Capital in the Twenty-First Century* (2014) is that inequality of wealth will grow in the twenty-first century because the rate of return on capital will significantly exceed the growth rate of the economy. Piketty claims that unequal distribution of wealth today is partly legitimised and driven by what he calls "meritocratic extremism."[11] This means that excessive wealth is to a high degree justified as being the rightful product of the labour and skill of an individual which is rightfully his or her own. But the major cause of increasing inequality will be due to what Piketty calls "patrimonial capitalism"[12]—a system where wealth is accumulated and

[10] The questions were as follows: "How has it come about that, in the major and most advanced capitalist countries, a tiny majority class—the bourgeoisie—rules by means of democratic forms?" and "In the nineteenth and early twentieth centuries, as both political practice and constitutional debate clearly demonstrate, prevailing bourgeois opinion held that democracy and capitalism (or private property) were incompatible … In modern times, however, since at least the outbreak of the Cold War, bourgeois ideologists have maintained that only capitalism is compatible with democracy." See Therborn, Gøran, "The rule of capital and the rise of democracy," *New Left Review*, Vol. 1, No. 103 (May/June, 1977).

[11] Piketty, Thomas, *Capital in the Twenty-First Century*, Belknap Press, Cambridge, MA and London (2014), p. 334.

[12] Piketty (2014), p. 173.

concentrated in few hands, and where the primary way to secure wealth is thus through inheritance or marriage because wages for the majority stay low.

As we have seen in this book, the idea that all individuals have a property right to their labour, which is a foundation for their freedom, was an essential feature of nationalism. This is foundational to the idea of the "meritocratic extremism" of which Piketty writes. This might be an indication of the continued prevalence of the fundamental ideas of nationalism today, and it shows how nationalism might legitimate such accumulation of wealth because it promotes the right of all individuals to enjoy the fruits of their labour. Nationalism might also be seen as connected to Piketty's thesis because nationalism had as its foundation the private property regime which makes possible the accumulation of private wealth in "patrimonial capitalism." Indeed, nationalism sees the right to such accumulation as one of the most fundamental of all rights: as the basis for the organisation of the political community.

Metamorphosis and Split of Capital

Two things are important to keep in mind when discussing nationalism, its property assumptions and the distribution of wealth in industrial society. One is what Piketty called the metamorphosis of capital,[13] and the other is what we might call the capital–labour split.[14] The two are related.

1. The metamorphosis of capital indicates that capital went from being primarily landed property (in agrarian societies) to being real estate or financial capital or assets (in industrial societies), but that its nature stayed the same.
2. The capital–labour split indicates the separation of wealth from the labour power it was created by—for example, the creation of surplus for a company by giving the workers wages but where some of the profit stays in the company with the owner. After the metamorphosis of capital the capital–labour split becomes more decisive and affects the understanding of property.

[13] Piketty (2014), pp. 113–116.

[14] I have also relied on Piketty for my description of the capital–labour split. See Piketty (2014), pp. 39–41.

These two changes also correspond with the changing understanding of property in agrarian and industrial nationalism. In agrarian society the right to property was understood to mean land, and the labour element of property was understood in large degree as the right to the potential wealth in land, and land was the main source of wealth. In industrial society the right to property is more complexly understood: it can mean the right to land or real estate, but also the right to financial capital or wealth and labour. In other words, there is a more decisive and clear split between the various elements of the right to property. This means that, for example, the right to labour can be a property right on its own (as in the national ideologies of our cases), disconnected from ownership of land or wealth. However, it also means that wealth or land is not necessarily understood as part of a universal property right. With these assumptions, as explained above, the right to property does not have to mean the right to actual wealth (as in the first form of the nation), but can simply mean the right to labour freely and to a wage. Because the *first form of the nation* was established before the "metamorphosis of capital" and the intensification of the capital–labour split, it would seem, paradoxically, that the assumptions of *the first form of the nation* are more favourable to egalitarian distribution of wealth than the second form.

Forms of Nationalism

Nationalism Versus Communism

In Chapter 1, I noted a Marxist and a liberal paradox in the way in which property rights and national democracies developed. The liberal paradox was briefly discussed above. In the following I shall discuss the Marxist one in more detail, and imply that one reason why Marxism has not been successful as an historical phenomenon is because it shares some of its fundamental property assumptions with nationalism—Marxism appeared as a form of *transvalued* nationalism. This comparison of Marxism and nationalism might seem slightly odd, but considering the preoccupation with property, wealth and labour in both worldviews, as well as the interesting similarities between them in these matters, a brief juxtaposition seems justified and relevant at this point.

Marxism emerged and formed roughly in the same time period in which the *transvaluation of property* happened: like the *transvaluation of property* in the national ideology, Marxist communism emerged as a reaction to the emergence of industrial society. Karl Marx himself was first a liberal who supported gradual reform, private property and legal constitutional states in the form that they had emerged in my cases as the first form of the nation.[15] Thus, he might have been coming from the same place ideologically as the members of the national movements of my cases. The similarity between these two worldviews lies in the wish of both to realise freedom for the individual by giving one the right to the property of one's labour. That this idea was so central to both worldviews must, at least partly, be contributed to the fact that both came out of the same intellectual milieu—the Enlightenment and the early Romantic period. Both Jean Jacques Rousseau and especially John Locke and Adam Smith had developed labour theories of value and property. Adam Smith, in fact, was to Marx "the Luther of political economy."[16] Such theories were at first applied by the members of the national movement in the US and Norway, and were understood in relation to the specific material relations there. Marxist communism could be understood as on a continuum with nationalism; it was an extension of it, and Marx posed his own transvaluation of the national ideals.[17] However, perhaps because Marx was not so strongly tied to one specific national tradition, and because he was already imbedded in an industrial world, his ideas of property were different from the national ones. The Marxian *transvaluation of property* transformed the inner and the outer meaning of both property and of freedom. Hence, Marx fundamentally challenged the idea that having the right to the fruits of one's labour made individuals free within the existence of the current private property system. Marx wrote in his *Economic and Philosophic Manuscripts:*

[15] There are many accounts of Marx's life and views. I found Francis Wheen's biography of Marx illuminating and interesting. See Wheen, Francis, *Karl Marx: A Life*, W. W. Norton & Co., London (2001).

[16] Giddens, Anthony, *Capitalism and Modern Social Theory: An Analysis of the Writings of Marx, Durkheim and Max Weber*, Cambridge University Press, Cambridge (2014) [1971], p. 35.

[17] I am not the first to point to the fundamental similarity between Marxism and nationalism. Two forceful statements of this are Greenfeld (1993); and Szporluk, Roman, *Communism and Nationalism: Karl Marx Versus Friedrich List*, Oxford University Press, Oxford (1991).

> The antithesis between *lack of property* and *property*, so long as it is not comprehended as the antithesis of *labour and capital*, still remains an indifferent antithesis, not grasped in its *active connection*, in its *internal* relation, not yet grasped as a *contradiction*. It can find expression in this *first* form even without the advanced development of private property (as in ancient Rome, Turkey, etc.). It does not yet *appear* as having been established by private property itself. But labour, the subjective essence of private property as exclusion of property, and capital, objective labour as exclusion of labour, constitute *private property* as its developed state of contradiction ...[18]

For Marx there was a contradiction between the labour of an individual and capital accumulated on private property. For this reason, private property had to be terminated and substituted with a positive form of property: "*communism* is the *positive* expression of annulled private property—at first as *universal* private property."[19] Marx elaborated:

> *Communism* is the *positive* transcendence of *private property* as *human self-estrangement*, and therefore as the real *appropriation* of the *human* essence by and for man; communism therefore as the complete return of man to himself as a *social* (i.e., human) being—a return accomplished consciously and embracing the entire wealth of previous development. This communism ... is the *genuine* resolution of the conflict between man and nature and between man and man—the true resolution of the strife between existence and essence, between objectification and self-confirmation, between freedom and necessity, between the individual and the species. Communism is the riddle of history solved, and it knows itself to be this solution.[20]

Communism, like nationalism, promised to give the individual freedom through property, and saw itself to be the fulfilment of a long historical process ("the riddle of history solved"); but instead of private property as the end goal, Marx saw communal property as the fulfilment of history. Communism and nationalism can thus be seen as two distinct, yet

[18] Marx, Karl, *Economic and Philosophic Manuscripts,* Progress Publishers, Moscow (1959) [1844], p. 42. https://www.marxists.org/archive/marx/works/download/pdf/Economic-Philosophic-Manuscripts-1844.pdf (accessed 19.08.2015).

[19] Marx (1959), p. 42.

[20] Marx (1959), p. 43.

related, answers to the same question: how to organise property in order to maintain freedom for the individual.[21]

Nationalism and communism were related, but the organising principles of each may be seen as a perversion of the other. In the national ideology, individual private property was sacred and the source of freedom. In communism, it was the root of all evil: for example, "private property is but the final and most complete expression of the system of producing and appropriating products that is based on class antagonism, on the exploitation of the many by the few".[22] In theory, the difference was smaller between nationalism and communism during the *first form of nationalism*, when, although individual property was the core of the ideology, at least it was postulated that one had to have a right to property over actual wealth to be free. However, in *the second form of the nation* an irreconcilable antagonism emerged between nationalism and what became Marxian communism. This conflict was, as indicated earlier, based on the understanding of labour and its relation to propertied freedom. Marx asked in the *Manifesto of the Communist Party*:

> Does wage labour create any property for the labourer? Not a bit. It creates capital i.e. that kind of property that exploits wage labour ... property in its present form is based on the antagonism between capital and wage-labour.[23]

It was because labour produced capital for the owners of the means of production that Marx saw private property, as it was in his time, as an evil. This assertion is in total opposition to the transvalued notion of property in nationalism, where it was claimed that every man was free by virtue of having the property one has in one's labour. To Marx, this is only half the truth, because:

[21] Marx wrote, like the nationalists of my cases, that the right to property in the fruits of one's labour was essential: "We by no means intend to abolish this personal appropriation of the product of labour, an appropriation that is made for the maintenance and reproduction of human life, and that leaves no surplus wherewith to command the labour of others. All that we want to do away with is the miserable character of this appropriation, under which the labourer lives merely to increase capital." See Marx, Karl, and Friedrich Engels, *Manifesto of the Communist Party*, New York Labour News, New York (1908) [1848], p. 33.

[22] Marx and Engels (1911), p. 25.

[23] Marx and Engels (1911), p. 25.

> Capital is a collective product and only by the united action of many members, nay, in the last resort, only by the united resort of all the members of society can it be set in motion. Capital is therefore not a personal, it is a social power ... in bourgeoisie society capital is independent and has no personality, while the living person is dependent and has no personality.[24]

In short, to only have the right to one's labour made one "dependent," not free, according to Marx. Although this highlights the difference between the property assumptions of communism and nationalism, it also highlights the similarity between the two. The above quote from Marx resonates both with the prevalent ideology of the first form of the nation (although the assertions about capital were not so theoretically sophisticated, but rather played more on analogies to feudalism) in which it was held that an individual was not free if subject to a labour relation—and with the pro-slavery ideology of the US. Fitzhugh's assertion that "capital commands labour as master does slave" is striking when compared to the passage from Marx.[25] This brief juxtaposition of Marxist communism and nationalism in the US and Norway may highlight the fact that the property assumptions in nationalism may take a variety of political and social forms. In this book I have explored only two (the first and the second form of the nation)—the communist alternative might be a third form.

The Specificity of National Propertied Society vis-à-vis Communist Society

It must be specified that, although the property assumption of nationalism might have the potentiality of many forms in it (including a communist one), it is also dependent on certain specific characteristics without which it would not have made sense to call it nationalism. These

[24] Marx and Engels (1911), p. 26.

[25] That Marx's views sprang from a soil fertilized by nationalism should not be a surprising statement considering that he came of intellectual age during the springtime of the peoples. Greenfeld, for example, has asserted quite forcefully the original and fundamentally nationalist foundations of Marx's vision. See Greenfeld, Liah, *Nationalism: Five Roads to Modernity*, Harvard University Press, Cambridge (1993, pp. 387–395). Greenfeld again builds her assertion on Krieger, Leonard, *The German Idea of Freedom: History of a Political Tradition*, University of Chicago Press (1972).

characteristics are naturally thus absent from Marxist communism. The property assertions of nationalism, as it appears in the US and Norway, were distinguished from Marxist communism in the sense that freedom and its property assertions were seen to be historically anchored to a specific tradition—nationalism connects its assertions to a specific sovereign people. It was also this specificity that formed the property assumptions of the ideology—it was because of widespread landownership and lack of feudal institutions that the property assumptions of nationalism became what they were. Marxian freedom is historical only insofar as it is to be realised in historical time, and is seen as a product of universal historical developments. National freedom was seen not only as a product of historical developments, but of historical development in specific places, to be realized only through the sovereignty of a chosen people. When national freedom became understood by its advocates as reality, all subsequent notions of freedom became tied up with that moment and that specific freedom. This is opposite to Marx's understanding. Marx wrote in the *Manifesto* about the labourer and national character: "Modern industrial labour, modern subjection to capital, the same in England as in France, in America as in Germany has stripped him of every trace of national character."[26] Marx saw an overarching homogeneity from which a new form of freedom could be created. It may have been true on one level for the cases investigated in this book that those living there were subject to the same forces of capital, and thus had no national uniqueness. On another level, however, this was not true—the labourers in the US and Norway had a national character: it was to be free and to have property, understood as a freedom inherent in their specific history. In the second, industrial form of the nation the members of the nation were seen as free precisely because they were embedded in capitalist labour and property relations, and connected to national sovereignty through a labour and property relation.

Other and Future Forms

With the short discussion of Marx above, I have hoped to indicate the wide resonance that the original national ideals about property achieved in the modern world. The national ideologies of the US and Norway represent a specific way of organising property and sovereignty.

[26] Marx and Engels (1911), p. 27.

Marxism may represent another. Furthermore, other nationalisms (ethnic, collectivistic, etc.) may have organised and legitimised property in different ways, but in one form or other most, if not all, nation-states have maintained a private property system akin to that which was established in the US and Norway. Even though they were geographically far apart, and even though the national revolution in Norway happened almost 40 years after the American Revolution was initiated, these cases reflect a common spirit that became pervasive in the Western world. The American case was the obvious one to look at to explore this spirit, given all its peculiarities as a "new world" nation and the fact that it was the first revolution of its kind. It proved, however, that Norway was not so different from the US, despite being situated in what would appear to be a very different historical context (the Old World). The fact that landownership was also widespread in Norway (as in America) at the time of the national revolution, combined with the lack of traditional feudal institutions in both places, contributed to the development of a similar ideology. That these cases were far apart and embedded in quite different historical contexts, and still produced similar institutions and ideologies (liberal democracy, private property, popular sovereignty, etc.) which now seem to be pervasive all over the Western world, might indicate that the main trends (i.e., *the first* and *the second form of the nation* with the centrality of property and the shift from land to labour) might also apply to other cases. Naturally, the account of nationalism given here is not an exhaustive account of all nationalisms, but the property rights perspective might also be applicable to other cases and times. The model is probably particularly applicable to other cases in the same geographical and historical time period to which I have confined my investigation. It seems reasonable that the model developed here could be a general theory of the emergence of nationalism in the West, seen in relation to the demise of feudalism, absolutism, etc., and the rise of industrial societies. The French Revolution would, for example, be an interesting case to look at in this regard. In fact, in most of the Western world between 1776 and 1884, feudal land ownership disappeared, giving rise to private property regimes, and it is probably not a coincidence that this time period is also generally seen as the heyday of nationalism in this region. It would require further research, of course, to investigate how property rights and sovereignty of the people were understood by different forms of nationalism, emerging at different times and under other class (property) relations than in the cases investigated here. It would require further research also to be able to determine how various historical and social conditions affected this consolidation and development of property and sovereignty in the long term. There are clearly many different trajectories: one can mention the Fascist regimes of interwar Italy and Germany, or the communist interlude in Eastern Europe, while Western Europe will probably be similar to the US and Norway. The Latin American developments, which in a way must be considered a type of Western nationalism, are also interesting cases where property relations and national development became both dramatic and, for a time, different from the North American and Western European developments, but where land rights and reform have also been a key issue. It could be very interesting to research further how different understandings and assertions of national property rights led to different political manifestations under different conditions, and how the property rights of individuals were legitimised. Finally, it must be said that to fully understand the development of nationalism in the US and Norway, one would need to also investigate the subsequent phase of national development there: the coming of the welfare state and its retrenchment in the twentieth century. But, that is for another occasion.

Literature

Buck-Morss, Susan, "Hegel and Haiti," *Critical Inquiry*, Vol. 26, No. 4 (Summer, 2000).

Falsen, Christian Magnus, *Som man raaber I skoven faar man svar*, Dhal, Enke og Søn, Bergen (1815).

Furstenberg, François, "Beyond freedom and slavery: Autonomy, virtue, and resistance in early American political discourse," *Journal of American History*, Vol. 89, No. 4 (March, 2003).

Gellner, Ernest, *Nations and Nationalism*, Blackwell, Oxford (2006) [1983].

Giddens, Anthony, *Capitalism and Modern Social Theory: An Analysis of the Writings of Marx, Durkheim and Max Weber*, Cambridge University Press, Cambridge (2014) [1971].

Greenfeld, Liah, *Nationalism: Five Roads to Modernity*, Harvard University Press, Cambridge (1993).

Koth, Halvdan, "Trongen til demokrati I 1814," *Historisk tidsskrift*, No. 38 (1947).

Krieger, Leonard, *The German Idea of Freedom: History of a Political Tradition*, University of Chicago Press (1972).

Langeland, Nils Rune, *Kveldsseta: historiske essay*, N.W. Damm & Søn AS (2003).

Marx, Karl, *Economic and Philosophic Manuscripts*, Progress Publishers, Moscow (1959) [1844]. https://www.marxists.org/archive/marx/works/download/pdf/Economic-Philosophic-Manuscripts-1844.pdf (accessed 19.08.2015).

Marx, Karl, and Friedrich Engels, *Manifesto of the Communist Party*, New York Labour News, New York (1908) [1848].

Morgan, Edmund S., *Inventing the People: The Rise of Popular Sovereignty in England and America*, W. W. Norton & Co., New York (1988).

Piketty, Thomas, *Capital in the Twenty-First Century*, Belknap Press, Cambridge, MA and London (2014).

Scott, William, *In Pursuit of Happiness: American Conceptions of Property from the Seventeenth to the Twentieth Century*, Indiana University Press, Bloomington and London (1977), p. 77.

Wheen, Francis, *Karl Marx: A Life*, W. W. Norton & Co., London (2001).

Index

A

B

C

D

E. M. Fuglestad, *Private Property and the Origins of Nationalism in the United States and Norway*,
https://doi.org/10.1007/978-3-319-89950-3

FSC
www.fsc.org
MIX
Papier | Fördert gute Waldnutzung
FSC® C083411

Kolibri 360 GmbH
Ferdinand-Jühlke-Straße 7
99095 Erfurt, Deutschland
produktsicherheit@kolibri360.de